Your Life
Is
Calling

Answer to happiness, health and wealth. Put the *LIFE* back into your life!

KAHLA KIKER

Copy Editor: Elizabeth M. Johnson

Book Cover Art: Cora Graphics

ISBN-10: 0692230548
ISBN-13: 978-0692230541 KWorld Ventures

This is a work of fiction. Names, characters, places and incidents either are the product of the author's imagination or are used fictitiously, and any resemblance to actual persons, living or dead, business establishments, events or locales is entirely coincidental.

DEDICATION

To all those seeking enlightenment and abundance. To you.

CONTENTS

Introduction

Section I: Happiness

Section II: Health

Section III: Wealth

Introduction

Everyone has been at a place in life where they felt completely alone, when it seems everything is going wrong and there is no way out. Hope seems lost and it's impossible to see a light at the end of the tunnel.

Are you there now? I want you to know you are not alone. You are not the first person to experience these feelings and you won't be the last. There isn't a human being on this planet who hasn't found him- or herself at a low point in their life, lacking energy, feeling unloved, or going through great misfortune. Inside these pages you will find stories of people very much like yourself who have endured different natures of hardship and have come out stronger in the end. No matter where you are, remember that someone else has gone through something worse and come through it. You can too.

EVERYTHIING you want in this life is possible.

These stories will show you by example what you can do to overcome the doubts and fears that plague your mind and although this book is about recognizing the Law of Attraction's theories and how they exist in our lives, it does not go into detail – like so many other books - about the Law of Attraction itself. What you do need to know before you read this book is that if you have never heard of the Law of Attraction before, my definition is very simple: the Law of Attraction is about like energies attracting like energies – whether they are positive or negative.

This book contains a variety of short stories focusing on different struggles that people experience in life concerning their happiness, health, and wealth. Each of these stories start with the struggle and move on to show you the moment of awakening that occurs when a person realizes what they hold inside themselves. Finally, we see each of these people free themselves from doubts and fears and embrace their destiny full of abundance, love, and success.

Using theories from the Law of Attraction, each of these individuals are examples of how our minds, mentalities and energies are the driving force of our manifested destiny. Here you will see how others changed their minds, changed their attitudes, and in turn changed their lives forever.

Ask yourself today, what are you manifesting? Have your thoughts and fears landed you in a position you feel you can't escape?

Whether it's a marriage you think is headed for divorce, a past you are struggling to overcome or a financial situation that is leading you down the road to bankruptcy – these stories will leave you taking stock of what types of energy you have been putting out into the world. You will see how negativity attracts negativity, positivity attracts positivity and be able to make these connections in your own life. Through these examples you will see that anything is possible, beginning by looking at things from another angle. How changing your perspective and changing one tiny thing in your life each day can change the entire course of your destiny. You'll see exactly how that happened for each of these everyday people.

This collection of stories will both inspire and amaze you as you see individuals who have hit rock bottom rise up once again, showing that the power to overcome resides within us all. They are all examples of situations that may look like the end, like there is no rising up and taking life back, only to find that through the Law of Attraction they were able to come back to life and reclaim their futures.

In this book I will show you how these individuals put the life back into their lives. It is never too late – not for them and certainly not for you. As you continue through these pages keep that in mind. You were meant for more. There is a bright, shining light inside you and by directing your energy you can overcome anything and achieve the desires of your heart.

SECTION I

HAPPINESS

"Happiness is not elusive and it definitely is not difficult. You just simply have to want to be happy."
~Kahla Kiker

YOU ARE NOT YOUR PAST

"The secret of health for both mind and body is not to mourn for the past, worry about the future, or anticipate troubles, but to live in the present moment wisely and earnestly."
~ Buddha (563 ~ 483 BC)

I didn't think I had any choice. I knew it was wrong. I'm not stupid. I just didn't see that I had any other choice. And it is that belief, that world view, which propelled me down a very dark road. It was a long time before I truly understood how dark the road would get.

I remember my five-year-old wailing, as she had been all afternoon. Like her older sibling, she was past starving. Jeff wasn't coming back, that was clear. Not a word, not a note. Left me with rent I couldn't pay and two kids I couldn't take care of.

Jeff was the last of three men attracted by my loser magnet; each a little sorrier than the last. My abysmal taste seemed to be genetic, inherited from my mom and her mom before that. Something in the Burke family bloodline, we couldn't hang onto our men. My great-grandmother Alice was married to Ted Burke. He had been quasi-responsible. At least when he took off he'd had the good grace to get himself killed in a work accident right away. With his insurance, Alice ended up with her house paid off and a little extra.

She was still working at Sears & Roebuck in Missouri when she was seventy. Between her salary and what she could carry home in her purse she helped her three children and whatever offspring they drug with them. Her son Bennie had been hurt in the war. He never had been quite right. James was also in the service. Career military, his wife and kids often stayed with Alice while he toured Korea and Hawaii. Her daughter Lois, my mom's mom, fell for several servicemen. One of them knocked her up. Lois said she really couldn't be sure what surname to use. So when mom was born, she became a Burke too.

My mom, Doris Burke, followed in her mother's footsteps and had me out of wedlock too. Apparently, he had a violent streak. Beat the hell out of mom when he found out she was carrying me. Mom didn't want me sharing his name either. She was a Burke, so when I finally arrived, that meant I was too.

I met Bill in high school. He was a senior when I was junior. He was tall and dreamy and going into the Navy. He had big plans for us. Before he left for Florida and boot camp we had a memorable evening. I got pregnant and I never heard from him again. He was the sweetest boy I ever met; he just didn't stay.

After my daughter Jill was born, we stayed with Mom and Grandma Lois. It's what Burkes do. There was always some generation of Burke to look after her. I waited tables at night, then after a couple of years I got on my feet. Turns out, I had a good memory for customers, orders, likes, and preferences. I made good money waitressing and was always able to move up to nicer and nicer restaurants. I finally worked my way up to the Velvet Tortoise, the nicest restaurant in the city. My tips alone were more than $100 a night. I was a good waitress and a popular one. We wore these really short uniforms and exceptionally low blouses. I was blessed with long legs and a nice chest. I always said, "This uniform is going to make me a wealthy woman."

One of my regular customers Jeff Abrams was a heavy tipper and a heavy drinker. Fortunately for me, the more he drank, the more he tipped. I was happy to bring him as many drinks as he wanted. He only drank beer, asked for them two at a time. Jeff was a car salesman. Did well. He even bought me a car. We dated for almost a year and then he asked me to move in with him, Jill too. He said he was the luckiest guy in the world, got to have a ready-made family. Not long after Jill and I moved in, I got pregnant with Tammy. Jeff wasn't very happy to hear his ready-made family was growing. He said he was worried the pregnancy would wreck my figure and I'd lose my job. He stopped coming by the restaurant and started getting his drinks elsewhere.

When I started showing, my manager, Mr. Armijo moved me behind the bar. He thought my bust line, which seemed to grow by the night, was good for business, even if my thickening waist wasn't. The tips I got bartending were even better than the ones I'd gotten as a waitress.

I was feeling pretty good about my situation until the night Jeff beat me up. He'd gotten raging drunk and started accusing me of sleeping around. The fight woke Jill up. She tried to break it up, even getting between us. When Jeff brought his arm back to hit her, I grabbed an ashtray and hit him on the side of his head and knocked him out. We packed up and moved back in with Mom and Grandma.

That was as good as life ever got. The money I got from selling the car Jeff had bought me covered the bills and got the girls and I into a little studio apartment. I was getting by at the Tortoise. But then the baby started getting sick a lot. High fevers, strep throat. A neighbor lady was watching my girls at night until Tammy got worse. I started missing work, calling in at the last minute. Mr. Armijo let me go.

I went back to waitressing days, but never made the kind of money I had been. Every month some bill went unpaid then two bills and then I started writing hot checks to keep everything current until payday. It was a lot to keep up with. I kept two checking accounts going, depositing into one and writing checks off another to make deposits to the other. I depended on that day or two of float to buy me enough time to keep the lights on and the repo man away. It worked for a while.

Tammy got sick again, a fever of 104. We ended up in the hospital and I didn't make it to the bank. All of the checks hit and bounced all over town. The bookkeeper at the bank did some research and caught the kiting pattern and reported me. The district attorney was new and trying to make a name for herself. I plea-bargained my way to a misdemeanor conviction and community service.

When Les showed up at the coffee shop, I owed the hospital for Tammy's emergency room visit and x-rays. I owed the pharmacy. I owed my landlord a month's rent. I didn't have a car and the economy had tanked. I had one girl in first grade and her sister in sixth. I felt two thousand years old.

Enter Les. Les was a truck driver. He had a nice smile and always left me a five-dollar bill for his cup of coffee. We struck up a friendship and started seeing one another. He drove over-the-road. He was often gone on a four-day turn around. He said he'd been living out of his truck. When he was in town, I let him stay over at my apartment.

Turns out, Les was a pretty good cook. When he was home, he'd load up on groceries and we ate really well. The girls liked him. He started helping me with my bills, taking care of the rent, paying the utilities once and a while. I started giving him my paychecks and I turned my tips over to him from each shift.

Les started picking up more and more jobs and was gone more than he had been. I came home and saw a disconnect notice from the light company. Our utility bill hadn't been paid in three months. I confronted Les about it and he said he would handle it. First thing the next morning he left to straighten it out and never came back.

I don't suppose I'll never know what Les did with the money I gave him. I only know what he didn't do with it. By the time the smoke cleared I had an eviction sign on my apartment door, the power company was going to turn our electricity off, an empty refrigerator, and two sick little girls.

I had no choice. I found some old checkbooks for long-closed bank accounts. I went to the Super All-Mart and loaded up my cart with medicines, food, paper goods, pajamas, and dresses for the girls. I don't know why or how my check was accepted, but it was. Emboldened, I dropped off one to the electric company for the full amount due. When I got back to the apartment, I ran into my landlord, he wasn't happy.

"I'm calling the Sheriff. It's past time."

I convinced him to take my check for the back rent, and promised to bring him cash money the following Friday. I thought he was just going to hold the check, but he didn't.

I was arrested at work, midway through pouring a refill for my favorite customers. Without money for bail or bond, I was immediately processed and jailed. I was arraigned and I watched at a distance as perfect strangers decided my future. When the rent check bounced, along with the others, the hot checks totaled more than $2,000. With my record, the district attorney saw a chance to throw the book at me. She charged me with the state felony.

They said later my judge was, under the circumstances, lenient. He convicted me of a lesser misdemeanor, sentencing me to 180 days jail time. The sound of both my daughters' cries as they led me from the courtroom was the worst sound I'd ever heard. I watched my mother and grandmother comfort them. I couldn't even make eye contact. I was transported to county jail and taken to a cell I would share with one other prisoner for the duration of my stay. Six months. The last thing I remember was the sound of the cell door closing.

Apparently, I collapsed – crying beyond control. The caseworkers decided my behavior warranted psychological attention and I was assigned a therapist. Our first session was memorable. I was seated across from DeeAnn Wallace, a woman in a crisp cream-colored suit, hair perfectly done, nails polished a solid red.

"I understand we're having some problems adjusting to our new situation," she started.

Her notes would later say I was belligerent and uncooperative, unwilling to listen or participate in my recovery. All I knew was I couldn't take some precious, educated chick in a suit using the "our" pronoun and that condescending tone. "We" weren't in jail. I was. I spent the first session with my arms crossed, glaring at her as tears streamed down my cheeks. "Whatever" was my one word mantra.

After the session, alone in my stale cell, with no air conditioning, I felt my own sweat trickle down the inside of my scratchy, gray jumpsuit. My cot smelled sour. I stunk. I had all these odors in my nose – commercial grade pine cleanser, my dirty hair, perspiration. I began to cry again until I couldn't anymore.

The next session, Ms. Wallace changed her tone. She asked me if I could think of one thing I could do that could make my life worse than it was right now.

"Sure," I whispered, "I could haul off and hit you. I could throw your stapler at you and they'd add more jail time. I could never see my girls again."

"Excellent," she said. "Then perhaps you're open to the idea that there's something you can do to improve your situation.

"Whatever."

Back in my cell, my roommate Sandra was on her bunk reading. She smiled when I came in.

"How'd that go?"

In her defense, she had tried to be friendly. I'd rebuffed every gesture. She was a trustee or something. One of those favored prisoners that got privileges and worked in the office filing. She closed the book and handed it to me.

"Read it." Sandra said.

"I'm not –"

"I know you're not interested. I want you to read it. Your attitude, whatever got you here, you need this."

I put it on the shelf above my bed, curled up and went to sleep.

In therapy, Ms. Wallace asked me to explain to her how I'd ended up in her office. Too worn out to fight her anymore I just told her.

"Do you know how some people are born lucky? That's not me. I was born unlucky. I come from a whole family tree full of unlucky women. Go back four generations and you've got the same thing. Every man we love leaves us. It's our destiny. The first man I ever met got me pregnant and disappeared. The next womanizing alcoholic made me his punching bag. The last predator took everything I had and got me thrown in here."

Ms. Wallace only nodded.

"That's it. That's all there is to say. I tried and tried and tried to make a good life for myself. I've been waitressing since I was fifteen, about all I could do without any higher education. So? I decided to be the best one I could be. But every time I pulled myself an inch off the floor, some man came along and knocked me right back down. I'd try again and wham! Down I'd go. I can't wait to see how much further I can fall in life, Ms. Wallace. I'm 33 years old, in jail, my kids are taken from me, my own family wants nothing to do with me, I can't --"

"Donna. Stop. Just stop. Whose fault then is it? If we're going to place blame, where do we place it?"

"Let's make a list!" I offered sarcastically. "We could start with my family, my mom and her mom and her mom for the great example they set, the great start they gave me in life. Then we could go through all the sperm donors. Oh, then, Mr. Armijo who wouldn't give me a chance just because my kid got sick; that creepy landlord,

7

the DA. Pick one. There's plenty of blame to go around.

"Huh," she said. "So, you're a victim of circumstance."

"Yes, I guess I am."

Back in my cell I was angry and frustrated. At least Sandra had a job. All I had was useless therapy to get me away from the tiny chamber a couple of hours a week. I was going to go out of my mind long before my six months were up. I picked up her stupid book titled *"The Secret"* by Rhonda Byrne.

"Oh, please." I moaned. It was probably some bodice-ripper romance about a pirate and a captive. Still, there weren't a lot of options. I started browsing. It was worse than I thought. It was a self-help book. I set it down.

At the next therapy session, Ms. Wallace was all business. "Donna, let me ask you a question. Is there anything you could have done differently?"

"Like be born to a different mother? That would've helped."

"No, seriously. I want you to make a list of choices you've had and choices you've made. Next time we get together I want to discuss those with you."

"Dr. Wallace, I don't think you've heard a word I've been saying. I haven't had any choices. I got dealt a lot of sorry hands. End of story. Just help me survive this and get out of here. That's all I want from you."

"Ah, but Donna, I want so much more from you."

I went back to my cell crying and barely able to breathe. I told Sandra about my assignment. To my surprise she broke out in a big grin. I asked her what was so funny.

"The Universe, girl. The Universe. When She wants your attention, She's going to get it. Right now, I think she's got yours. You've got to work on your list. If you want to talk, I'll listen. Have you started reading the book?"

"It's not really my thing. Maybe later."

"That's okay, girl. You'll read it when you're ready."

It took a couple of days to finish my list of choices. I didn't like what I saw. I shared it with Ms. Wallace.

"What did you see when you made this?" She asked, after reading my list.

"That I had more choices than I realized. That I made some really crappy choices. Those stupid choices led to stupider choices. That brought me here. So, I guess you could say, I brought this all on myself. So, when -- if -- I get out of here, I can look forward to a life of crap."

To my surprise, Ms. Wallace laughed, long and loud. Beaming, she said, "That'd be a choice, then, wouldn't it, Donna?"

This was getting me nowhere. I got back to my cell emotionally drained and Sandra had moved the book from the shelf to my pillow with a note by it. "Try again."

And I did. Having spent so many hours looking at my life choices, I found myself very receptive to the idea that I could make new ones. I chose to read the book with an open mind. I read until mealtime and after. I read until Sandra came in and we talked about the book until lights out.

In the middle of the night, I was still awake thinking. I sensed Sandra was awake. I climbed on her bunk. "So it's possible, right? If I'll change the way I think about my life, about me, I can change what happens in my life?"

"Yes, Donna. I believe you can. I've been working the Law of Attraction for a year. Hard work. Faith. Believing a better future for myself than circumstances say I can have. I was transferred from the women's prison upstate to here. I was given a position of trust. They've already shaved several months off my sentence. A year ago I would have told you none of that was possible."

"You've been lucky, Sandra." I whispered.

"No, Donna. It's not luck. I'm fortunate – but I believe the good things that have happened have everything to do with my concentrating my mind and thoughts on good things happening for me."

I couldn't wait to tell Ms. Wallace. See what she thought.

"I'm very familiar with the book 'The Secret' and the Law of Attraction. I think it dovetails nicely with the work we are doing here, Donna. Either you are a victim of your circumstances or you orchestrate them. Do you want to lead the orchestra of your life or sit in the audience and just see what plays out?"

In the weeks that followed, my therapist and cellmate helped me heal and grow. I read and re-read the book. I didn't make any overnight changes but I did become very aware of my thought patterns. I recognized that I was a very negative person. I dwelt on the dark side of everything. I hadn't ever considered how good my life had been, when at one time, it was very good. I needed to forgive my family and myself.

"Donna," my therapist asked, "why didn't you just move in with your mom and grandma when things went south?"

"Seriously? You mean again? How many times had they already bailed me out? How was I going to go back and ask for help again?"

"How many times would you help your two daughters if they needed it?"

"A billion times. All they'd have to do is ask." I said.

In that instant, I realized, I had underestimated my mom. I hadn't even tried to talk to the girls or her since I'd been jailed. I couldn't face them, didn't want them seeing me here. I was so ashamed. In Ms. Wallace's office the weight of that shame and the loss of my girls overcame me again. I cried from the depths of my heart. From the deepest depths where hope resided and gave me the optimism that I could make my life great.

Later, I called my mom. I begged her to forgive me.

"There's nothing to forgive, Donna. There's nothing you've done your grandmother and I haven't done or worse. We'll help you. The girls are fine. You'll be fine. You'll stay with us when you get out, just concentrate on getting out, okay?"

I did. I concentrated on getting out and the life I wanted to have when I did. I focused on creating a good life with my family. Not a mansion on the beach, but a nice, safe home. With a puppy and a yard. And a good job. In our last meeting, Ms. Wallace made me promise to make small improvements every day.

"Just focus on the next choice, Donna. Our lives are comprised by our choices. One right choice, woven with another and you'll have a beautiful tapestry. Remember, you are not your past."

I'd been in jail 90 days when my Grandma Lois passed away. On Dr. Wallace's recommendation I was given permission to attend the funeral and a provisional early release. Mom inherited the dilapidated family home and was stunned when a realtor told her how valuable the land was. Mom sold it and bought a nicer place with a little yard, and my daughters, Rex the puppy, and I moved in with her.

Mr. Armijo was more than happy to help me get back on at the

Velvet Tortoise where I'm now night manager and doing exceedingly well. Sandra will come to work for me when she gets out next month.

I thanked her for changing my life.

"You made that choice, Donna. You made that choice."

Closing Thoughts

Ah, the blame game. It can be so much easier to blame others for the failures in our lives than to take responsibility for them!

Please don't take that statement the wrong way. When you are born into generations of family that have played the blame game, you may have never thought that there was any other way. Like all those before you, you truly believe you were born unlucky. What you don't realize is that, like Donna, you are making a choice. In adopting the attitudes of those who came before you, you are forecasting your own ill-fated destiny.

Go ahead and make a list like Donna did. Examine your past and review your choices. Is it possible that if your attitudes and actions had been better, you might be in a better place right now? I'm sure you'll agree that the answer is yes. But please, don't beat yourself up. You were brainwashed. You were surrounded by negativity and you didn't know that living could be any other way. So really, a lot of what happened to you was not your fault.

However, from this point forward, you are one hundred percent responsible for the outcome of your life and happiness because you read this book. You know that there are other possibilities out there – good ones with happy endings. And those happy endings are yours for the taking. All you have to do is use the power of your mind and consciously make each choice for the betterment of your future.

Right now, at this very moment, you can begin to change your life. This is not to say that if you put a smile on your face today you will win the lottery tomorrow, and the entire future path of your life will be a bed of roses. Think baby steps. Challenge yourself to have a positive attitude one day, all day long, no matter what comes your way. When you've been programmed to think otherwise, being able to do that can be a mammoth accomplishment. Break it down. Take it hour by hour.

When something in your day throws you a curveball, that's when you have the power to make a choice. You can either say, "See? This positive thinking stuff is a crock," and go back to your old ways, or you can decide that you're going to get through it with a positive mindset and do whatever you can to achieve the best possible outcome at that very moment. I know it's not easy to stay positive in challenging moments, but what's the alternative – continuing to live your life like an unhappy victim?

It's time to wake up. Stop right now and take a few deep breaths. Inhale all the abundance you want to see in your life and exhale the negative past. It's time to start your life again. Make the choice – today -- right now – to claim the happiness and good karma that the Law of Attraction and the power of positive thinking can bring. It's yours for the taking. It's up to you.

GRATITUDE CHANGES YOUR LIFE

"A thankful heart is not only the greatest virtue, but the parent of all other virtues."
~ Cicero

"You're not leaving already? You just sat down."

"No, man, I gotta get some sleep," Kenny said, swallowing the last of his second beer. "Maybe you can stay up half the night and greet the commuting public, but not I, good sir, not I." He gave me a very dramatic bow and walked away. Then he turned back and said, "You might want to consider turning in yourself. Nothing good is going to happen here after a third beer, hear me?"

"Yes, Mom," I said, in a suitable whine.

Damn, like I needed one more person weighing in on how I should be living my life. I could've stayed home and gotten another lecture from Princess Tina. We'd already been married five years and it seemed like a death sentence. Who could blame me for wanting a little sedation at the end of the day?

Kenny. Wow, had he changed. Mister straight and narrow. Ken and I had practically grown up together and we both started at the railroad shortly after we turned eighteen. His dad had been with the old Santa Fe line forever. He brought Kenny on and then Kenny brought me on. We'd both be able to retire with a boatload of pension and benefits before we turned forty. "If we live that long," he used to say.

For years, Kenny and I were frick and frack, the dynamic duo. We called each other "Scorp" because we were just like scorpions, if you saw one, the other had to be close. We stood up for each other at one another's weddings, no matter how many times we were asked to. We bid on the same jobs so we could work together. We had almost seniority dates, so that wasn't hard to arrange.

I liked the overnight turnarounds best. We'd leave the station about 5:30 p.m. carrying commuters down the "Corporate Corridor" to their suburbanite cul-de-sacs one to three hours away. The next morning we'd schlep them back to their cubicles and desk jobs in the big city. It was easy work, easy money. We only put in about eight hours total, but got paid for two full days plus the night shift differential. It was like earning double time all the time.

Kenny didn't like being away from his wife overnight and of course, Princess Tina has a royal fit about it. She sure liked the money I brought in, so the way I saw it, she could keep her mouth shut.

I ordered another beer and a whiskey shot chaser. Kenny was right, I did need to call it an early night at least once this week. Mornings could be brutal. Sometimes I barely got to bed before the alarm went off. We had to be at the station at 4:00 a.m. which wasn't that big a deal, the hotel they put us up in was right around the corner, but that still meant getting up around 3:15 a.m. to get cleaned up and ready to go. Sometimes, I didn't even bother to change uniforms.

I surprised Kenny getting to the station before he did. "Whoa," he said, feigning complete shock. "So hell did freeze over, look who's on time for once."

Our shift went smoothly. All the passengers were in a good mood. They usually were on Fridays. No problems. No lost tickets or rail passes. No one trying to pull anything. As I walked up and down the aisle I played my usual game in my head, picking up my next conquest. I hadn't actually pursued anyone since Tina and I made it official, but I was always looking.

That's how Tina and I met. She was a non-rev passenger on one of my turnarounds. When I asked her to show me her ticket, she smiled her million-dollar smile, batted her long lashes and said, "I'm afraid, Mr. Conductor, I can't find it right now." She was coming on to me and we both knew it. I was used to being the aggressor. I hadn't even come up with a good opening line.

I told her I was going to give her a pass and went on to collect the rest of the tickets in the last two cars. When I came back I asked if she'd found her ticket. That's when she showed me her railroad I.D. I grabbed a coffee from the club car and came back and sat next to her. We talked the rest of the trip into the city.

In the beginning, I don't think any two people could have fallen harder or faster than we did. I'd already been married twice and was definitely not looking for anything serious. She'd just broken up with a married man and wasn't looking either. But, chemistry, man, what can I say. She got me. She was volatile and high energy and funny. She had a good job working for one of the railroad execs and she'd been with the company about as long as I had. She wasn't sending out those needy cloying signals.

Both Kenny and I had kind of a reputation for being players. Before he'd gotten together with Connie he was even worse than I was. He was always on the hunt for an attractive female bed partner. If a new passenger boarded, someone we didn't recognize as a "reg" or regular commuter, he'd get my attention, point her out and mouth, "Dibs."

He always liked to tease me that he'd said "dibs" first about Tina. But there was no question I saw her first. She was petite and small-framed. She had long, curly brown hair and super long eyelashes fringed over these big brown eyes. She could stare right through me. From the second I saw her I felt something different. Something possessive, like she was some kind of a china doll and I had to have her.

We met on my last shift before my two-week vacation started. We made plans to have dinner that night. We went to a steak and lobster place right on the water and right from the beginning I know we both felt something. We both kept saying we didn't want any big deal relationship but our relationship became a big deal fast. We slept together that night and every night after. Since I was on vacation, I'd pick her up when she got off the train from work and we'd spend every minute together. I'd ride with her back to work in the morning and then take a train back home and get some rest then we'd do it all over again.

She was impulsive and reckless and crazy too. She'd get on the train with me after she got off work and ride whatever route I was on, just as long as she could be back to work in the morning. She kept a bag packed always, ready to go. I loved that about her. She never pressured me to be with me. She didn't have to. I wanted her with me. Until I didn't.

I don't know what happened, really. She had invited me to a big company dinner party, some retirement deal for one of her bosses. It was very la-di-da and invitation only; black tie, the whole nine yards. I told her I'd go.

Maybe it was the whole showing up as a couple thing. I suddenly felt like I was going to be her Ken doll for the evening. I wasn't a formal wear kind of guy. It was all getting too serious too fast. I was supposed to meet her for drinks downtown before the soiree and I didn't. I called in sick to work and then made arrangements with a buddy in scheduling to bid on a route where we'd never run into each other.

I ignored the dozens of calls and texts and the next day I changed my number. I'd ditched chicks before. The guys on the job kind of covered for each other. We had sort of a code, no information to wives or girlfriends without express permission. We could be very hard to find.

Of course, I forgot all about her working on the job. She had all kinds of connections and had no trouble finding me. She waited a couple of weeks and showed up on the station right before my train was leaving. I was just pulling up the steps when I saw her. All she said was, "Can you at least tell me why?"

I couldn't even think of a reason. The doors closed and I didn't have to come up with one. I went back to my former life, drinking with the guys after work, picking up girls. I really didn't miss Tina, but she missed me. My condo was on the other side of the city about an hour away from the train station. One day I got a call from a number I didn't recognize. When I answered, it was Tina. She was taking a training class nearby and wanted to know if I wanted to get a drink. I met her at a bar downtown and we just picked up where we left off. She didn't bug me about what happened and we just moved on. Until we didn't.

And that became our pattern. We perfected the on-again-off-again relationship. I initiated every break up and I got pretty good at getting

16

her back. But then, once we were back together I didn't want her around. She used to say, "Damn it, Cale. Just as soon as it starts to get good you throw a switch and wreck it. You can't stand to be happy. You must be allergic."

We probably would have been done for good. Each time we broke up my behavior was a little worse. Almost like I wanted to do something so bad she'd never come back. I had a fling with a waitress at the hotel where the crew stays. She was cute, convenient. She sexted me some pretty hot pictures of her. I never deleted them. Tina found those and ended it. I've never seen her so mad. "You're a loser, Cale. That's bad enough. But you're making me one too."

A few months later she called. "Here we go again," I thought, smiling. We agreed to meet at a coffee shop, instead of a bar. She said she wasn't doing alcohol. I wondered what that was about. I hoped she hadn't gone all religious on me.

The hostess took me to her table. As Tina came back from the ladies room I could see we'd have one topic to discuss. It was out of my mouth before I could stop myself. "You've been busy, whose is it?"

"Not funny, Cale." She sat down and very calmly explained she was five months along, keeping the baby, thought I should know. She expected support, but didn't want to make a big production of it. She'd been hoping we could handle it without a lot of drama.

In that moment, all I could think of was I was going to have a kid. It was a typical, how can I make this an all-about-me-moment. I haven't done a lot of things right and my first two marriages were disasters, but a kid needs a father and parents should be married to one another. I asked her to marry me right away. She was less than ecstatic.

"I'm not sure, Cale. What would be any different if we got married? We get back together, you'll be all Mr. Romance, until one day you wake up and decide you want to be single again. This was a bad idea. I never should have told you." She threw a twenty on the table and got up to leave, saying "I got breakfast. I don't want anything from you, Cale. You just don't have it to give."

You might say that I took that as a challenge. I decided to win her back and I did. I surprised her at her office with a ginormous stuffed teddy bear with a ring on a ribbon around its neck. We got married

17

on the train, took a long honeymoon and settled down. Until we didn't.

I was opening the mail one day and came across a credit card bill from a company I didn't recognize. When I saw the balance on it I couldn't believe it. I confronted Tina about it and she said she had responded to a credit card offer that'd come in. It was at a great rate with no interest the first year and she didn't think I'd mind.

"It's in my name, you stupid idiot," I screamed.

"And, I'm paying it with my own money you Neanderthal control freak!"

That was one of our calmer exchanges.

We stayed married. Five long years and a kid in first grade. We stayed together. She ran up credit card bills and wouldn't tell me. I'd pay them off and then cheat on her. Then I think she cheated on me. Then Tina just got too tired of the game to play anymore. "Look, Cale. I don't know that we can make this right, but I'm going to stop everything I've been doing to make it worse."

I went back working turnarounds so I'd be gone over night. Tina worked part time days but she never came with me on the overnights anymore. I was behaving myself but didn't think that was going to last much longer. I was lonely and resentful.

That's what I was talking to Kenny about that night in the bar. Every night, it seemed, I was complaining to Kenny about my marriage.

"You know what your real problem is, Cale?"

"No. O wise one, what pray tell is my problem? Enlighten me."

"You can't you get you off your mind."

"What are you talking about? Been watching Oprah again?"

"I'm serious friend. Night after night you have the same story to tell. You know, if nothing ever changes, nothing ever changes."

"Quick, bartender," I said. "Some paper and a pen please, I gotta write this down."

"Just saying', Cale. Sometimes, when the same things keep happening to you no matter who you're with? Maybe the problem's the guy in your mirror. What is this, marriage number...?"

Suddenly, I didn't feel like drinking anymore and I didn't want Kenny's wisdom, advice or company. I went up to my room and fired up my laptop. In a minute there was a knock at that door. It was

Kenny, he had a book in his hand.

"Look, you don't want to hear it, I know. But this book helped me more than I can ever tell you. I wouldn't be your friend if I didn't at least pass it on to you. That's all I'm going to say on that."

"*Love Dare* by Stephen & Alex Kendrick?" Whatever. I shut the door, threw the book on the couch and went back to the computer. I'd much rather check out some chicks on the on-line dating sites than curl up with a dumb book some Dr. Phil wannabe wrote. I guess I had the book's title on my mind, because I entered "Love Dare" into the search engine instead of "Love Match." Here we go. It was a bunch of hocus-pocus about doing something nice for your spouse every day. Great. I'll just bring Tina a dozen roses every day and we'll live happily ever after.

I turned off the computer and went to bed. But I couldn't sleep. I kept hearing Kenny: "If nothing changes, nothing changes." I turned on the lights, picked up the book and read until it was time to get ready for work.

I got home and Tina was out. I sat down at my desk and opened the mail. Another credit card bill, I thought she'd stopped that. It was only $20, but the point was she'd said she'd stopped. When she got home, I forgot all about the exercise I was going to try from the book Kenny had given me. All I could think of was how mad I was about the bill.

I hit her with it before she even set down her purse. I went on for five straight minutes without drawing a breath. She never said a word. I asked her to explain herself.

"I didn't charge anything, Cale. I haven't charged anything on any credit card it your name or mine for more than three years. If you'll look close you'll see it's the renewal of the annual fee. I'm going to go pick up Jeremy from the sitter."

The door closed behind her. She was right. She had bent over backwards trying to make me happy. She never looked at another guy, and I'm not sure she ever even cheated on me. I think she had an emotional affair with a guy at work, just a friend she could pour out her heart to. But when I threw a fit she transferred to another area. That's how she was, I'd throw a fit and she'd do double back flips to fix it, but I'd always find one more thing that was wrong with her.

That night I asked Kenny more about the book. I'm not a big reader and it seemed so complicated.

"Let me break it down for you, Cale. Even you can do this, Bro. All you have to do is watch and be grateful. Tina's not working tomorrow, right? Great. As soon as you get home tomorrow morning start paying attention to all the things she does for you and Jeremy. See, Cale, you can focus on the good or the bad. It takes the same amount of effort. Instead of picking fights or looking for problems where there aren't any because you're in some sorry mood, look for something, some one thing good. Focus on that and say 'thank you.'"

"That's it?"

"Yeah, that's about it. I imagine even you can't screw that up. Oh, and think about switching to days, man. These nights wear me out and Connie really likes me home in the evening with her."

When Kenny got up to leave, I went with him. I got a good night's sleep and went straight home from the station. Tina was vacuuming when I walked in. She couldn't hear me over the noise. I watched as she went about her housework, unaware that I was home. She had her earbuds in, rocking out to her music as she dusted the living room. As she picked up one of Jeremy's toys off the floor she did a little twirl. She carried it into his room and started straightening his bed. I watched her happily singing along to some song.

She looked up and saw me and sort of jumped back. "You startled me, I didn't know you were home. Was I making too much noise, are you trying to rest?"

I caught how her face fell when she'd seen me, and how all the light went out of her eyes. "No, not at all. No. Just, just do what you do. Don't let me stop you."

"Okay, if you're sure," she said carefully. We stood there awkwardly.

"Uh, Tina." I wasn't even sure how to say it so it didn't sound completely lame. "Thank you for vacuuming."

She stared back at me like I'd just grown a second head. After a moment, she mumbled, "Okay."

I went to the den, shut the door and called dispatch and scheduling. "Hey, Cale Barton, ID 6868019. Yeah. Let's see if we can find me a day shift."

Kenny, as expected, was thrilled to be back on days. "Connie calls

20

it her twelfth honeymoon," he said. But, he added with a grin, "She's wearing me out. How's project thank you coming along?"

I explained how uncomfortable it felt. He told me he'd felt the same way. "You know, I think tough, macho, don't-need-anybody guys have a gratitude muscle, but it's all weak and wimpy because we never exercise it. Like any muscle, the more we use it the easier it gets and the stronger it gets. Make sense?"

"Well, sort of. I guess I'm only discovering what a complete jerk I've been. We've been together this long and I'm only starting to say thank you?" Is that what the whole book is about? One hundred and one ways to say thank you?"

"Well, sort of." Kenny said, laughing. "More, it's about what we talked about. It takes the same amount of effort to focus on the good as the bad. It's about making choices. Choosing the good. In everything—your job, your marriage. I think it also taught me to consider Connie, first. You know, my whole life I've always acted like the world was one big party being thrown for Kenny Hardigan's benefit. Now, I try to think a whole lot less about Kenny and a lot more about Connie."

It's been two years since I switched to days and started exercising my gratitude muscle. The whole thank you practice just snowballed. The more I found to be thankful for, the more thankful I became. It took time, but slowly the light's come back in Tina's eyes.

Now, I have more to be grateful for than ever. The uncommonly beautiful woman you see parking that SUV is my talented wife Tina, next to her is our handsome and brilliant fourth-grader Jeremy. Oh, and in those matching pink car seats? Our twin blessings, Kinsey and Cassie.

Closing Thoughts

Gratitude. When was the last time you gave the word any thought?
It's a funny thing, gratitude. It's easy to remember we want it, but it's hard to remember to dole it out. It's sad, in a way because gratitude is paralleled to our happiness. It's like every day we're the little kids at a special holiday occasion, and we haven't learned manners yet. How old were you before you realized that, when it came to gifts, it really

could be better to give than receive? Now, apply that concept to gratitude. Are you there yet? On most days, many of us aren't anywhere near there. How else would an entire generation in America have been dubbed, "The Me Generation"?

I here today to tell you to start small. Pick one person to thank today. Thank them again the next day, and the next, and the next. Once it becomes a habit, start again with another person. Practice this habit enough and you will innately realize that you feel grateful for all of the good things that have been done by the people around you. Your outlook will change. You will begin to see life's glass as half full, when it used to appear even less than half empty.

Yes, the world can be a terrible place. There is no shortage of violence, hunger, illness, and crime. Your spouse, your kids, your job – they all can have bad moments, for sure, but if you choose to focus on that at the expense of all else, you will never know what it is like to live, for even one day, as a positive and fulfilled human being.

So thank your partner. Thank your children. Thank your parents. Thank your bosses, your co-workers, your subordinates, and your friends. Can it change your life? Well, it worked for Kenny and Cale, and I know it will work for you too. In fact, it will change your life.

THE SERENDIPITY OF TIMING

"Sometimes our fate resembles a fruit tree in winter. Who would think that those branches would turn green again and blossom, but we hope it, we know it."
~Johann Wolfgang von Goethe

As promised, my precious daughter Jennie gave a shout when she was ready to head back to college. She had just stopped by to pick up a few more things. The family and I had tackled the big move-in earlier in the month. Classes had already started and she just now had her first long-weekend break. She'd been a tad homesick, but couldn't wait to get back. "I don't want to miss a minute," she'd said. Dave and I had raised a pretty independent kid.

I could hear her voice ring out from the driveway as she was pulling out: "Mo-om, I love you, I'm leaving." I sat at the kitchen table sipping on the dregs of my morning coffee, her words echoing in my head. Words I'd heard when I was almost her age all those years ago.

At Jennie's age I should've been in college too. That had been the plan. My earliest memory was of wanting to go away to a big name school with a great football program. I earned good grades and had a stack of acceptance letters from several schools. I had scholarship offers to most of them. For a while the biggest decision I had to face was which one I'd pick and what colors I should get for my dorm room.

In fact, I was shopping for pillows when I pulled into a parking space in front of a popular upscale retail store promising all things bedding and more. So was Jake—the very *same* parking space. Had I not pulled the steering wheel hard to the left I would've hit him. I may not have hit Jake, but he sure hit me, like a ton of bricks; every dreamy, good-looking, bad-boy-on-a-bike inch of him. He was tall and when he pulled his helmet off, he revealed the prettiest long brown hair I'd ever seen on a guy or a girl.

He told me I had to take him for coffee. It was the only decent thing to do since I'd almost killed him. Laughing, I reminded him it was the other way around. "Lucky for you, I'm a good forgiver." We went next door and I can still remember how the waitress stared at him when she took our order. She never even acknowledged me. She kept finding reasons to stop by and ask if he needed anything. He, on the other hand, couldn't seem to take his eyes off of me. He had a way of staring with this laser focus, like he was absorbing my being. No one had ever looked at me like that.

I had dated in high school, not a lot and not anyone seriously. I was always too busy for a relationship. I ran around with a big group of friends and social life revolved around class functions, choir, my part-time hostess job and church. Looking back, it seems like my life was all P.J. (pre-Jake) and after. Almost like two different lives. We didn't have much in common, but I found him fascinating. He regaled me with all of these exciting stories of traveling around the country on his bike and all the odd jobs and odd people he'd encountered. He was irreverent and bold and made my whole life seem so unadventurous, predictable, and boring. My life up until then had been pretty predictable. I came from a great middle-class family. Dad worked, Mom stayed home and raised the three of us kids. She volunteered and had a million hobbies, but it was so...common. I was looking for a lot more adventure than a cul-de-sac, a husband, and two-point-five children.

So, when Jake nearly collided into my life, I was ready for some "unexpected." He gave me that. From that first coffee we were inseparable and it wasn't long before our relationship got physical. I had no sexual experience to speak off, but he made me feel like the most alluring seductress ever. I found him irresistible. What little time we were apart I spent thinking of the last time we were together and what we were going to do the next time I saw him. My mother said,

"You're becoming obsessed with this boy," and I was.

The week before I was to go up to college for freshman orientation, Jake asked me to move in with him instead. He convinced me school could wait six months, but we would never have our "new love rush" again. "That's the best part of real love, Marley," he'd tell me. "We can't miss this." So the pretty new sheets I'd bought for my dorm went on the bed in his room at the cramped, messy rental house he shared with two other guys. I told myself it was cozy. My parents were crushed and expressed their disappointment in me loudly and often. Jake convinced me to stop calling them and taking their calls. "I just don't want them to hurt you, baby. If they really loved you they'd be happy for you. Don't worry about them, I'll take care of you." And he did.

He moved us to an even smaller apartment, about an hour further away from my family, closer to the city where he said it'd be easier for him to find work. He worked crazy hours, nights, mostly, temporary shift-work. I'll give him that, Jake was a hard worker. Sometimes he'd work seven days in a row or take double shifts, telling me he had to because the overtime pay was too good to turn down. I felt so guilty. Him, slaving away, paying all the bills, rent, and utilities while I contributed nothing.

Once, I suggested that I start looking for a job. That didn't go over well at all. Jake got real upset, saying he wanted me to be available to spend time with him whenever he was off work.

"Listen, babe," he'd tell me. "My job is work, your job is to keep me happy." When he suggested I sell my car it just made sense. It's not like I needed the transportation, he reminded me. The almost new Nissan my parent's had given me as a graduation gift would really help us out. He drove the car to a dealership downtown and I handed over the money to him, hoping he wouldn't have to work so hard.

After we made the deal, we rode his motorcycle over to one of the classiest restaurants in town and he treated us to a lobster and steak dinner and a bottle of wine. I drank most of the wine while he kept ordering whiskey and water. We were both pretty tipsy when we left.

I woke up in the hospital. I had a broken arm and a concussion. They kept me overnight for observation. My first thoughts were, "What happened? Where's Jake?" The nurse told me he had refused treatment and left. She said they'd called his pager number several times. Sedated, I slept most of the next day. When they released me, I waited around in the reception area for two hours before Jake finally walked in. I was never so glad to see anyone in my life. He swooped me up his arms and saying, "There's my princess, let's go home." We took the bus. His bike was impounded. I never got on it or any other motorcycle ever again.

After the accident, Jake worked harder than ever. He explained most of the money from the sale of my car had gone to hospital bills. We didn't have insurance. The rest went to his attorney to fight the DUI charge. He was convicted, had to pay a huge fine and that ate up the rest. With a DUI on his record, he was disqualified from several of the driving jobs the temp agency had been giving him, he said. That's why he had to work more hours than ever and there never seemed to be any money.

When he got off work he'd come home, eat something and go to sleep. Then he'd get up, we'd watch some television or play Scrabble. Jake loved to watch sports—boxing, car racing, and soccer. Every once in a while, as he was flipping through all the channels on the remote, I'd catch a bit of a college football game. That always made me a little sad. I tried not to think about that part of my life – P.J. I didn't like to dwell on what my life could have been. I was with Jake. It may not seem like we had a very romantic life, but to me, at the time, it seemed so. We were in our own little world. Jake was my world. As long as he was around, I had everything I ever wanted.

When he wasn't around I was terribly lonely. Jake hadn't moved us to the safest neighborhood, and I didn't feel comfortable walking around it by myself and I didn't like riding the buses at all. Besides, where was I going to go? All my friends were away at college or had married and were starting to raise families. I spent my time reading, cleaning our apartment, preparing meals and scouring the newspaper for coupons, trying to stretch our money so Jake didn't have to be gone so much. I worked crossword puzzles, watched old movies on TV and waited for him to come home.

Money was tight. We couldn't afford a telephone, as much as I wanted one. He'd say, "It's a luxury we can't afford," or "Are you trying to make me feel guilty for not providing you every extra? Aren't I doing enough?" He used to give me spending money, but all of a sudden he stopped, saying he was getting a handle on our finances and trying to save up for a surprise he had for us. I was losing myself, diving deeper and deeper into solitude. I had no friends, I blended into my life like a still image of art on the walls.

One night, he didn't go to work like he usually did. When I asked him why, he just went crazy. I'd never seen him like that. He just exploded, yelling, calling me names. "After everything I do for you, it's never enough, is it? I try to take one day off and you are on my case. Well, you want me out of here? That can be arranged." He stormed out, slamming the door behind him.

It was our first real fight. I tried not to argue with Jake. If I disagreed with him, even over something minor, he'd raise his voice or sulk. Sometimes he'd pout for a day or two. It was just easier to go along and get along. Besides, working non-stop had to be draining. No wonder he was so touchy. I could always find some excuse for how he acted. When he didn't come home, I started to get anxious. I asked our neighbor a few doors down if I could borrow her phone. She was surprised I didn't have one in our apartment. No one had a cell phone back then. If you had a mobile phone in your car then you really had money to burn. I called Jake's pager over and over and over. I waited at the neighbor's for hours. He never called me back.

I stayed up all night, scared to death that something had happened to him. Before I left my neighbor, I'd checked with the local hospital to see if he'd been in another accident. I was always terrified he was going to lay down that motorcycle again. I was almost going to call my parents, but what could I say? "Hi, it's me, your darling daughter. You know, the one that gave up her dreams and is shacked up with a guy who just called her such a bad name she can't even tell you what he said. Yeah, the one who sold your graduation present, the one who..." No, I didn't call my folks, I just sat on the couch panicking. What if he didn't come home? I didn't have any transportation, no money.

I was so relieved the next morning when I heard his key in the door. I didn't know whether to run and throw my arms around him or pick up an ashtray and throw it at him. One look and I could tell he'd been drinking. He couldn't even look me in the face. I lost it. I started hurling a million questions at him like some kind of crazed interrogator. He just ignored me. My voice kept getting louder, more

27

and shriller. I watched as he pulled a duffle bag from his closet and start emptying his bureau drawers, tossing socks, undershirts, underwear into it. My stomach tied in knots, all my attempts to thwart his packing were useless.

He moved to the closet and calmly started pulling out hangers with shirts and pants, putting them on the bed. I stood up on the bed and started jumping up and down, hysterical. Screeching and sobbing now, "What are you doing? Tell me what you are doing. Where are you going? I love you."

He never stopped moving. He just kept putting clothes on the bed, selecting some and putting those in his bag. He looked up at me finally and said, "I love you, but I can't take this anymore. I'm leaving."

I don't really remember the rest very clearly. I remember the begging. I actually got on my knees and begged him not to leave. Even after he told me he was moving in with an ex-girlfriend. Shannon something-or-other. Apparently, that's where he'd been the night before—and many nights before. He was very casual, very matter-of-fact, and then very gone. He mumbled something like, "It sure was a great first love rush."

Sometimes, all these years later, I can actually feel that feeling – that knot in my stomach. I can still hear my howling.

There would be more to cry about in the days ahead. I spent the whole first day leaving tearful messages with every friend of his I'd ever heard of. I knocked on every neighbor's door. I called the bartender at his favorite haunt. I paged him thousands of times. I cried until I brought on a migraine and cried through it. I went to medicine cabinet for an aspirin or something stronger and found it cleared out. I cried some more.

I heard a noise at our door and leapt to it. I knew he'd come back. Instead, it was our landlord. He had just finished posting an eviction notice on the door. "I didn't expect anyone was still here," he said. "Y'all keep taking down this sign, doesn't stop the clock you know. Thirty days is thirty days and you're down to four. You better have your stuff out. Next time I come back it will be with the sheriff and we'll lock you out and sell your possessions for what is due. That's the law. That's what I told your husband."

I didn't correct him. I thanked him, politely, and shut the door.

Wearing the same clothes I'd had on for two days, I finally went to bed. I didn't get up for a while.

When I did, my first thought was the trouble I was in. No car, no job and now, no place to live. I didn't even have the funds to grovel my way back to my parents. Jake clearly was not coming back. I can remember wanting to cry, trying to cry, and not being able to get any more water out of my eyes. I was utterly cried out. I knew in that moment of hopeless loneliness that I needed to find myself again.

I went to the bathroom and opened the cabinet under the sink. Way in the back was where I kept my personal hygiene supplies. I emptied the box of tampons and found the $20 I secreted away for emergencies. "I think this qualifies," I said.

I showered, dressed, and went to the local convenience store and picked up some groceries and a Sunday newspaper. I needed a job, a place to live, and a way to get to both. I went home and made a plan – something I had never done before. In the morning I would start with the temporary agency that had helped Jake.

Bright and early I headed out. I mustered the courage to board the bus to downtown where the temporary agency was located. When they called my name I was ushered into a tiny cubicle. A woman about 40 asked me how I'd heard of them. I told them about Jake. Imagine my surprise. They'd never heard of him.

The agency may not have helped Jake find any work, but they certainly helped me. They tested my secretarial skills and apparently I could 10-key, keyboard, type, add and subtract enough to render me "highly place-able" – at one dollar over the minimum wage, less state and federal taxes, FICA and insurance. "You are very bright, Miss Wilbanks" the placement counselor offered. "Did you ever consider going to college? College graduates are eligible for premium pay hourly rates."

I didn't cry over Jake for a while, but I did cry for myself. I cried for the woman I was supposed to be, the woman I knew I was, and the woman that I lost along the way. I had no choice but to get busy cleaning up the mess he left me in. My life became a matter of urgent priorities. First, I needed some place to live, then I needed some way to get to the jobs the agency would send me on.

Some might say I was courageous, I just think I was desperate and desperate people can get pretty brave. The temp agency said they could arrange it so that all of the jobs I'd be sent to were in the same geographic radius. I found an apartment complex right downtown that had a sign reading: "Ask About Our Free Move-In Special." I asked and moved in. Everything happened in robot mode until I walked into a car dealership nearby. As I waited for someone to see me, a guy around 50 came out of his office, hand out, big smile on his face. He looked familiar. "I remember you!" He said. "You're the Nissan Maxima kid. I helped you sell your car a few months back."

"Can I have it back now?" I said, forcing a smile. And then, holding back tears, I told him everything. He must've felt sorry for me. I left there with a gently-owned, 13-year old Buick and the chance to work the car lot on weekends. "You seem like a bright girl. I think you could have a future here, but if I were your dad I'd suggest you go to college and get your degree first. And if I'm not overstepping my boundaries, I think your boyfriend leaving you was the best thing that could have ever happened to you. It may not feel like it now, but one day it will."

I drove home that day as his words marinated in my mind. As I parked out front of my own little apartment, I looked at my reflection in the mirror and for the first time since Jake walked out that door, I actually believed that I would be okay. That night I cooked myself a box of macaroni and cheese and sat on my living room floor. I was completely alone, but there was a new energy in the air—a new energy of possibilities and I no longer felt lonely.

For months I worked 7 days a week, just like I thought Jake had been doing when he was obviously out doing something else. He'd left me with more questions than answers and a stack of unpaid hospital bills. He'd taken out credit cards in my name and it was months before I had could arrange to settle those. The longer I went without seeing or thinking about Jake, and believing in myself the stronger I got. I immersed myself around people and slowly regained a new outlook on my life.

Turned out, I was really good at sales. Eventually, I made enough money on the weekends and didn't have to work for the temporary agency. I went to work full-time for the car dealership. My boss kept encouraging me to go back to school and finally offered to pay half my tuition. I studied business at the local community college. One of my professors was a man I had worked for on one of the temp assignments. His name was Dave Anderson. He taught economics and used all these neat analogies to explain concepts. "Life is all about economics," he'd say. "Whatever you want in life, you trade something else for it. The secret to life is to make really smart trades."

I graduated with my associate's degree and went on to earn a bachelor's too. My parents proudly attended both graduations. I kept working my way up the ranks of the dealership. One day, I saw Dave Anderson in the lobby. He was ten years older and looked just the same as I remembered. I recalled he was married, with two little girls. "Don't tell me the little one is ready for her first convertible?"

"I remembered you said you worked for this dealership," he said. "Thought I'd see if you and I could make a really smart trade." Dave bought an Audi and would stop by regularly to have it serviced or with some question. He'd been widowed two years before. He and I started dating—slowly. This time I was financially independent with a hard lesson under my belt, so it was comfortable and easy and right. We married and together we raised his two daughters and added two more to the brood.

Sometimes I shiver with the goodness of it all. Occasionally, I'll think of Jake and wonder what happened to him. I confess, once I tried to find out about him on the Internet. Morbid curiosity, I suppose. Once, I thought I caught a glimpse of him outside a bar downtown. Mostly, I wondered how I could have lost myself so completely for such a lying loser.

I took a big detour on my life path. Gratefully, the Universe is very generous with second chances. Course corrections are just a matter of making the next right choice. That's what I learned on my journey and in Economics 101. Along the way I made some pretty stupid trades. I traded in a lot for Jake—my independence, innocence, my car, my self-esteem. But then I started to make better trades. I learned to invest in me. I traded long hours and little sleep for a degree and a great career. The sign outside the dealership now reads, "Wilbanks Classic Cars: When You're Ready to Trade Up."

Closing Thoughts

Are you waiting for "serendipity of timing," for something

31

unexpected to bring you good fortune? Maybe that's not the best idea. It certainly wasn't for Marley. For certain, Marley thought her chance meeting with Jake was serendipity. What were the odds of the two of them meeting any other way? Of course, as a young girl wanting adventure and romance, this chance meeting seemed as if it was meant to be.

Marley most likely would have been much better off considering the economics of life. Had she thought about the fact that she was trading her college education for "new love rush," she may not have made such an impetuous decision. You might argue that Marley's life wound up fine in the end – she wound up getting her college education, married a wonderful man, and happily raised her brood. Regardless, Marley most likely could have taken a much less painful route to a happy life had she not misinterpreted her chance meeting as serendipity.

Conversely, who would have thought that Jake's leaving Marley was, in fact, serendipitous? At the time, Marley felt that Jake's leaving was the worst thing that could ever happen to her. But as awful as it seemed, it was this act that initiated Marley's brave struggle to reclaim her life as her own. If he had never left, Marley could have lived captive to a verbally abusive man for the rest of her life.

So back to the question . . . are you waiting for "serendipity of timing," for something unexpected to bring you good fortune? Are you at a low point in your life, hoping that good fortune will bail you out? Forget about hitting that lottery, be brave like Marley, and make your own luck before you are forced into the change.

YOU ARE LIMITLESS

"Twenty years from now you will be more disappointed by the things you didn't do than by the ones you did do. So throw off the bowlines. Sail away from the safe harbor. Catch the trade winds in your sails. Explore. Dream. Discover."
~ Mark Twain

I'm not sure how much time had passed. I'd had my index finger poised over the SUBMIT button for a while. It sat just to the left of its twin, the SAVE button. I'd been opting for the right side of the screen for days.

Good grief, you'd think there was a million dollars riding on the outcome of this one action. I exhaled. It's not like I didn't make decisions every day. That's all life came down to, wasn't it? Decisions and choices, one right after the other. For the life of me I couldn't understand why this one had my gut in such a knot.

I don't know how long I'd been holding my breath. I exhaled slowly and practiced my deep breathing. In, one-two-three, out, one-two-three-four. For some reason I couldn't make myself just hit the stupid graphic and be done with it. There was nothing more to tweak, nothing more to research, perfect, analyze or obsess about. Still, my long manicured digit hovered.

While I waited for my breathing to work its magic, I thought about my journey here. It'd been a great life so far. Some might say, charmed. I grew up in a typical suburban community. I was raised by parents that found each other late in life after failed marriages on both sides. They were, for lack of a better word, "ga ga" over each other. If I had any complaints about my childhood, and I would have to dig to come up with some, it was they were so over the moon for each other there wasn't always room for me. An only child, I spent a lot of time in my room, day dreaming, playing with my dolls and my imaginary friends.

Both my mom and dad worked. He was an engineer for the space program and mom had a successful home-based business selling all-natural cosmetics, vitamins, essential oils, and household cleaners. We never wanted for money. They had the resources to send me to any university in the country and I certainly had the grades for admission, but they insisted I pay my own way. That wasn't a surprise.

My parents always encouraged me to work for the things that I wanted, first, saving up my weekly allowance I received for completing a dozen chores like laundry, carrying out the trash, setting the dinner table, loading and unloading the dishwasher.

I used those funds to buy the Bob Mackie designer edition Barbie, my first iPod, and makeup. At 15, I talked my way into an interview at a new coffee shop opening up in our town. I was the first in the line of applicants. I may have changed the last digit of my birthday by a year. I worked as a hostess 20 hours a week, earning minimum wage. I felt like a rock star.

When I really was 16, I was accepted in a bank internship program. It was a way to earn partial college credits while gaining experience in the work force. It seemed like a very important job. I got to dress very professionally and learned all of the back room duties like research, bookkeeping, and customer service. I worked part-time after school until I graduated.

I was working for the biggest banking company in the country, First Union. I got along with the branch operations office and she made a place for me when I graduated. I worked for her as a full-time teller my first two years of college, saving enough to transfer to a bigger university a couple of hours away. With the help of student loans and a transfer to a branch near campus, I was able to continue my education and the job I enjoyed.

I carried a full load of classes and worked 40 hours a week. It never occurred to me I couldn't do both. I was a pretty determined

34

young woman and I never expected anyone to pay my way. It made a difference in my outlook, that's for sure. I stayed in the dorms my first year away at school. Most of my dorm mates were partying into the wee hours most nights and I rarely joined them. I was too tired when I got off work if I'd wanted to and when I wasn't working at the bank I was in class or studying.

Just before graduation, I was recruited and qualified for a management training position at the bank. I would spend six months in San Francisco at their corporate headquarters. It was a fast-track exposure to all of the financial institution's key departments: trust, lending, leasing, and operations. After the six months, I would be assigned a junior management position in one of the branches.

After working full-time and going to school for so many years, "just" working seemed so easy. I never complained about the hours and often volunteered for projects and assignments no one else wanted. I loved the hum and energy of working at the company headquarters. The offices were deluxe – like something out of a movie set. There was travertine marble on the walls and floors; gilt elevators moving sixty floors up.

Early on, I entered a company productivity contest and won first place and a chance to have lunch with some of the bank executives in the private dining room at the very top of the First Union building. The dining room only held about 30. I was seated at a linen-draped table set with baccarat crystal, sterling silver utensils and fresh roses. The china looked like it could chip if I sneezed. I sat straight back in my chair, hands folded in my lap, scared to breathe.

I'd asked my mom what she thought I should wear. "Blend, blend, blend," she said. "Now's not the time to stand out, blend. You are being offered a rare opportunity, just watch and learn. And remember, you can never go wrong with navy blue.

My father suggested a bolder choice, "First you want to dress for the job you want, not the job you have. Wear red. You want them to remember you. And wear the pearls I bought you. Always wear the pearls." I could see the wisdom in both their approaches and went for the middle ground and the pearls. I hoped I made a good decision.

A group of executives were ushered in – commanding men – all silver hair and Armani suits. Gold watches and collar stays. I was glad

I had splurged and spent money I didn't have, using every bit of credit on my store account buying a black sharkskin suit, a cream silk blouse, stockings and three inch leather pumps. I'd be a year paying off that bill.

When everyone was seated I found myself between two of the highest-ranking executives at the bank. Linn Hargrove was on my left. He was the Executive Vice President and head of all of the bank's branches. On my right was Geoff Caldwell, Senior Vice President and Director of Personnel. I certainly knew them by sight. I had made a point of memorizing the names and profiles of all the executives.

I have what you could call a chameleon personality. I guess it stems from having such diverse "blend, blend" versus "stand out" parents. Whatever situation I'm in, I naturally find a way to stay comfortable and make those around me feel at ease too. That day at the executive dining room, I tried to play the role of modest newbie, just thrilled to be there.

Apparently, I held my own. A couple of days after the luncheon, my training manager, Nancy Morgan called me into her office.

"Sit down, Steph," she said. "Got some good news."

It turned out the personnel guy had noticed me. So had some of the other execs and not because of my wardrobe as it turns out. My employee suggestion, the one that had won me the nice luncheon had apparently saved the bank a ton of money. Geoff Caldwell phoned Nancy to discuss an opening he was working in branch facilities. He thought I had the background and personality for it. It was an entry-level position doing a lot of number crunching. Branch facilities handled every aspect of opening and closing the bank's then 3,000 branches nationwide.

I went to work in the Methods Research area, basically a think tank for devising uniform standards and implementing cost saving measures. If you could find a way to save money at one location and multiplied it thousands of times, you could really make an impact.

Hard to believe that was eighteen years ago. I was blessed to find a job I was good at that paid me so well. The promotions and raises came before I could even dream about, want or appreciate them. For the past several years I've headed the facilities arm of Mergers and Acquisitions. When First Union takes over another financial institution, and it seems like that happens every Monday, I look at the redundancies – the overlap. Sometimes First Union already has a branch in the same location as the bank we acquired and we need to shut one of the branches down. Or, we'll be acquiring a branch in a whole new territory and I need to oversee training the other bank's staff in the First Union operations and culture.

It's challenging work. When I first came to the department, I worked closely with Geoff. He was adamant that we find "homes" for the displaced workers, absorbing them somehow rather than laying them off. Geoff was one of the most considerate corporate types I'd ever run across. When he accepted a position and promotion with another bank, he invited me out for dinner to say goodbye.

Which turned out to be hello. "Since we're no longer going to be co-workers," he suggested, "there wouldn't be any reason we couldn't see each other, would there?"

It was a natural progression of a great friendship and that segued into a wonderful marriage. Geoff and I have a ten-year-old daughter, Julie, who has inherited all of our good qualities and none of our bad. If I have a problem with her it's that I miss her so much. My job takes me away from home way more than I'd like.

Doing what I do means crazy hours, overnight travel and weekends away from home. I'm not proud of the fact that I have missed almost every important event in Julie's life. When we acquire another institution, sometimes it's by government order. A bank may be in trouble or on the verge of insolvency. When that happens we have to be onsite to change the locks and change the name. It's all very regulated and not subject to schedules and planning. I've missed many first days of school, plays, and winning soccer goals. As Julie approached her tweens, I worried about not being available for her.

One morning I heard her talking with her Dad. He has the luxury of a regular schedule and never misses an event. I envy their closeness. She was filling him in on a summer soccer camp she was hoping to attend. I was finishing my makeup and walked in to the breakfast room where they were making toasts with the smoothies Geoff has made. "To soccer camp!" Geoff said, touching her glass.

"Soccer camp? Well, tell me, what am I missing?" I asked, unprepared for Julie's response.

"Everything, Mommy." She said. "You always miss everything."

I turned before she could see my expression, but I caught Geoff's. He winced like someone had hit him. He knew what that comment did to me. My precocious daughter wasn't being cruel She was just stating the facts.

In the bathroom I pressed a hand towel to my face, trying to staunch the flow of tears. I had to finish packing, I had a flight to catch and two back-to-back "ramp ups" to handle. Those were the fun assignments, readying a brand-new facility for their grand opening. They were a lot of work but everybody involved was usually excited and enthusiastic. It was the best part of my job that offset a lot of the sacrifices, yet I couldn't quit crying over Julie's words.

I remember clearly that particular flight. I had been so distracted by Julie's remark I left my iPod and reader on the kitchen counter. Normally I used the time in the air to get caught up on my reading for work or pleasure. I always had about for four books going at a time. It was going to be a long flight.

My briefcase was in the overhead. I could get it down and pour over the ramp-up protocols, but I knew every step by heart. I reached into the seatback pocket for one of the airline magazines. That'll kill at least 30 minutes, I thought. When I reached for it, I noticed a paperback stuffed down at the bottom of the pocket. I pulled it out and read the title: "Infinite Possibilities" by Mike Dooley. I liked the title. I was hoping it wasn't a steamy romance novel. I wasn't in the mood for that kind of reading.

The flight attendant came by to make sure we were all buckled in. He noticed the book in the seat beside me and asked if it was mine.

"Actually, I just found it. I was going to turn it in." I said, handing it to him.

"No, don't worry about that," he said, refusing the book. "Go on, keep it. You're in for a ride. That book right there changed my life. I always wanted to be doing this, but never dreamed I could." He said, gesturing about the cabin. "I read that one book and here I am. Listen, my name's Jim, and I'll be back to check on you."

Well, thankfully that ruled out bodice ripper, I thought to myself. Once we were in the air I picked up the book and started reading.

My flight landed in the early afternoon. I'd been so engrossed in the book I hadn't even noticed our descent. No meetings were scheduled for today, it was a slug of free time to rest and prepare for an early call in the morning. Everyone was to be downstairs for the shuttle to the bank at 6:45.

I'd already decided I'd be staying in. I could run like the energizer bunny but I learned to take advantage of downtime and recharge this bunny's battery. I stopped at the hotel gift shop for a couple of bottles of water and some ibuprofen. I always got a headache when I flew and I'd left my bottle of pain relievers on the kitchen counter with my reader.

The gift shop was very nice. It had everything I could ask for, including some tasty-looking croissant sandwiches. I grabbed one of those. Next to the travel-sized shampoos and razors I saw a display of stationery items. There was a darling journal by the artist Leigh Stanley. On the cover was a drawing of a giant peacock and a caption that read: "Have only one rule: Be your wild, courageous, brilliant self every single day. No matter what."

Huh. There were three adjectives I'd never use to describe myself. I bought my sandwich, the water, and the journal, and went up to my room for the night. My head was throbbing. I remember wondering whether that was really due to the flight or my thoughts tumbling around like a large-capacity dryer.

Dooley's book had given me a lot to think about. How we have choices and options and sometimes all that's stopping us is our perception of what's stopping us. Years ago, before life got so crazy busy, I used to keep a journal. I'd use it to write down the events of my days or to sort out my big life questions. I was looking forward to some sorting out. The thoughts running around in my psyche were so confusing to me I wasn't even ready to discuss them with Geoff, and we discussed all our deepest thoughts and fantasies. I couldn't even describe the stuff I was thinking about. If I had to label it, it was dark, whiny, what-am-I-doing-here angst. I felt foolish and ungrateful for even having discontent.

I had a great marriage, great daughter, and a great job. People like me? People blessed with everything imaginable? No, I don't think we get to whine. I was too tired to read and too tired to write. I channel surfed and caught the last few minutes of Joyce Meyer, the popular televangelist I liked to watch from time to time. She always had some practical wisdom on living a better life. She was talking about thoughts, too: "Where the mind goes, the man – or woman – follows." Then, "You know you can spend your whole life climbing that ladder of success and discover all the time you've had it leaning against the wrong wall."

That did it. It was like the whole universe was provoking me – first Julie, then that book "Infinite Possibilities" by Mike Dooley, now Joyce Meyer. All my life I'd done the right thing. I worked hard, made my way in the world. Why was I in a hotel room in Cincinnati, Ohio with tears streaming down my face? I loved my job, but what was I missing?

The rest of my life.

Still crying, I ran a hot shower. I hoped the water would wash the tears and this increasingly down mood away. This was ridiculous. When I got home I'd talk to my doctor. Maybe I was having some super early pre-menopausal meltdown. I had a great job with a fabulous salary, a 401K that matched 50% of my contributions, health, dental, and vision insurance, a company car, five weeks paid vacation. "Yeah, crybaby." I scolded myself. "Walk away from all of that."

I had been either/or-ing for years. To me, I could trade my current life for another one. This or that. All or nothing. I could see now I hadn't been making a place for other possibilities and there were lots of them. I picked up the journal and started writing down everything I wanted in my life. Instead of "or" I made myself think in terms of "and." And, and, and, and, and.

For six months I wrote my wild thoughts and crazy imaginings. Some "ands" were fleeting. Some of my hopes and wishes were tenacious, appearing day after day. I rediscovered what writing did for me, not only was it a release, it was like oxygen. I was positively buoyant when I wrote. No, I couldn't quit my six-figure job and just write, but as I learned long ago, I was good at doing both – I worked *and* went to school. I worked *and* raised my daughter. Why couldn't I work *and* write or work and change the world?

I seemed to be flying all the time. Often Jim, the flight attendant, would be on board. We'd talk about "Infinite Possibilities." He was very encouraging. I filled journal after journal with dreams. I saw how often I wrote about wanting to spend more time with my family. I underlined every time I wrote about that. Other familiar themes were

40

writing and travel then out of nowhere another pattern. Significance. The work I was doing was important to the bank directors and stockholders. Sure, my work impacted the employees, but it didn't make a difference in the world. I realized, I wanted my life to matter.

I bet a lot of people were feeling exactly like I was. I started writing about that. I wrote a blog about the search for significance in an ordinary life. I wrote every day. I wrote about finding life-changing books on airplanes, about collecting journals. I wrote vignettes about life and lessons learned and questions that still looked for answers. I built up a respectable tribe of about 1,000 followers.

I had written more than two hundred blog posts when the email came in. It was from the editor of a popular women's magazine asking for permission to publish one of my blogs as an essay in an upcoming issue. She encouraged me to publish a book of my essays and told me she thought there'd be a real market for them.

Last week I was traveling to Raleigh, North Carolina for another branch opening. I was excited. This was going to be my last ramp up. In two weeks I start my new job heading up a brand new division. I'm going to be Senior Vice President of Corporate Giving. In addition to having regular hours and being home for my family, I'll be spending my days brainstorming ideas on how to raise money and then allocate those funds to help various charities in a host of ways.

As I boarded the plane, I saw Jim. I had a feeling we'd be running into each other. Giggling with delight I reached into my briefcase for a surprise I'd been carrying around just for him. Inside the front cover I'd written: "to Jim in the skies, a really great dreamer and a very good friend."

The book I gave him was mine. That day at the keyboard? I was trying to decide whether to submit it for publication. It seemed like such a big and crazy dream then. Turns out, it was, and it also made a terrific book title.

Dream Big, Dream Crazy by Stephanie Gruber. It's been on the New York Times bestseller list for eleven weeks now. Because life doesn't have to be either/or. It can absolutely be both.

Closing Thoughts

Are you looking for purpose in your life? Perhaps you've had to make your own way in life and you've been too busy just trying to make the rent each month to even worry about purpose. Perhaps you've spent most of your life fostering the success of others. Perhaps you've had a smashingly successful career path like the banker in this story. There are many paths that may lead us to that moment in our lives when we notice that something is missing, but I'm here today to tell you that you are limitless.

Very often this point in time, when you realize that you want your life to have more meaning, can be thought of as the "tombstone revision" moment in your life. Someday when all is said and done, do you want your tombstone to read: "Your name here – he always got the rent paid?" "Your name – she raised kids and helped her husband climb the corporate ladder?" "Your name – she helped a bank make money?" It's not that any of these accomplishments aren't worthwhile. It's much better that you got the rent paid than if you hadn't, it's a wonderful achievement to successfully run a household, and good performance at your job brings us full circle – it's an essential thing to do so you can pay the rent. But now you're at that point in your life, like our banker, when you feel like you're at a crossroad and you need to do something more.

Good news – no matter what your current circumstances, you have the power to invoke change and find that purpose and happiness in your life! First, think about what it is you'd like to accomplish and identify a few possible goals. What is it you'd like to do? Only you can answer that question. Just as our banker wrote in her journal, take some time to search your heart and soul. Gather your ideas and determine a few avenues you might like to pursue. Then pick the one that is nearest and dearest to your heart.

Next, sketch out a path to your goal. How can you envision accomplishing your goal? What changes would you have to make in your life and are they realistic? Who among your friends and family might be excited to share in your vision and help support you along the way? If you think and think and you can't see a way to accomplish your goal, then perhaps your starting goal is too demanding. Scale your plan back and determine the very first step you would have to take to make progress toward your ultimate purpose. Our banker didn't set out to change the whole world at once; she simply started with the idea of writing a blog. Make accomplishing that first step your mini-goal for success.

Finally, you need to take action. Rome wasn't built in a day, and it certainly wasn't built by workers who sat still and watched the world go by. Write your first letter, make your first call, step your first step, blog your first blog. You may be amazed at how quickly the baby steps you take add up. And even if you find that you have to do some side-stepping and backpedaling along the way, you will realize that in taking these steps, you are living your life with the intention of making a positive change in the world. You will, in fact, be living your life happily with purpose.

LOVE YOURSELF AGAIN

"We are not lessened by our past – nor is our future's evolution limited because of it."
~ Kahla Kiker

It was a while before her tears stopped. We'd just spent 30 minutes we didn't have trying to find my littlest one's report card. She said she'd set it out for me to sign a couple of days ago, but couldn't remember where she'd put it. We looked everywhere and couldn't find it, which made her miss her bus and then I had to stop and get dressed to drive to her to school.

As I started digging through the pile of clothes spilling out of the laundry basket onto the floor next to my closet, Cindy started whining. "Where'd you put it, Mom? Teacher said we had to bring them back today or we couldn't go on the field trip." I tried to assure her we would find it, but she wouldn't let up. With her going on I could scarcely concentrate on finding something to wear. I finally found a white t-shirt but I couldn't wear that with the black bra I had on.

"Hurry up, Mom," Cindy said. "We're la-ate."

By now her whines were louder and every word was becoming two syllables. I heard my husband grumbling from the other room, "Like I can get anything done in this madhouse."

I stepped over the clothes, went into my bathroom and found a shift I could throw on. I'd put on so much weight lately it was hard

44

to find clothes that still fit, if I could find my clothes. I spied one sandal, but couldn't find the other. Fine, I'd go barefoot. I went out to the kitchen to grab the car keys. I'd started keeping them on the floor by the garage door so I'd always be able to find them. "Mo-om," Cindy wailed, "Hurry up." The keys weren't there.

"Would you two just get out," my husband hollered. "I'm trying to fill out an application here." Glenn has been out of work three months. He'd had a management job with one the local Save-Mart, but got crossways with his new boss and gotten fired. Ever since it'd happened he was always on edge and irritable.

I turned around to answer him and must have tripped over the dog's food bowl, sloshing water everywhere and scattering kibble in all directions. I went to the utility closet to get the mop, but when I opened the door everything stuffed away in there tumbled out. A can of cleanser fell, landing on my head just as I slipped on the wet floor landing face first by the dryer.

"What, now?!" I heard my husband, yell. I didn't know whether to laugh or cry. Picking myself up, I saw the car keys sticking out from behind the washer. I picked them up, put the wailing 2nd grader in the car and drove her to school. Even though I was a mess I stopped to talk to Cindy's teacher and explain about the report card. She gave me a withering once-over that made me want to disappear.

"I can bring it tomorrow," I offered.

"Tell you what, let me just print one out here for you to sign. Papers never seem to make their way back here when we send them home with Cindy. You know, in class she does real well, but the assignments we want her to work on at home, she never completes those."

I was going to try and explain but didn't have the energy. On the way home I decided to spend the whole day cleaning, no matter how long it took. I walked in the back door and surveyed the house. I didn't even know where to begin. I could start with the kitchen. I needed to get to the stacks of dishes in the sink; they were getting pretty rank. Before I could tackle those I needed to empty the dishwasher, but I needed to clear the counter first so I would have somewhere to put the clean dishes... I stopped. This was what always happened. There never was a place to start.

I went into the den and found Glenn rummaging through his

45

desk. "Can't we even keep a freaking pen around here? One that writes?" The desktop was littered with job applications, files, unemployment forms, mail, bills, potato chip bags, books, crushed soda cans, classified ads, half-empty coffee cups.

I walked back out shutting the door behind me. He could have his man cave. I went over to my son's bedroom. It wasn't any better. Kenny was in Middle School. He loved sports and was good at both baseball and basketball. I almost wished he wasn't. Both activities required special gear, uniforms, helmets, bats, gloves, balls, shoes -- and laundry, tons of it. That kid was a sweating machine. With games three times a week it seems like all I ever did was wash his stuff. I never could get the clothes from the dryer folded before he'd need them again.

On the floor was his basketball shirt. He hadn't been able to find it in time for last night's game. He wore one that didn't match and really stood out on the court. I overheard one of the other mother's make some comment about how she'd never make her son come to a game dressed like that. Made me feel terrible. He was such a good kid. I wished he could keep his room straight, but he was so busy with school and sports, when he came home all he could do was fall into bed.

I picked up all the clothes from the floor and went to his bathroom to see if there were any more. One look and I gave up on that idea, I'd need a hazmat suit to work in there. I took the clothes in my arms to the laundry room. I couldn't tell what was clean or dirty so I'd have to do them all. The spilled dog food, water, and everything that had escaped from the utility closet awaited me. Ugh. I moved into the family room and surveyed the scene. Every surface was buried in stacks of unread magazines, newspapers, fast food paraphernalia, plastic and Styrofoam and paper. I went over to bookcase. It was an antique Glenn and I had found on our vacation to Cape Cod, cherry hardwood with a pretty glass front. It used to be such a showpiece. Now it was just another place to catch debris.

I reached over to pick up one of the takeout bags someone had thoughtfully left on a shelf almost out of my reach. I smelled it before I saw it move. "Oh, my God," I shrieked. I dropped the bag and days old, unrecognizable half eaten food product spilled out. Tacos I think. The maggots were moving.

Hearing my scream, Glenn came running in. To his credit, he grabbed the mess without a word and carried it outside. He came back to find me on the floor, rocking back and forth, tears streaming down my face. "When did this happen? When did this all change? Why would anyone want to live this way?" I asked him, arms spread wide, gesturing around the room of filth and trash. He sat on the floor and held me while I cried. I didn't get any cleaning done. I spent the day depressed in bed.

The next morning I got up before the alarm went off and instead of going back to sleep, I felt the need to escape the hoards of mess in front of me. So, for the first time in forever I put on my walking shoes and went outside. The skies were just clearing from an overnight rain and the sun was coming up. I breathed deep taking the fresh air into my lungs. I had only walked about a block when my neighbor Carrie caught up with me.

"Hello, stranger," she greeted me. Carrie was probably the most cheerful woman I had ever met. I liked that about her, but sometimes it just was too much to take in. Nobody could be that happy all the time.

"It is so great to see you," she continued. Carrie and I used to be involved in a lot of school activities together. She was raising her grandchild who was a year ahead of my Kenny. Since my brother passed away I didn't do much socially. Truthfully, since my twin died I hadn't done much of anything.

As if reading my mind she asked, "What's it been now? Three years?"

"Almost. Will be this June 13th."

"Damn cancer. How are you doing?"

"Well, up until yesterday I might have said okay." With that little opening I began to cry. As we walked I told her all about the events of the day before – the report card, the fall in the laundry room. I left out the part about the maggots, I couldn't handle any judgment.

Carrie suggested I was probably overwhelmed and thought it'd be a great idea for me to get out of the house a little each day. She volunteered to be my official walking partner. We agreed to meet early every morning at the park.

I met her there the next morning at 6:00. "I'm a little out of shape," I warned her.

47

"We're going to take this real slow," she said. "I've helped a lot of folks start exercising or get back into their walking habit. The secret is to take small steps and make a little progress every day. Set baby goals before you set the big ones. The important thing is to set a goal and then start working towards it. Today, let's just try to go a half a mile.

That first morning we went the half-mile and I was so proud of myself I could have clapped. Carrie was encouraging like that, made me think I could do anything. She told me, "Tomorrow we'll go just a few steps more."

When I got back to the house I felt great. Just that little bit of exercise in the fresh morning air made me feel so good. I grabbed a giant lawn and leaf bag from the pantry and started pitching every bit of trash I could find. I set another small goal of filling up one bag and taking it outside to the trash. Only it turned into 4 bags and I could finally see my dining room.

The next morning I told Carrie how her "coaching" had helped me. For just a second I saw the look of alarm flash across her eyes when I described the amount of trash I carried out. If only she really knew what the inside of my house looked like – every room.

"Yep, that paper can be a beast. Sometimes I think it reproduces overnight. That day we walked a half mile and, true to her word, just a little bit more. "Remember," she said. "Baby steps."

I went home and filled up another three trash bags, did a load of laundry, cleared a small space on the counter, emptied the dishwasher and washed all the dishes in the sink.

It seemed morning couldn't come fast enough. I didn't realize how starved I was for conversation. Glenn and I somehow lost our ability or desire to talk anymore. First my brother Gary died and I didn't feel like Glenn had been there for me. Then he lost his job and the money problems started. Carrie was so easy to talk to. I started to open up to her about my marriage, the depression I'd been in since I lost my brother, and the house.

"You know, I hear you, Nicole. You've been through a lot. Sometimes when we get a lot of problems all at once all we can see are the problems. Tell you what, tomorrow's Saturday. Do you think you could come over to my house after we walk?"

I told her I could and then she made the strangest request. She

48

told me she'd make us brunch if I would bring her a dozen magazines. That seemed like a fair trade to me. Little did she know I probably had a hundred of them scattered around my home.

The next morning, after our one-mile walk we went to her place. I had brought over twenty magazines, curious to see what she wanted them for and thrilled to have at least that much stuff out of my house. I could actually see some of my living room coffee table.

We walked into her house and I almost cried. Her home was beautiful, like something out of one of my magazines. Absolutely immaculate, perfectly decorated, welcoming. The sad part was I could actually remember a time when my own house had looked like that.

As we were finishing a wonderful brunch, her husband Jeff came in from playing golf. He gave her a big kiss and then started clearing the dishes and running water in the sink. I jumped up and offered to help, but he wouldn't hear of it. "It's my job," he said. "Takes me no time at all. You girls go do your art thing."

We went into Carrie's den where she had a table all set up with neatly arranged craft supplies. White poster board, glue, scissors, tape, beads and all kinds of interesting pens and decorations. Also on the table were my magazines we'd unloaded from the car. "Ready to get to work," she asked?

Carrie had me flip through every magazine page by page and tear out every picture I liked or would want to be part of my imaginary perfect life. "It doesn't matter how outrageous, expensive or unrealistic. If you like it and would like to take it into your new life, tear it out. If you see a phrase or a word that appeals to you, tear that out. It might be a slogan from an ad. If it makes you smile or think, cut it out."

She worked beside me with some magazines of her own. Once in a while she'd look over and make a comment, like, "good job," or "don't think, just tear." Two hours later I had quite an assortment of images. There were pictures of pretty rooms, vacation destinations, beaches, jewelry, fragrances, furniture, bedding, dishes, gardens, and automobiles. I had all kinds of great quotes too. My women's magazines had all kinds of features on exercise and diet. Most of them with great slogans like: "What are you waiting for?" She then had me cut out the pictures and phrases from all my torn pages.

"We'll work some more if you want next Saturday," Carrie said, putting all of my pictures and word snippets neatly in a folder and sweeping the scraps and magazines into a trash sack and carrying it outside.

We continued to walk a little over a mile each weekday and on Saturday we met again for brunch. As soon as we were finished eating, Jeff came in to clean up. "You've got to teach them how to treat you." Carrie said. "We're always teaching others how to treat us, whether we know it or not."

We went to the den and she said, "Ready to play?"

She had a white poster board laid out for each of us. Beside mine was my folder full of clippings and between us all the craft supplies.

"I'm not very artistic, Carrie." I laughed.

"You can glue, can't you?" She went on to explain we were going to be creating vision boards. A visual way of organizing everything we want to have in our lives. I noticed she had cut out airplanes, cruise ships and pictures of luggage and cameras.

"You can put anything you want on your vision board, Nicole. But right now, I'm all about Paris. I've never been and I just think that needs to happen before I get too old to climb the Eiffel Tower.

As I started pasting my pictures onto the white board, I noticed how so many of my images were of clean, sparsely decorated, uncluttered rooms. I mentioned that to Carrie. I told her it was odd that that seemed to be what I wanted, but I sure didn't do a very good job of keeping a pretty home. I broke down. Sobbing, I told her how awful the house had become. The mess and how I'd try to get it straightened up and it had only gotten worse and worse in some terrible downward spiral. I even finally told her about the maggots. "God, Carrie, just don't bring in the cameramen, I mean I am not a hoarder."

With that, she laughed. She snorted and giggled until she was holding her stomach. Then I laughed. Then we both got into that crazy kind of infectious hysterics where you can't stop and you don't know why and the tears just fell.

"Okay. Think of it like this," Carrie offered. "You know how your mind can get jumbled with a whole bunch of thoughts going every which way? That's like mind clutter. And we both know, it's hard to find anything in clutter, am I right?" We both laughed some more. "First get your head clear and you can get your house in order, I

50

guarantee it. Now, back to gluing."

When I'd finished I had a mish-mash medley of beautiful images. As instructed, I glued them randomly. Interspersed among the pretty pictures were great thoughts. "I got this," was one of them. "Declutter Now" was another I'd cut out from the cover of one of the magazines. It was lettered in bold purple on an orange background. I centered that on my board.

We worked all day. Carrie had arranged for the kids to go to the movies together while Jeff and Glenn went to the driving range nearby. Surprisingly, when I broached Glenn with the idea of a grownup play date he was all for it. "I've always liked Jeff," he said. "He's fun to be around."

Carrie poured us a glass of wine and announced it was "time to sparkle!" With that she brought out a spray can full of some kind of adhesive and opened several vials of glitter. "This may be what's missing from both your vision board and your life right now, Nicole. You need some glitter. Get your sparkle back." She sprayed our boards and then showed me how to dust the shimmering speckles over my board. I loved the result.

Just as we finished, the men came in with the kids. Glenn was just beaming. "I forgot how much fun it was to hit a bucket of golf balls. And the driving range just happens to be right next door to Wally's pizza," he said, setting down three extra-large pies.

We took the pizza, some soft drinks, and a bottle of wine outside to the patio. Jeff and Carrie had a gorgeous backyard with a pool, lush gardens, even a waterfall flowing over rocks and stones. It was breathtaking. Carrie went inside and came back with a huge photo album.

She set it down where we could all see it. It was old and some of the pictures were faded. The tape on some of the images was cracked and brittle. "I've had this a long time," she said.

As she turned the pages of the album, my jaw just dropped. There were pictures pulled right out of magazines. Shots of couples playing together, golfing, riding horseback on the beach. Pictures of children at a park. There were ads for Hawaiian vacation rentals, homes, campsites, cars.

"For as long as I can remember I've been cutting out pictures of what I love and saving them. I look at them often. I really enjoy seeing what's happened over the years." As she turned the page she revealed an obviously dated picture of a scenic pool, rocks and a waterfall. "This was taken from our hotel room on our honeymoon. We always said one day we'd create something just like it."

"Yeah, I'm sure there's a picture of a guy in one of her high school dream albums that looks exactly like me," Jeff said.

"Yes, sir. I conjured you right up, my dear. That's what happens when you focus your energy on the positive. Now, Nicole, you need to find a spot for your vision board. Display it someplace where you'll look at it every day. Then, you just watch what happens."

That day I resolved to clean up my act, my attitude and my home permanently. Carrie suggested I set a kitchen timer for just 30 minutes and only work that long on any particular task. The first day after our pizza party I spent a half-hour cleaning around the fireplace, clearing off all the junk on the hearth. The timer went off and I kept going. I dusted and waxed and polished the mantle until it gleamed and it was there I put the vision board.

I continued meeting Carrie every morning for two and then three mile walks. Jeff and Glenn got to be close friends too. Jeff introduced Glenn to one of his suppliers and Glenn ended up going to work for the guy. He's making way more money now than he was at Save-Mart. Next year the four of us are going to France.

The kids loved the change in their mom and soon were volunteering to help out around the house. "I love to see you happy, Mommy," my baby girl told me one morning. "You sparkle."

"Yes," I heard my husband say from the other room, "she does." In the year since Carrie and I started walking, I dropped thirty pounds and have a home I can be proud of. I went from cleaning to de-cluttering to totally redecorating. I'm always amazed when I finish a new room and see how much it looks like one of the images on the vision board.

The original vision board, that is. I have several now. Every few months Carrie and I create new ones. "Always keep dreaming, Nicole," she tells me. "And pass the glitter."

Closing Thoughts

Are you a hoarder? Chances are, according to the textbook

definition, you are not. If you are a compulsive hoarder, a person who accumulates things with the inability to throw anything away, it would be good for you to recognize that and seek professional assistance. However, there are other forms of hoarding. Nicole was an emotional hoarder. For three years, she hung on to the sad feelings caused by her brother's death and refused to let go. She believed it was okay to live amongst the trash and chaos or rather she maybe deserved to live amongst it because her emotions were negative and depressing. This emotional hoarding drained Nicole of energy and motivation, which led to many other problems in her life. Her house was a disaster, her relationship with her husband was suffering, and her behavior had a negative impact on her children's lives as well.

What are you emotionally hoarding that is holding you back? Like Nicole, have you experienced an emotional trauma that has left you feeling empty? Has someone in your past treated you poorly, leaving you to feel unlovable or unworthy? Have you felt taken advantage of, to the point that it left you feeling unable to accomplish goals? If this is the case, you may be living with a victim mentality. The self-thought process of a victim is that, due to some emotional pain experienced in the past, you have lost your sense of self-empowerment; in turn, your impaired sense of self-empowerment devalues your sense of self-worth. What's worse, this victim mentality often takes the path of a vicious downward cycle. You feel incapable of progress, therefore you fail; this failure further bolsters your negative feelings, so you withdraw further.

Lucky for Nicole she found a friend in Carrie, a wonderful mentor who helped her learn to regain control and direction in her life. Most of us, however, do not live down the street from a friend with the gifts of insight, patience, time, and nurturing that Carrie shared with Nicole to get her back on her feet. So how do we fix things without a Carrie? It all begins with self-love.

Once you acknowledge that your sense of self-worth is not where it should be, the best way to counter that is to simply tell yourself that it is time to stop hoarding the feeling of worthlessness. Tell yourself that it is time to take out your mental trash. Kick it to the curb and move on.

This is not to say that you will instantaneously feel better and be able to leap tall buildings in a single bound. However, this positive self-talk will enable you to take a first step, just like Nicole. What is the first thing Nicole did? With the process of creating her vision board, Nicole cleared her mind, looked at her life, and figured out what she needed to do to change. She created a vision of her first end-goal: a well-organized, clean home. She also gave herself encouragement that she could accomplish the goal by latching on to phrases such as, "What are you waiting for," and "I got this." She then capped off her vision with glitter, symbolizing the beauty of the emotions she would feel when her goal was accomplished.

Once Nicole determined her vision and found her motivation, she set out that very day to tackle the whole problem at once, right? Wrong! Each day she looked at that vision board and each day she took baby steps toward accomplishing that goal. Before she knew it, Nicole had accomplished what she thought was impossible.

I know it can be overwhelming, so do what Nicole did, start with a small counter. Start with something – anything – big or small. Maybe the answer is not to do anything with the mess you're in, just walk away for a day and decide you won't add to the mess for 24 hours. That is still success!

So what is holding you back? Does some pain in the past cause you to feel a lack of self-worth? Let it go! Love yourself enough to envision the change you want in your life, and recognize that you are capable of accomplishing it. Take a moment or take a day, but then get up and create your vision board, find your motivation, and take those baby steps. Before you know it your true happiness will have returned and you'll be living the life you imagined, and you will realize that you are a person worthy of self-respect and love.

LIFE IS RIGHT IN FRONT OF YOU

"To live is so startling it leaves little time for anything else."
~ Emily Dickinson

It was a Tuesday when my 3-year-old grandson woke me up and changed my life. The late morning sun was already streaming through my bedroom window when I heard my cell phone chirp, announcing I had a text message coming in. I rolled over to check the time. Even without my glasses I could see the super-sized red numbers on the digital clock by the bed. They read 9:50. Good lord, I hadn't intended to sleep the day away.

Gary must've been extra quiet when he left, I thought to myself. I'd slept right through. I attributed it to the prescription the doctor gave me to help me sleep. The medicine worked but left me feeling so tired and groggy. I grabbed my glasses from the nightstand and read my message. It was from my daughter Annie. "Carston wants some face time with you. Are you up?"

I connected us on the app Annie had installed on my smart phone. Face time, space time, something. It allowed us to physically see each other while we talked. In about a minute I could see Carson's beaming face. He was waving at me wildly saying something like: "Gwammy, Gwammy, wuhtzdinzahwooldzgwointowiddu?"

"Well, he's just as precious as ever, Annie," I said. "But I can't make out a word. What's he trying to say?"

"Listen hard, Mom. He's been practicing it all week."

The 3-year-old was certainly doing his very best to be understood but I hadn't a clue. "I give up, what?"

He's saying, "Grammy, What in the world's going on with you?

Annie must have been teaching him that expression. It used to be my favorite, my signature phrase. That had been my greeting to my own children from the time they were in the crib. That's how I woke them for school and the first thing I'd say when I'd see them again. I would be so animated and excited when I'd say it. I hadn't been animated or excited in a long time. I never even saw my kids anymore.

You would've thought at least one of my five grown children might have settled down close to home, at least in the same state. Annie's a stay-at-home wife with four kids of her own. Her husband Bob is career military and stationed overseas. The twins, Dennis and Danny, live about four blocks from each other on the other side of the country. They had a family business and all of the in-laws and outlaws played some role in it. Terry's an attorney in D.C., he's always in court or getting ready to be, and Leslie, my youngest, is a pharmaceutical rep. She travels so much she really doesn't live anywhere at all.

I took a few minutes to pseudo-talk with my daughter and the baby. I'm normally pretty vain about my appearance, but when those two want to get face-to-face I don't care what I look like, just so I can see them. I know from experience how quickly 3-year-olds turn 30. Hard to believe my baby has been on her own this many years. Where in the world did the time go?

I knew Gary and I certainly spent a lot of it traveling. Gary owned his own professional placement service, jetting all over the world recruiting hard-to-find specialists in medical technology and research. Over the years he'd racked up more frequent flyer miles than we could ever use in a lifetime. He loves his work and it's unlikely he'd ever retire, "I'd be crazy to give up a job I like mine. I love chasing great talent. I'd do it for free."

Our 44-year marriage was, by most standards, a good one. It certainly had been a good pairing of our talents. I always wanted a big family and felt exceedingly blessed to have children that grew up healthy and smart. Not that the teenage years weren't a challenge, they were, but everyone survived and as I liked to say, "So far, no one has a psychiatrist on speed-dial."

I was often asked if I thought I gave up a lot for Gary and the kids. What was there to give up? Motherhood was my life's calling, I was good at it. I was a good wife too. Gary never had to worry about the house or the bills. I did all the scheduling and entertaining. I kept everything in order, took care of all his travel, made all the arrangements. I even handled all the bookkeeping for his company and our family until his business got so big we needed to hire a full-time CPA.

Gary has always been generous financially, I never wanted for anything. When the house was full of the kids and their friends, I never really got a chance to miss him – even though he was gone an average of 300 nights a year. But once the last bird flew the coop, I began having bouts of real loneliness. I never would have thought loneliness could feel so awful.

Sometimes, after Gary left for the office or to meet some of his buddies at the club and I knew he'd be gone all day, I'd go back to bed. I mean for the day. Yes, I'd seen a doctor about it. First it was some sort of menopausal malady and then it was empty-nest syndrome. Then it was anemia and then I was tested for Epstein-Bare, fibromyalgia, multiple sclerosis, Parkinson's. I was scanned and poked, x-rayed, MRI'd, prodded and had my blood tested dozens of times. No one could come up with a diagnosis. But whatever label you wanted to put on it, I didn't really feel like being awake.

I tried to snap out of it. But every morning I woke up to the emptiness that had become my life. "The void" I called it. That morning, when I ended the call with Annie and Carston, I dragged myself to the bathroom to get ready for the day. Annie said I dressed like an old woman. I didn't need to hear that. I thought I dressed fine for my age. I chose simple tailored, classic clothes from popular designers. I stood in front of my walk-in closet for I don't know how long. I had all the clothes a woman could want, but all I saw was another decision to make. I went over to the bathroom sink to splash water on my face and caught my reflection in the mirror. God, I wondered, when did I get so old.

The face staring back at me was drawn and haggard. Dark circles lined my eyes. My skin was gray my hair was gray. I was a gray old woman. And I was too tired to wash my pathetic face. At that moment all I could hear on continuous loop was little Carston's voice asking me, "What in the world is going on with you?" Not a single thing, I thought. Not one single thing. I went to bed, pulled the covers over my head and stayed there.

I woke up and could hear my husband on the phone with our son Dan. It was dark outside, I could tell. I didn't even want to know what time it was. I burrowed further beneath the covers, straining to catch some of their conversation. Gary's voice was full of concern and frustration. "I don't know what to do, Danny. She's having another one of her spells. I thought today was going to be a good day. But then, I always hope she's going to have a good day." And, then: "No, there's nothing you can do. Heck, the doctors don't even know what to do. I'll see if she wants to go somewhere. Sometimes she rallies when she has a trip to look forward to. But I don't know if that will even work. She won't discuss the future. She won't discuss anything. It's bad son."

I wished I hadn't overheard any of that. The last thing I needed heaped on top of me was guilt. Did every one think I wanted to feel like this? I wanted to cry but that was going to take more energy than I had in me. I took another sleeping pill from the bottle on the nightstand, rolled onto my stomach and went to sleep. My last thought was: "See, Carston, this is what in the world Grammy's doing."

The next morning I forced myself out of bed and feigned as much of a smile as I could. I assured Gary I was feeling better. That's what he wanted to hear. His sigh of relief confirmed he'd believed me. I drug myself through the process of bathing, dressing, and eating breakfast with my husband. He was leaving for a four-day trip and I didn't want him worrying about me. I made as much small talk as I could stand and sent him off to airport.

I made myself get out of the house. I needed to pick out a wedding gift. The couple was registered at a nice boutique in town. I'd get the present taken care of and come home. I was looking at some of the bride's selections when I heard my name.

"Mrs. Lindale? Is that you?"

I turned around to see Ashley Davenport, Annie's best friend from forever, all three of her kids in tow. She said, "Wow, I almost didn't recognize you." She must have seen my face fall for she quickly caught herself, covering and saying, "I mean, how long has it been, right?"

I knew what she meant. I saw her expression. She'd recognized me all right; she just couldn't believe I looked like I did. I let her off the hook. "It's okay, I've been under the weather. How are you? Chasing after those three must be exhausting."

She said they did keep her pretty busy, but she was also quite involved as a board member for the Chamberlain House, a privately funded facility for special needs kids and young adults.

Now, I was the one to look surprised. Why in the world would she waste her time there? Her children were perfectly healthy and probably kept her plenty busy. As if reading my mind she volunteered, "It's a pretty important project. I mean, here I am blessed beyond measure and right here in our very own town there are so many families suffering. Believe me, I can find time to help them. In fact, I better find time right now. I've got a board meeting starting less than an hour. Hey, it was great to see you, Mrs. Lindale. Tell Annie I said hi."

I watched her leave the store, her brood following her out like baby ducks. It made me think of my own kids when they were that age. My own five baby ducks. Suddenly, I didn't feel like shopping anymore. As soon as I got home I stretched out on the couch and went to sleep.

Days passed, and then months. My moods did not improve. I thought, briefly, of going back to the doctor or getting another opinion, but there just didn't seem to be any point. I felt like I was literally disappearing. My husband was doing great, my kids were all healthy, happy, and busy with their own lives. I was – irrelevant. Invisible. Nobody needed me, nobody saw me. I was just taking up air and space. Happiness, I decided, is for someone else.

From time to time I thought of Ashley. Ashley was not invisible. She was a tour de force. Too bad her enthusiasm for living wasn't contagious. Well, she'd find out when her kids were all grown and moved away. We'd see how enthusiastic she'd be then.

I was out buying Christmas presents for the grandkids at the boutique where I'd seen Ashley. It wasn't far from the Chamberlain House. I thought I'd stop by, take her to lunch. I'd just talked to Annie and could fill her in on the latest in her life.

I parked the Mercedes in front of the restored two-story colonial.

The foyer was welcoming. A young woman, probably college age, came out to greet me. I explained I was there to take Ashley to lunch. Ginger told me Ashley didn't work there every day. She'd come in and out for board meetings and as needed to fill in.

"We all wear a lot of hats at Chamberlain House, Mrs. Lindale." Ginger explained. There's a lot of want to and a lot of willing, but right now we don't have a lot of money or staff. We depend on the private sector, corporate donations, that sort of thing. Actually, right this minute I have a class going. It's a reading hour we do. I'd love to have you come back and join us."

I couldn't find a way to politely refuse and I was curious. I followed her through the French doors down a hallway with rooms on each side.

"This is such a neat old house. The widow, Sandra Remington left it to us in her will. Her son was special needs and she cared for him here all her life. She's left enough for a skeleton staff and we've had a few events to raise some money. We're lucky. We have volunteers helping us slowly rehab the place. You should have seen it when we got it. It's pretty cool, but I wish we had more of it."

I noticed easels with posters promoting a silent auction with proceeds to go to the building fund.

"Yes," Ginger said. "If we can raise enough money we can add on to the classrooms and the living quarters. That'd allow us to help even more kids."

I was reticent to go into the classroom. I wasn't sure what I was going to find. Much to my surprise the room looked like a library in someone's home. There was a wood-burning fireplace, draperies. Very cozy and inviting. Around the fireplace sat a dozen children and young adults. Some in wheelchairs, others in club chairs.

Ginger handed me a book and said, "Why don't you read for a while. This is one of their favorites, and mine. She handed me a well worn, oft read copy of Dr. Seuss' classic: "Oh, the Places You'll Go."

"Just read it?" I asked.

"Yes, please. Loudly. Some of our gang won't understand the words but they love the cadence and beat of the sentences. Go on."

And so I began. This had always been one of my children's favorites. I knew it almost by heart. "Congratulations! Today is your day. You're off to Great Places. You're off and away!"

Some of the kids recited parts of the book aloud as I read, just like my kids had. Those that could occasionally clapped. Every child there smiled.

I was smiling too, until I got to one verse: "And, when you're in a Slump, you're not in for much fun. Un-slumping yourself is not easily done." I looked to Ginger with tears in my eyes, she smiled and rescued me.

"That's good for today, gang. I think it's just about snack time. Who's ready for a snack?"

I was rattled. I thanked Ginger for the opportunity and was starting to leave. On my way out I ran into Lois Albright, the director at Chamberlain. She was breezing in the door, a rush of sound and flurry and color and light. She and I had gone to high school together. I hadn't seen her since the last reunion, but she hadn't changed. The woman never aged. She was vibrant and perfectly made up, her hair cut short and spiky with highlights. Her nails were long and painted a day glow fuchsia. She had on white paints a flowing tunic in about seven colors of orange and pink, giant sunglasses and sky-high sandals. Lord, how did she walk in those?

"Bev Lindale, oh my gosh, how are you?" Lois burbled, sweeping me into a huge hug like I was her best friend ever. At the same time she checked her messages and quick-stepped down the hall, high-heels clicking on the hardwood floor. "Have you seen everything? What do you think? I'm so glad you've come. We need all the help we can get and you'll be perfect."

"But – what –?

"You are here about the assistant director position, yes?"

"Why, no, I just came by to see Annie."

"Oh, I'm disappointed. You'd have been the ideal candidate. Well, think about it anyway. Come back when you can and I'll give you the full tour."

Driving home that day my mind raced. I never saw that coming. I wasn't sure how I felt about making a commitment like that. I wasn't sure if I was up to it physically. Almost as I had that thought I remembered the passage from Dr. Seuss I'd just read. Maybe that was my problem. I imagined my doctor breaking the news to me:

"We're sorry to have to tell you, Mrs. Lindale, but you have a very severe case of acute chronic Slumpitis."

With that, I started to giggle. Then I was laughing out loud. I hadn't heard that sound come of it me in ages. Laughter. After all those experts and specialists, maybe the only doctor I really needed was one named Seuss. When Gary called to let me know he'd arrived safely in Newark, I couldn't stop talking. I told him all about Chamberlain and Ginger and reading and Lois.

"Wow," he said. "You have had an eventful day." Then, "You know, Beverley, if this is something you'd be interested in you have my complete support. I'd do absolutely anything for you."

After we hung up, I started making notes of ideas I'd had about the place. I had a library full of children's books I could bring them, they had a very few. I decided I would go back the next day and drop them off.

When I did, Ginger, Lois and Ashley were all there. The greeted me warmly and I couldn't miss the exchange of conspiratorial glances that passed between the trio.

"Feel like reading some more?" Ginger asked. I did.

Start from the beginning, that's what Ginger suggested. Soon, I got to one of my favorite parts, and leaned in and read a little louder with more animation in my voice: "And when things start to happen, don't stew. Just go right along. You'll start happening too."

All the children and young adults started to clap, and I looked up to see Ginger, Lois and Ashley at the door beaming and clapping too. "Ladies, meet our new Assistant Director." Lois said.

It happened pretty much like that, all at once and out of the blue. Lois was a cheerful, enthusiastic and positive leader. She had complete confidence in me. So did Gary.

Even though I had never been officially employed, I did have more than 35 years experience in bookkeeping and administration. I'd organized many a bake sale, helped market Gary's business, and found ways to cut costs. Lois gave me free reign to make suggestions and implement improvements. Through Gary's business we were able to bring in consultants and experts to help Chamberlain House in diagnostics, assessment, and treatments.

Before long I could feel myself "start happening too." My days became a whirlwind of meetings and activities. There just never seemed to be enough time to get to all the ideas I had circulating. I'd fall into bed late at night and fall sound asleep, no medication required. I woke up each morning with energy and purpose. I was un-Slumping.

Together, Gary and I put a lot of our time and personal resources into the facility. Both of us felt like we had been given so much it was important to give back. Our kids were all successful. We had more than enough and couldn't seem to do enough. One of my favorite special projects was overseeing the restoration of the flooring at Chamberlain. We had the hardwoods redone, along with the two mahogany stairways. We installed tile in the foyer with a stunning mosaic in the center. In the middle of that I had a local artisan create a custom granite engraving.

The floors weren't the only projects to be remodeled and overhauled. Lois made me her pet project. "We want Chamberlain to feel alive and vital and electric. We can't have you drab out the place." She set her stylist on me with clear instructions to "fix her." And he did. When Larry Jordan was finished with me I had long layers of red tresses and a wardrobe of fun fashions. I retired my pairs of sensible pumps and even showed some toe from time to time.

We held a combination gala and fund-raiser to invite the community to see the remodeled and expanded facility. It was well attended. All of the Lindale kids and their families were able to come and all of the Chamberlain kids were there too. Everyone gathered around the foyer and together, Lois and I revealed the space in front of the French doors to reveal the custom mosaic in the center of the floor. Inside, it read, "Every Need is Special."

As Gary drove us home from a very successful event, I texted Annie, "Got time for some Face Time?"

In a moment Carston was on, excitedly uttering his well-rehearsed and much improved version of: "Hey, Grammy, 'What tin the worldz going ton wid you?'"

"Oh, precious boy," I said. "Just wait until I tell you!"

Closing Thoughts

Are you at a point in your life at which you feel like happiness is for someone else? Are you motivated to get out of bed in the morning only because others expect it of you? If so, know that you are not alone. You are not the only person who has experienced this. Just like Beverley Lindale, it is very common for people to feel sluggishness, depression, and even worthlessness after significant life changes, especially those in which your responsibilities are significantly reduced.

Many people look forward to the day when they are no longer directly responsible for their children, or the day they can retire from work, only to find themselves unpleasantly surprised that their children or their workplace can manage to survive without them. These changes can leave you wondering what the purpose is for the rest of your life, now that those who needed your direct service for all these years are managing on their own. You may feel like you've served your purpose, and now there's just nothing left.

Well you may not know it, but there is somebody else out there who needs you. The full life you have lived to this point has given you a unique set of strengths and talents that can be used for the good of others. Stop, listen, and look around you. Every day in the media there are ads upon ads requesting donations for abandoned pets, underprivileged children, the homeless, and people with special needs. There are literally thousands of charitable causes that you can support, and if you think that the only thing these organizations need is money, you are mistaken. Many need manpower as well.

Just like Beverley, you've probably spent many years helping your family and/or helping your employer. Why not use your talents to generously help others? Research the needs of your community, and when you feel like you've found the niche that's right for you, get going! Dig in with both hands! Will you feel better on day one? Maybe a little, maybe not. Day two? Maybe. But the day will come, with enough dedication, when you feel like you've made a measurable difference for the good of someone else. It is that feeling that, without a doubt, will be fulfilling enough to get your happy back.

So if you're lying in bed, feeling like there's nothing left for you to do, think again. Life is right in front of you. Take advantage of and explore your new found freedom and reach out and help others. I promise it will help you too.

HOPE IS NOT LOST

"Joy is a flower that blooms when you do."
~ Author Unknown

I was trembling. As I waited for Leslie to finish introducing me, I felt my mouth go dry. This is ridiculous, I thought. It's not my first trip to a podium.

"…tireless efforts, energy and devotion to raising the awareness…" Oh, my. Leslie did like her time at the mic. I just hoped she wouldn't put the crowd to sleep before I got a chance to speak.

It may not have been my first presentation but it was certainly my first in front of this size crowd. The convention center's Leonard Auditorium was at capacity with more than 2,500 guests. Leslie was wrapping up. "…my pleasure to introduce your keynote speaker, Ms. Avery Severin."

The unexpected ovation was generous and lasted long enough for me to situate myself, adjust the microphone, and take a couple of deep breaths. It's not like I didn't have my remarks prepared. I knew every syllable by heart. I'd delivered some variation of this address more times than I could count, and it was, after all, my story.

But I'd never presented it to this large an audience before or in front of such prestigious company. Thankfully, my assistant Nancy had made sure I had within reach a tumbler of water, extra reading glasses, (I never could keep track of mine) and a box of tissues. You never knew.

I was addressing the best of the best – the top movers and shakers in the world of charities, corporate giving, scouting, and government types from FEMA and other agencies. The heads of the American Red Cross, Salvation Army, Heart Association, Interfaith Relief Organization and every imaginable service organization were on hand for the kickoff off of the three-day convention: "Great minds working together to solve great problems."

The Vice President of the United States was supposed to be attending with his family. Although with the lighting I couldn't distinguish the audience members from the stage. Just as well. Okay, show time. I paused to be sure I had everyone's attention and began to speak.

"If you will, think back to your most favorite day ever. Close your eyes and picture it as clearly as you can. You know the kind I'm talking about. Those days when all the planets align, the weather cooperates, your hair turns out okay. Those out-of-the-ordinary, perfectly extraordinary magical days. The days and moments that leave their own kind of indelible imprint on our minds. I can remember my most favorite day so vividly.

"I knew at the time I was having a favorite day. It was just that incredible. I'd just recently found out I was pregnant, a little more than five months along. That was really great news, since I had just thought I was really getting fat!"

I let the audience enjoy that. "Seriously, it was a blessing I never thought I'd get again in my life. The doctors had told me after our first one was born I probably couldn't have any more children. I'd accepted that. I already had the most wonderful kid in the universe. When he heard the news, my big old strong teddy-bear husband Adam cried like a baby. Our eight year old daughter Susie shrieked with delight. "I get a baby brother or sister!""

Like I said, our little family was already pretty perfect. We had reached that point where we had all these fun routines and traditions. Friday nights were movie nights; Sunday afternoons meant family nap times. We'd all bundle up in the bed together, watch animated Disney shows, doze off and on and have tickle fights. Tuesday nights were spaghetti nights. We'd cover the dining room table in newspapers so we could be as messy as we wanted. We had lots of pasta and salad and garlic bread, Susie's favorite food. Afterwards we'd play a board game, Monopoly or Life. Susie used to say: "I wish everyday was Tuesday."

So, that one particular Tuesday, I was especially excited. Before I'd left the house for work, I saw Susie setting the table. She was setting it for four. She looked up at me just beaming, "I'm practicing for when the baby comes."

That morning, Adam was in charge of getting her to and from school. I straightened up the house, grabbed my briefcase and left for my office. I'd had my own consulting firm for about ten years. We designed and delivered customized training programs to Fortune 500 companies all over the country. I helped executives with their presentation skills, coached on team building and leadership. I loved every minute of it. When the operation started getting too big for me, I enlisted help. I wanted to be out in the field, not pouring over spreadsheets. My friend Zenith introduced me to Adam. He was a CPA and an operations genius. I liked him so well I not only hired him, I married him."

I paused while the audience laughed.

"Both of us wanted to start our family right away. Right from the start it was the three amigos, our pet name for our little gang. Since we had our own business, Adam and I were able to adjust our schedules so one of us was almost always with Susie.

"Anyway, that favorite day was turning out to be an outstanding one at work too. My early afternoon meeting went especially well. I landed a big client, one of the nation's largest banks. They'd contracted with us to handle all of their senior management training programs. I couldn't wait to tell Adam. As I walked to my car the sun was shining. It was a perfect February day, blue skies, with fluffy white clouds. Happily, I dialed Adam's number.

I reached him just as they were headed into the grocery store.

"Hey, babe." He said. "Glad you caught us. We're just on our way to get some last minute things for tonight. Need us to pick anything up?"

Before I could answer I heard Susie's high-pitched squeal: "Butter bread!"

"Yeah," I said. "Butter bread...and vitamins."

"Vitamins?" He'd laughed. "What kind and what for?"

"Whatever kind you need to keep you going, Mister." I said, announcing excitedly: "We just landed All American Bank!"

His whoop of excitement was loud and heartfelt. "Oh, Avery. Are we not the luckiest people in the whole world? I'll pick us up a bottle of that cabernet you like. We are going to have to do some extra-serious celebrating tonight."

"Oooo. Extra-serious..." I whispered back in my best breathy tones. "I like the sound of that!"

"Butter bread!" the shrill little voice rang out. "Love you, Mommy!"

"Love you, Avery!"

"Love you back! I'll see you two at home."

I paused my remarks there. I took a sip of water, grabbed a tissue – just in case – inhaled deeply and continued speaking, my voice now flat, even.

"But I didn't... I didn't get to see them at home. The Highway Patrolmen said the axel somehow separated from the 18-wheeler, careening into the SUV and sending it into the guardrail. Adam and Susie were killed instantly. The officers didn't tell me right away of course. They didn't even call me on the phone. They came to the door, said there'd been an accident and escorted me to the hospital. But I knew. You don't get driven to the hospital in a police car if everything's okay.

"They wouldn't let me see them. I heard the doctors and police talking together in hushed sounds. I only made out snippets and word fragments. Dead at the scene... impact... unrecoverable. I went into shock. Shock helps. I really don't remember much.

"My mom swooped in and just handled everything. I sort of remember her dressing me the day of the funeral. Holding me up at the graveside. She slept with me that night. We both woke up covered in my blood.

"The stress. I lost the baby, too. So you see, when someone tells you they've hit rock bottom? I'm here to tell you, there is a place so much farther down than that, way below those rocks. I found a crevice deep down under those rocks. I crawled into that space and stayed there. All I wanted was to be with Avery, Susie and the baby, but I couldn't even summon enough energy to die.

"Thank God for Mom's huh? Let me tell you, mine definitely has angel wings. She moved in with me, took care of me, made all of the funeral arrangements, handled all the hospital bills; then all the insurance. It was a circus—reporters on the lawn and phones ringing off the hook. She ran interference so I didn't have to get involved with all the lawyers. Lord, they came out of the woodwork. Everyday another attorney showed up wanting to bring another lawsuit against somebody else. There were lawsuits filed against the driver, the transportation company, the axel manufacturer. Everyone smelled money. Mom spared me all that.

"She sorted out the legitimate agents from the ambulance chasers and was instrumental in negotiating a sizable settlement without having to drag me into court for hearings or testimony. For months if there was a decision to be made she made it. My business partner Zenith stepped up in and kept my company going. I couldn't imagine a time I'd ever go back to work. I couldn't even get out of bed.

"The doctors kept me pretty sedated, but they couldn't numb me enough. The pain was visceral. Physical. My gut actually ached night and day. Nothing I took made that go away. Or the guilt. Why couldn't I have gone with them? What was the sense of letting me live? Why take the baby too?

"My emotions ran the same gamut over and over. Guilt, sorrow, anger. I fell asleep crying every night and woke up screaming with nightmares. I never saw the photos from the scene. I didn't have to. My mind played ghoulish tapes of its own creation over and over and over.

"I refused visitors. I didn't want to see anyone and I especially didn't want to hear anyone's stupid empty platitudes. I never wanted to see flowers again as long as I lived. I didn't want condolences and I sure didn't want to hear about 'God's plan.' Heaven help the next person who tried to tell me they knew how I felt. I waded through the motions of each day, sleeping through as many hours as I could manage.

"Eating was almost out of the question. I couldn't eat. I had no appetite and when I did manage to take a bite I could barely keep it down. There wasn't one thing that wasn't a clawing reminder tearing at my open wound. Especially food. Poor Mom. She wanted to get me out of the house so one evening she took me to a neighborhood Italian restaurant. We walked in the door and there was a big black easel with the feature of the night. In white lettering it read 'Spaghetti Night.' Needless to say, we didn't stay. I went to bed that night in agony. All I could wail over and over again was 'butter bread.' I didn't come out of my room for days.

"About three months after the tragedy I caught my reflection in the hallway mirror. I was unrecognizable. 'Look at me, Mom.' I said. 'I'm not pudgy now. I'm Zombie girl. The incredible walking dead.'

"Honey, we need to talk. The insurance money came in, Avery." She said.

I waved her off. "Don't want to hear it."

"I know you don't, baby girl, but you should know. It's a lot. We should probably discuss what to do with it."

"Tell you what, Mom," I started in, sarcastic, hurting, and hysterical. "Why don't we stack it all up, put it in a big pile, count it over and over and let's just see if it's enough that we can pay somebody to bring my family back. Why don't we do that?"

"The doorbell rang before I could say anything more I'd feel guilty about. I remember gasping when I opened the door to see her standing there. My, God. For a second, I'd thought it was Susie. I blinked back tears, pulled myself together and said, 'Hi.'

"Now, I'm here to tell you, that child was on her game. She went right into her introduction, features and benefits and closing, ending with: 'How many boxes would you like?'

"That did it. It reminded me of how I'd worked with Susie on her sales campaigns. I just collapsed on the front porch steps, sobbing. I'm surprised the little girl didn't turn around and run. Instead, she sat down next to me and put her little arm around me, and –

This was always the hardest part of the speech for me to get through. I coughed, sipped some water and went on.

"When I looked down at her and saw her looking up at me with such compassion, it was like looking right in to Susie's eyes."

The little girl looked at me and said, "It's okay Lady, it's going to be okay." She sat with me for several minutes and then quietly got up and walked away. I went back inside and went to sleep. I didn't wake up until the next morning. Mom must have gone out shopping. I got up, showered, brushed my teeth, dressed, and faced the day. I was going to take one of my tranquilizers, but decided to skip it. Barefoot, I went to go to the mailbox by our curb. When I opened the front door, I found a box of Thin Mints on the step. Adam's favorite. On the box was a note. In perfect cursive it read:

70

I am sorry you are so sad.
My mom says if you smile you will feel happy.
I hope these cookies make you smile.
No charge.
Your friend, Lisa James.

"I can remember that morning so vividly. That sweet gesture. The thin mints. It was like some cosmic love letter. For the first time, I smiled. For the first time, I thought I might make it. Oh, yes, I started crying all over again, but I was smiling as I wept. I took the box into the dining room. The table was still set for four. I wouldn't let mom touch it. I put a cookie on each plate. First, I ate mine. Then I ate theirs. I told you, I was feeling better."

I've learned in making presentations, you've got to lighten the mood once in a while. Admittedly, mine is a pretty sad story. I let the audience release some tension, and went on with the tale.

"Now I'm not saying Girl Scout cookies are magical, although we all know they are. I am saying that my life turned around that day. Every time I saw that box of cookies I thought of the note and the wisdom in it and the kindness behind it. I forced myself to smile at first. It was hard. But I kept trying, out of respect for the little girl who stopped everything to reach out to this pitiful wreck.

"That was 2002. Who knows what happened to the stock market after 9/11? Well, my smart mother. My super smart, brilliant, Mother is out in that audience with you somewhere right now, my investing guru genius, she put the insurance money into a few blue chip stocks. Please stand Mom. You did real well.

She stood briefly, waving off the attention, mouthing an "I love you, baby girl" to me.

I continued my story. "Okay, so the next year, my doorbell rings and to my delight, it was Lisa. I had meant to look her up and thank her but never had. There she was smiling from ear to ear and still looking so much like my Susie. Lisa dropped her clipboard and pencil and threw her arms around me. Do I need to tell you? I bought every box she had.

"Lisa became a good friend. I looked forward to each April when cookie season kicked off for the chance to see her, thank her. I'll always be grateful to that little girl and her uncommon kindness. And fortunately, I get to tell her that almost every day. Ladies and Gentlemen, it is my profound honor and pleasure to introduce you tonight to that very special little girl, Miss Lisa James."

As the now grown, stunning, Lisa walked to the podium, the crowd was on its feet. As I waited for Lisa to make her way up to the stage, I felt tears well up in my eyes. I was so proud of her. She truly was one in a million.

"As many of you know," I continued when the applause finally died down, "Lisa made sure I was a repeat customer! The only way I survived the anniversary of the tragedy each year was because of this gal right here. She corralled me into helping her with her cookie campaigns each year. She gave me a purpose and a reason to just keep pressing on. It took some time. When you are as far down as I was you can't get up by yourself. You can't even imagine how you could. Lisa was right. You have to sometimes do the hard thing before you feel like doing it. For me, it was forcing a smile until I felt like smiling. It was a first baby step in moving forward. And, I guess we did all right, huh, Lisa?"

Lisa beamed and stepped to the microphone. "We did all right. When you agreed to help me with the cookie sales I wasn't sure what was going to happen. You had all these great ideas and brought all that training and marketing background and taught me so much. Together we sort of blew the roof off every sales record in the country.

"We sure did," I added. "And, you taught me a lot in return. Like, how to act and behave the way you want to feel, even when you don't feel that way yet. That's what you taught me Lisa, the power of yet."

I continued, telling the audience how Lisa and I had remained close through the cookie years and after. When Lisa finished college she came to work at my company. Then together we wrote, "Pressing On, It's Not About the Cookies" which became a bestseller. We started touring, giving motivational speeches all over the country. Between the book sales and insurance money, which, thanks to my mother's brilliant investing, had grown to a sizable amount, I was able to launch Susie's Legacy, a charitable foundation helping victims and survivors of tragedies come back and start over.

"So whether you're a Girl Scout or a girl Friday, CEO,

philanthropist, homemaker or rocket scientist you can make a difference. Somewhere right this minute someone is hurting and absolutely desperate for something only you can do. Right this minute all over the globe people are having their 'favorite day.' Tomorrow, calamity may strike. It could be a car accident, terminal illness, a fire, tsunami, or tornado.

"Until you lose everything, you never think about everything you have to lose.

"Twelve years ago, an eight-year-old girl taught me everything I never wanted to know about loss. Twelve years ago another eight-year-old girl taught me everything I needed to learn about moving on. We all have losses. Thankfully, most of them aren't as catastrophic as mine or the people Susie's foundation helps. But the world is full of heartache and hurt. You probably have known some yourselves.

"The secret to pressing on? In sales? In life, in achieving your goals? Lisa James showed me you get over your own hurt by reaching out to someone else. You press on by caring more about someone else's pain, even a complete stranger's, than you care about your own.

"I didn't know much about Lisa's mom that day we first met on my doorstep. The one with the advice, 'If you smile, you will feel happy.' I didn't know that Lisa's mom had passed away the year before after a long battle with cancer."

Now it was Lisa's turn to grab a tissue. I continued, "Lisa didn't have a mother and I didn't have a daughter, and it's worked out very well."

"Don't forget about Dad," Lisa added.

"Well, of course! Ladies and Gentlemen, Lisa's Dad is with us tonight, Mr. Gary James. Please stand, Gary." Gary James was seated in the front row. The tall, silver-haired and distinguished global philanthropist was well known in this circle. He stood, turned, and waved to the crowd, as I continued my introduction.

"I can tell you I've had the pleasure of watching this guy for many years." I said in a familiar tone. Let me just say he's a terrific role model and father. Oh, yes. And, I'm especially proud to call him my husband."

That always comes as a big surprise to audiences. The announcement, as expected, had them cheering.

"So, you see? I told you all, it's not about the cookies." I said.

73

"Philanthropy, service, charity, even scouting is about so much more than fund-raising and programs and knocking on doors. It's about knocking on hearts. Every single day we have an opportunity to reach out to the broken, wounded and hurting. We have no idea the impact we can have on someone when we are willing to give of ourselves. I hope you all have a million favorite days. Keep pressing on!

Closing Thoughts

I hope, dear reader, for your sake, that you have not suffered tragedy akin to that which Avery suffered. I realize that in writing that, I am judging the magnitude of some tragedy you have suffered versus the magnitude of another's suffering. Who can do that? Who can measure pain?

It does not matter whether death is expected or unexpected; either way, its impact can blow a hole in the path of existence that is seemingly too large to surpass. One only needs to look at the fact that many elderly people die within weeks of their spouse's death to understand that even the expected death of a loved one can be devastating.

It does not matter whether your loved one is 13, 33 or 83. It does not matter whether your loved one is part of your daily life or stationed at a far-away outpost. When death is done rearing its ugly head, it can make those of us remaining feel like rolling over and lying down right along with our loved one.

Is that what Avery did? Yes, for a while it was – and who could blame her? It seemed as though just about everything good in her life had been taken from her. What Avery realized when young Lisa came knocking at her door, is that where there is life, there is hope. She reminded her that, despite great loss, there are reasons for going on. I hope you find your reasons for going on and living a life that you and the ones you have lost can be proud of!

You may not think so now if you are currently going through this hardship, but your happiness does return - stay open enough for it to find you.

SECTION II

HEALTH

"A journey of a thousand miles begins with a single step."
Lao-tzu (604 BC – 531 BC)

75

YOU ARE IN CHARGE OF YOUR DESTINY

"Tell me what you eat, and I shall tell you what you are."
~ Anthelme Brillat-Savarin

"Hey, Dad," my 11-year-old son called from the kitchen as he came running into the living room. I looked up from the presentation I was putting together for a client on my laptop to face him. Kevin's eyes were wide and concerned, and I hated that he looked at me like that on a regular basis.

Putting that out of my head for the moment, I asked him, "What's up, slugger?"

He stopped beside my makeshift desk beside the couch and hesitated. I waited, always and forever patient with the boy, and finally, he asked, "Are you going to be able to come to the Lookout Point on Astronomy Night with me? Everyone is bringing their dads, but it's a little bit of a hike up the hill. If you can't come, I can ask Mom to go."

It broke my heart that he had to ask me that, to know that he understood just how dangerous my health was and that he was willing to make sacrifices for me. Wasn't it supposed to be the other way around, with a father making sacrifices for his son? Feeling sad and unworthy, I forced a smile. "I'll come, Kevin. I'll just be extra careful on the way up."

Looking relieved and excited, Kevin threw his arms over me – not around me. His arm span wasn't long enough for that. At 425 pounds, I shopped online or at the specialty stores for my 60-inch waistline. I'd always been heavy, but admittedly, I'd let it get out of control in the last few years, and I'd paid the price for it.

I patted my son's back and sent him back to finish his homework, unable to look him in the eye as I remembered that horrible day six weeks ago. I wasn't sure I'd ever forget it. The words the doctor spoke to me haunted me to this day, and try as I might, I couldn't escape the truth of them.

"Mr. Rowland, you died."

He'd spoken them with such emphasis that I knew he wasn't lying, and I knew it hadn't been some quick, skipped heartbeat. I lay in the hospital bed, stitches in my chest and several monitors hooked up to me and a very strict diet of hospital food without salt, and I wondered how I'd gotten there.

That didn't mean I couldn't remember the horrific moment the heart attack hit me. I was at my son's soccer game, and he'd just scored. I stood to cheer for him, screaming his name from the bleachers with my wife, Tabitha, right next to me and suddenly it felt like someone was stabbing me in the shoulder. I grabbed my shoulder, and a stinging numbness crawled down my arm as my heart beat out of control and felt like it was going to explode.

"Jonathan!" I remembered hearing Tabby cry, and the world tilted sideways as I toppled from the bleachers to the ground below. I also saw my son, as he rushed from the field to my side and the look of fear on his face was etched into my mind. I must have blacked out for a bit because the next thing I remember was paramedics loading me onto a stretcher and lifting me into an ambulance. After that, it was all a blur until I woke up from surgery with an oxygen mask on my face, a doctor and several nurses hovering over me like I was a specimen in a lab.

That's when the doc had told me. "Mr. Rowland, you had a serious heart attack and we found that two of your valves were 90% and 95% blocked, respectively. We did a double bypass surgery, replacing one artery with a stint and cleaning the other." He took his glasses off after reading the paperwork to me, as if I couldn't read for myself. "Mr. Rowland, your weight made this a very dangerous, very complex surgery. We nearly lost you."

I had rasped out a laugh. "Well, doc, good work. I appreciate you not losing me. You're a genius for keeping my heart beating."

His face grew grimmer, something I hadn't thought possible. "Mr. Rowland, you died. In the middle of the surgery, you flat-lined on the operating table. It took us over three minutes to revive you, to get your heart to beat again. Any longer and there could have been severe damage to your brain or to your extremities. I want you to know this is not a joke. You still have a 30% blockage in another valve, and just because we cleared the one we didn't stint doesn't mean it won't clog again. You have to change your lifestyle, Mr. Rowland, or you'll end up back on my table with a good chance of not surviving the surgery. I don't like losing patients."

I swallowed hard at the seriousness of his voice. He'd actually cared, and his concern scared me. Of course, I'd been there for a week for recovery, and then I'd come home. While I'd cut down the salt in my diet, and my wife wouldn't let me eat red meat, I hadn't really pursued a hardcore change to my diet. After all, I was 44 years old, not 60, and I had issues with the thought of taking the joy out of life, which is what I equated dieting to. Besides, if I went through with that sort of change, I couldn't even go to barbecues or out to most restaurants. I would become antisocial, and my work would suffer with the inability to share a meal with potential clients. I was in sales. A lot of times it took some wining and dining to get the sale.

But as I looked at my son in the kitchen, concentrating on his homework, I knew I was lying to myself. I was lazy and I needed to find a new attitude. I just didn't know where to start looking. If I didn't adjust my outlook, I would never be able to convince myself to get on the wagon and get healthy. I watched my wife as she picked up the living room around me, and I smiled. Tabby had been a little overweight after having Kevin, but she'd stuck to her guns and come back down to her ideal weight again. I admired her, but I also knew she had a lot more willpower than me.

Still, I owed my family something better than a round man who got winded walking out to the curb to check the mail. I shut down my laptop, deciding I'd finish the presentation later, and turned on the television, looking for a movie I could enjoy with my family. I'd decide what to do about my weight tomorrow.

But the next day, I had to go into the office for yet another big sales meeting. Attendance was mandatory, or I would have headed to a client's, checked in with them, and taken the rest of the day off. I just wasn't motivated to work today. Nonetheless, I dragged myself out of bed, stuffed my bulk into a shirt and tie with slacks, and drove in.

When I arrived and took the elevator up to the conference room, I was surprised to see an unfamiliar face at the front of the room. I elbowed Gabe, one of my fellow salesmen, and asked, "What's going on? Are we taking a lesson in sales or something?"

He shook his head. "No, that's Spencer Fulton. He's a motivational speaker. He's got a couple books out, and my wife read one of them, said it was really good. We'll see what he has to say about happy, healthy work lives." He rolled his eyes and laughed as we took our seats around the long conference table.

I wasn't expecting much, but a few minutes into his presentation, he had my rapt attention. It almost seemed like I'd been destined to meet this man today, my whole perspective thrown off balance as he spoke and I listened with more interest than I'd felt in anything for months.

"It's scientifically proven that mind over matter is more than just a saying. In multiple medical trials, several patients taking placebo drugs have improved health. Why? Because they *believe* they are going to get better. Obviously, the placebo isn't making the difference." It made so much sense. He continued, "How many times have you started your day off feeling grumpy, and you stub your toe as you get out of bed? That makes you grumpier, and you spill hot coffee on your favorite shirt. By that time, your mind is set that it's going to be a miserable day, and you get a ticket on the way to work because your registration is outdated. You get to work and lose one of your biggest accounts or get a lecture from your boss because you aren't meeting quota."

I knew those days. The truth was, they happened more often than not. I sank deeper into my chair, along with several of my coworkers, as we recognized ourselves in his stories.

"On the other hand, positive reinforcement in children has always produced better results than negative reinforcement. For example, once a child receives a disciplinary mark in school, they are likely to act out again, perhaps not finish their homework, and start a downward spiral. However, if a group of children is given an assignment and told that they can do something extra to get extra credit, the realization of that encourages them to continue down the positive path.

"Ladies and gentlemen, the point I'm making is that, if you hit the floor with a positive attitude, telling yourself that today will be a good day, you'll have a better day. If you face a client believing that you'll make the sell, then you'll get the contract. It always comes back to mind over matter."

The words meant more to me than just work. They reminded me that I had become a completely negative person. I woke up every day thinking that I'd start the diet tomorrow, or that going on a diet wouldn't do anything but make me miserable. And lately, it had gotten worse. I'd come to the conclusion, ever since the doctor told me I'd died, that true death was imminent. I went about my days thinking that any moment could be my last – thinking that my heart was finally going to explode.

I realized that was my biggest mistake. I needed to face each day like it was the first day of the rest of my life. Did I want to spend that life worrying that my heart would fail while I climbed the mountain with my son on his field trip this weekend? Was I ready to throw in the towel and just let things come as they may? I wasn't. When I faced the facts, I could admit that I'd dug myself into this hole, and the only way out of it was to climb back up. I had to do it on my own, and I couldn't give up, or I would simply get buried.

I left the meeting with a new attitude, and that night, after putting Kevin to bed, I sat down to talk to Tabby. "I want to make some really big life changes, and I'm going to need your support."

She took my hand in both of hers and told me, "I'm always behind you, Jonathan. I'm always here, cheering you on and ready to do anything you ask of me. So, tell me, what can I do to help?"

I was so grateful to have such a wonderful wife. "Let's cut salt completely from my diet. No more cakes and candies for me unless they're sugar free. I want to keep my portions down, and I'm going to start exercising." I fought back tears; after all, I'd always been taught that men don't cry, even if it was a 400-pound-plus man. "I don't want to miss out on my son growing up because I was selfish and stupid."

She shed a few tears but smiled. "I don't want to lose you, either."

I nodded. "I know. I'm also going to adopt a new attitude. I'm

80

sorry I've been so lazy and negative. From now on, I don't care how bad things seem. I'm going to find something to concentrate on that's good and makes me happy. I promise, I'll be a better person."

The next morning, I got up and made an egg white omelet with an English muffin and a glass of orange juice. I went to the store and bought a treadmill before going to work and I set the machine up as soon as I got home. I'd made two new sales at work, using the positive attitude method, and I was in a stellar mood. My wife stopped my work for dinner, which consisted of baked chicken, steamed broccoli, and white rice with lots of seasoning. It was fabulous and while I had to learn how to not be hungry with the smaller portions, I was satisfied.

The next morning, I used the treadmill. I had to walk, not run, and I only made it a half mile, but it was more than I'd done before, and I told myself that it was only the beginning. By the end of the month, I was walking fast for three miles every morning and I'd dropped six pounds.

There were times when I woke up, thinking that I'd never be healthy, never find that inner peace with myself. It took every ounce of willpower I had to keep trying. But like Peter Pan, I clung to my happy thoughts – my wife, my son, and a long life – and butted those up against the fear in my son's eyes when I collapsed and the tone of the doctor's voice when he said, "You died." I wanted one over the other for sure, and I was determined to make sure I earned it.

It was when Kevin came to me, one afternoon after school, with a bright smile on his face and asked, "Hey, Dad, can you come throw the ball for me? I've got to practice my swing if I'm going to make the softball team."

I was so proud that he felt I was ready to do something physical with him I nearly cried, but instead, I smiled broadly and nodded, telling him I'd be out in just a minute. I hadn't weighed myself in months, so I went and stepped on the scale. I'd lost 68 pounds. I felt lighter on my feet, and I had to have my pants taken up because they were literally falling off. I didn't buy new ones because I was determined to keep going.

Little by little, the pounds came off, and little by little, I felt better about myself, more confident about my life. I made more sales, and I got promoted at work. I smiled more, and my son and wife both wanted to spend time with me. I finally scheduled a vacation for us, something I hadn't done in four years because I was too lazy. It took me two years, but I found myself – the real me, who was thin and fit – at 195 pounds. My doctor's smile was the best thing I'd seen in ages as he told me, "I didn't think you could do it, Mr. Rowland, but your Type II diabetes is now under control. You have normal blood sugar levels. And you can stop the blood pressure meds. I want to keep you on the cholesterol meds for another couple of months, just to make sure, but otherwise, all your tests are clear. Nice job, Mr. Rowland."

I'd become such a believer in the mind over matter philosophy and had such success with a positive attitude in my life that I wanted to thank the person who'd opened my eyes. I contacted Spencer Fulton and asked him to meet me for lunch one day and I told him, "You changed my life. You came to my office to teach your methods over two years ago and I weighed more than double what I do now. I'm a better, healthier person because of you."

He was glad to hear it and gave me some more advice that was right on the money. "I appreciate your thanks, Jonathan, but you did the work yourself. If you want to show gratitude for the gift you've received due to your diligent effort, you should pay it forward. Share your experience so that others will unburden themselves. Help others climb out of their holes before they fall as far as you did. Be the hero who rescues them."

It sounded like the perfect way to pay my respects. I started putting together an inspirational newsletter at work, with advice for dieting, exercising, and other means of self-improvement. I included information from Spencer Fulton's books, and I asked for anyone with issues to send in questions that could be addressed. Several people joined in the production of the newsletter and before I really knew what was happening, I was the head of a new health and wellness department for our company. I helped with insurance, healthcare programs, and even psychiatric needs.

On top of that, I started giving presentations, not for sales, but for inspiration. I told my story at work, at other companies, and even at churches and seminars. I talked to people one-on-one who couldn't bring themselves to join the group sessions, and before I could blink, it became a regular thing. I was scheduling seminars of my own, where my story was used to help others. The audiences were always full. There were people who were overweight, dealing with disease, depressed, out of work, and they came from all spectrums of lifestyles. Some were rich, others poor, and I told them all where I'd come from.

I started getting success stories from people who had attended, and my company became an investor in me. I wrote a book, for those who couldn't make a seminar, and it was published, selling thousands of copies. I used the money to start my son's college fund and I maintained my day job for everyday expenses. It became my life's work, my passion and I grew happier and with each successful conference, with every person who sent me his or her story.

When my company asked me to travel around the globe, I agreed, but only if I could take my family with me. I wanted my wife and my son to experience all that life had to offer and to really see how I helped others. I was proud of my work, of my life, of my body, and most of all, my attitude. Kevin loved it, too, and he adopted the philosophy, sharing it with his friends. He'd always been a good student, but he graduated at the top of his class, getting a full scholarship to a prestigious school where he'd get an incredible education.

I was humbled by the respect people afforded me and I was glad I'd chosen my path. I looked back one night, just after Kevin had left for college, at pictures from our trip up the mountain to the Lookout Point. My son looked so much the same and yet so much younger. I, on the other hand, was barely recognizable compared to the man I was now. I couldn't believe I'd wasted so much of my life dreaming of being a healthy man rather than just making it happen.

The best moment of my life, though, was when my son opened his clinic. He became a therapist, specializing in eating disorders and other physical ailments in people who suffered from psychological problems. He dedicated it to me and asked me to give seminars at the clinic to help those who could benefit. I had set an example for Kevin, and he had decided to carry on my legacy. What more could a man want in his life?

Closing Thoughts

How do you feel today, right now, at this very moment? Are you encouraged by this story, or are you rolling your eyes sarcastically, thinking, "That won't work for me?"

Yes, I know, it's much easier for a character somewhere else in the world to drop a few hundred pounds than for someone like you – but that doesn't mean it can't be done – and people have done it. That having been said – do you think it would be easier to achieve goals like that with a positive, "can-do" attitude or a negative, "can't do" mindset?

What did your inner voice say the last time you attempted to accomplish a goal but failed? I bet it sounded something like this: "I'll give it my best, but this deadline's awfully tight. Or maybe it said, "I can get this done. I know it's going to be awful, dieting sucks, but I'll just have to suck it up and do it." Or maybe, "I doubt I can do this, I've never been able to in the past, but I know I should keep trying." Really, with negative self-talk like this, how do you expect to accomplish anything? You've failed in your mind's eye before you even started along the path toward accomplishing your goal.

I once went to a weight support group meeting with a friend. It was the first time I had ever been to one of these meetings. I had a positive attitude that this plan was going to help me lose weight. My friend came out of the meeting and asked me if I wanted to go out for nachos and beer. Seriously, guess who lost weight and who didn't? Four months later I was down 23 pounds. My friend never returned for the second meeting and she still weighed the same as she did when we went to that first meeting.

I challenge you, no matter what goals you are currently seeking in your life, to drop any negative thoughts you have and charge ahead full-throttle with a positive attitude. I know it may be challenging at first because you have had negative thought patterns for so long. In fact, at this point do you even still believe that you are capable of accomplishing your goals?

Of course you are! It's time to re-train your brain. Make a list of all of the goals you are working to accomplish. When you first wake up in the morning, think an "I will" sentence for each goal. Make sure you don't follow each statement with anything contrary – thoughts like "Yeah, right" will sabotage the process. Do this exercise again mid-day and at night before going to sleep. You will also want to do it any time you have a negative thought or temptation during the day,

84

but at those points you will want to do it twice – once to neutralize the negative thought and the second time to get back on track. Before you know it, you will not only be saying these positive affirmations, but also believing them as well.

No matter what your goal, be it weight loss, giving up cigarettes, career success, or some other personal challenge, retraining your brain to think positively about accomplishing your goal will help you every step of the way. Just like Jonathan and the thousands of real-life people who have applied the power of positive thinking to achieve success in their lives, you are in charge of your destiny. Think good thoughts and make your healthy dreams come true!

THE MAGIC IS INSIDE YOU

"There is no illness of the body apart from the mind."
~ Socrates

"Can you state your name for me?" the nurse asked as she began gathering supplies. I hadn't wanted to go to the hospital, but I had come to a point where I had no choice. I was deathly ill, vomiting, and nauseous for over a wee and I couldn't understand why.

"Rose Carter," I told her and recited my date of birth.

She continued her work, hooking me up to IV fluids, checking my pulse, temperature, and blood pressure. "Let me get you something for your nausea and the doctor will be in shortly," she told me. I nodded as the room swirled around me. My husband, Will, stood at my side, holding my hand, and I couldn't look at him. He'd convinced me to come here. I felt it was a sign of weakness of character. I didn't want him to see me like this and I certainly didn't want him to believe I was weak of mind or spirit.

I read a lot, far more than the average person. I read romance novels, and I read books on helping romances blossom or rekindle. I also read a lot of books about the law of attraction, mind over matter, and other nonphysical ways to improve yourself and your health. In fact, I read a little about everything, and so I knew a little about this and that and the other thing. But I was especially versed on the mind-body connection, and I knew this shouldn't be happening.

I'd taken in tons of information about it, and I was a firm believer in the law of attraction. I knew that, if my mind was healthy and

86

focused, my body would remain healthy. But I couldn't pinpoint a problem with my point of view, my state of mind, or any other aspect of my health that could have caused me to get so sick.

I'd been reading about this for nearly four years now, and I'd made a number of life changes from the start. I hadn't been healthy in college, so I'd looked for ways to repair myself. I'd found my answer in the mind-body connection philosophy and I'd immediately started actively pursuing the life changes needed to make a difference. Within a month, I felt like a new person. My diet was better, I was exercising not because I needed to but because I wanted to, I was taking all the right supplements, and my mind was focused on the goal of being healthy. I told myself every day that failure was not an option and that I would move forward in a positive way, no matter how much of a struggle it was.

When I was getting ready to graduate and putting my resume out there to get a job, I'd used the same philosophy, grinding it into myself that this was going to work. If I told myself that I'd land a great job right out of school, it would happen. Literally two days after graduation, I had an interview and got an amazing job that paid better than I'd hoped. I'd gone into the interview with the determination to make it work, and I'd come out golden.

Two years later, when I wanted to settled down and get married, I'd put it out into the universe with a positive vibe that I would find the man of my dreams. My husband, Will, had been at a party two weeks later. We'd been inseparable from the day we'd met.

I'd never let myself get depressed, even when Will had been laid off shortly after our wedding and it didn't look like we were going to be able to pay our mortgage.

Instead, I'd told him everything would be alright and we'd both been very positive. He'd landed another job that paid a little more within a month and we were fine. All the time, I continued to read up on how I could improve my mental health and have it affect my physical health positively. I'd been sick a lot in my life, having a weak stomach and a susceptibility to colds, but ever since I'd started working with the mind-body connection, I hadn't fallen ill a single day.

On the occasions that I thought I might be a little under the weather, I didn't seek out a doctor's help. They would just give me pills to mask the symptoms and patch me up. Instead, I looked to alternative medicines, ways to truly remedy whatever ailment I had. I used antioxidants to assist in a healthy immune system and I ate yogurt regularly and took probiotics to assure that my stomach was as strong as it could be. Green tea supplements, papaya, and other extracts helped my organs and my energy level. If I was feeling down, some St. Johns Wort did the trick. For sleepless nights, rosemary and lavender tea put me under.

Now, my methods had been failing me for nearly a week. I couldn't keep anything down, and I was weak and nauseous all the time. I finally agreed to go to the hospital when the scale showed I'd dropped ten pounds in the one week. My husband was scared and for all that he supported my lifestyle choices, at this point, he insisted on a second opinion.

I waited as the doctor came to assess my issue, and he ordered lots of blood work and a CT scan of my abdomen and intestines. I was nervous and frightened. I couldn't remember the last time I'd seen the inside of a medical facility and I hadn't had such intensive testing done in longer than that. I squeezed my husband's hand, telling Will, "I need you to stay positive for me, okay? I'm having a really hard time with this because it shouldn't be happening."

He nodded with a frown of concern and sympathy. "I know, Rose. You take incredibly good care of yourself, but sometimes, things are out of our hands, no matter how hard we try to keep them within our frame of control. I'm just glad you came in. I'm sure they'll figure out what's wrong and get you on a path to recovery."

I scowled. I didn't want a million prescriptions to get me on the road to recovery. I wanted to know why my own methods weren't working and, if I could at least be diagnosed, I could perhaps figure out what to do differently in my diet and exercise routine to fix the problem. I wouldn't just throw a bandage over it, the way doctors did by offering prescriptions for nausea and pain. I would find the source of the problem and treat it until it was healed.

It took longer than I thought it should have for the results to come back, and when they did, I was shocked, even irate. The doctor told me they couldn't find anything specific wrong with me and would have to run some more exams and tests. I looked at my husband and demanded he take me home, where I could figure things out for myself, and he started to protest. But even before Will could tell me what he thought, I was sick again, and I knew I wasn't going anywhere until the mystery was solved.

They ran x-rays and more CT scans, PET scans, and more blood tests. They ran urine tests and stool samples and still came up empty handed. All the while, I was getting worse and worse. They were feeding my nutrients through my IV because I still couldn't keep anything down, whether solid or liquid, and I became scared and discouraged.

I spent all my free time forcefully willing my body to get well, but all I seemed to be doing was putting more of a strain on my body and draining what little energy I had. Something had to change, or I was going to lose my mind and my faith. I'd been in there a week with no resolution when I finally gave into the emotions and cried. Will came to see me after work and found me sobbing, my face red and swollen, and my eyes sunken in, and my cheeks covered with tear streams. "I'm so tired, Will," I told him as I let him wrap me in his arms. I buried my face in his neck, and my words came out a mumble. "I've been willing my body to heal the whole time I've been in here, and I've put forward a positive attitude, guaranteeing they would find an answer. But I'm getting worse instead of better, and there's no end in sight. I don't know what to do anymore."

"Well, I'll tell you what you can't do." I raised an eyebrow at him through my tears. "You can't give up. It's not who you are, Rose. It's not how you've chosen to live your life, and it certainly shouldn't be the way you choose to end it. You're a believer and a fighter, and I want you to remember that and be patient." He ran his fingers through my hair, one of his typical signs of affection and I cuddled against him, not wanting him to go.

I barely slept that night and I asked the nurse for some herbal tea with lavender in it. She brought me some of her own personal stash, and I was grateful, but it didn't matter; I couldn't keep it down. It was a final straw for me, and I wanted to call it quits. As far as I could tell, I was dying, and there was no fixing me.

When my husband arrived the next day, I turned my head, not wanting to speak to him. I'd ignored the nurses all day, barely responding to them, either. I just wanted to be left alone in my misery. I was tired and frustrated, and I was so sick I couldn't stand myself any longer. I had to pretend I was somewhere else, someone else, just to keep breathing for the moment.

But he took one of my hands in both of his and said, "Rose, I need to talk to you. I did some reading of my own last night, and you know how much I hate to read and research anything." I didn't turn around, and he cleared his throat. "Come on, Rose, give me a chance here. I know you're going through so much right now, and I hate to see you hurting. But it's not just your body hurting right now. Your mind is hurting, too, and I think I know why."

I wanted to retort that of course my mind was sick. I was knocking at death's door. Anyone's mind would be a mess right now. But I didn't. Slowly, I forced myself to look at Will, swallowing my protests and skepticism. "What is it you think is wrong?"

I saw him flinch and knew I sounded sarcastic, as if I didn't trust him to know anything or at least not as much as I did. But to his credit, he seemed to put it up to my illness and the bad attitude it was creating in me. "I read about the mind-body connection, and I think you have a lot of it right. You focus on the positive, you maintain a positive course, and you believe that you're going to meet your goals. But something is lost in translation, and I think that's why you aren't getting better."

I tilted my head, not sure what he meant. "What might not be translating? The whole principle is that, if you think it's true, it comes true."

He shook his head. "Not exactly. You have to actually believe it, and that has to run through all of your energy, not just in your head. You can think it all day long, but that doesn't mean your body feels it. I think you're so busy trying to force a response that you're expending your energy in the wrong way." I must have looked at him like he was crazy because he rolled his eyes. How was I supposed to react? Will never studied up on this or engaged in conversation about it with me. When it came to the law of attraction, he mostly listened and nodded his head while I talked.

But today, he wasn't finished. "Hear me out, Rose. It's not about willing it to be so with your mind. It's not a matter of making up a story about going to New York, and just because it's in your head, a plane ticket to New York City falls in your lap. Your positive thoughts, your dreams and aspirations, your determination to be

90

healthy all have to translate from your head to your heart and soul. You can't make demands on your body and expect it to listen."

I thought about what he was saying and asked, "So, are you thinking that, just because I want to be a bodybuilder, it doesn't mean I can tell my puny little body to bench press 500 pounds and have it just happen? I have to have that goal in mind and work my body toward it until my body's ability is in sync with my mind's desire."

He nodded, smiling with relief. "That's exactly what I mean. You have all the goals in mind, and you want to reach them, but you're trying to bully your body into cooperation rather than persuading it to fall in line with your mind." He was getting more and more excited as he spoke. Maybe he had something, but I just didn't feel like I was doing it wrong.

At the same time, I appreciated that he cared enough to try to find the answer, and I gave him the first smile I'd had in days, even though I knew it didn't reach my exhausted eyes. "Thank you, Will. I'll look into it and see if there's some way I can intensify that connection. Maybe you could bring my iPad up here so I can look around and see what possibilities there are."

"Anything to help you, Rose. I love you, and I can't lose you. We'll figure this out, okay?"

I nodded and let him go. He came back later that evening with my iPad, and I dove in. I started with the internet, but I ended up downloading dozens of books and short publications that might shed some light on the truth of what Will had told me. I read until I thought my eyes might bleed, taking short naps in between, and over the next two days, I came to realize that he was right. I'd taken the basic lesson to heart, but I'd misapplied the directions.

I'd assumed that my mentality was like the general of an army that gave orders for my body to follow. I had been off the mark with that. In order to have the mind-body connection, both units had to make a decision. They couldn't work independently of each other and still achieve success.

It made me wonder how exactly I'd managed to get this far in achieving my desires when I'd been going about it the wrong way. If there was something my mind wanted, with my body not initially cooperating, I had to finesse it into agreement, and vice versa. There was no general, it was an orchestra. Each unit played a different role, but had to work together to create the beauty of a symphony.

I found a lot of information about how to make the first connection, to bring the two entities together, and I found a book on breathing. Breathing exercises were meant to calm the entire body and mind so that you could dive deep into your inner self, where the real healing needed to take place. I took the advice, actually picturing the world around me just coming to a stop and standing still so I could breathe and find that part of me inside. When I did tap into it, I felt better, if not whole and connected.

I began meditating daily, every morning, again at lunch, and in the evening before I slept. I was finally resting at night, and I no longer cared that I was stuck in a hospital. I was building a bond between my mind and my body that originated with my inner self, and I could feel the sparks flying through me, as if that was enough to heal me, all by itself.

Still, I struggled. I was weak from my illness, and my mind had been in the wrong place for a long time. When the two came together, I realized just how poorly I was fairing, but at least I was back on a path to results.

Within a week, I started keeping clear fluids down – herbal tea, chicken broth, and even a little gelatin. It made me stronger and I used that strength to build resolve. The doctors still didn't know what was wrong – they'd never found anything in the test results. It made me wonder if my illness was directly connected to my mental state. After all, if a positive connection could create health, then a negative mind-body connection or lack of one entirely could lead to sickness.

Meditation became easier, and I could put myself in that place with little effort. It helped me to focus on the here and now and forget just how bad things had gotten. The day that I managed to fire down some mashed potatoes and a few bites of baked chicken, I celebrated and cried tears of joy on my husband's shoulders. I'd done it. I'd found the real way to apply the law of attraction to my life and it had changed not only my outlook, but the truth of my well-being. It was a beautiful chemistry and after almost a month in the hospital, I was finally released.

I immediately started my yoga classes again, this time with a clear head and a way to reach that inner being inside me that was the at the core of my health. I enjoyed every minute of every day, throwing myself into work like I never had before, taking care of my home and my husband with no resentment, just making sure it was all in good order. My husband joined me in the practice, adopting my diet and finding his own exercise program while also connecting his mind and body with a positive outlook.

I was healthy for about six months when I started to feel a little under the weather again. I was nervous at first, but with a lot of meditation and focus, I managed to control it and try to find the core issue. When I discovered what was wrong with me, I set up a romantic dinner with my husband to discuss the situation. I could barely contain myself as we sat down; Will had been worried, too, for a couple of days since I told him I wasn't feeling up to par. He was anxious to hear what I had to say.

I looked at him and raised my glass of wine in a toast. "We've come a long way since I was stuck in the hospital, sweetheart, and we've earned every moment of happiness. Here's to us, having a happy, healthy life and a happy, healthy baby."

His eyes nearly bugged out of his head as my smile spread ear to ear. "You're pregnant?"

I nodded, fearing that speaking the words would bring me to tears. We'd talked for a long time about starting a family, but we'd never determined it to be the right time. Over the past several months, we'd simply put our thoughts and wishes into the universe and decided that things would happen when they should. To me, that meant this was the right time to have our first child.

Will seemed to agree as he whooped and hollered his celebration before catching me up in his arms and hugging me so tightly I could barely breathe. I didn't know what to expect during a pregnancy and the months that followed weren't the easiest of my life, but they were a breeze compared to the month I'd spent thinking I might die. This time I was prepared with my mind-body connection and I willed myself through that connection to stay well and manage the difficult parts of pregnancy.

William Aaron Carter was born the following May. As he grew, we taught him the importance of unity within himself and positive energy in his life. He was a very healthy son, incredibly smart, and a good student. For the next eighteen years, all three of us were reasonably healthy, with only a few short-lived illnesses that we worked our way out of with herbal supplements and alternative medicine.

On William's graduation day, I looked back at what we'd been through, where I personally had come from, and I knew that I had done a lot of growing during the worst moment of my life. I'd also continued to grow and learn with my family. I was so proud to see him walk across that stage, knowing that he would go on to college and make me even prouder to be his mother.

I went home with my husband, while William went to a graduation party. I sat down with a bowl of berries for dessert, next to my husband on the couch, and we watched a movie together. It was nice to know I'd been successful in my life and that I had so much more to live as my son started his own family and gave me renewed purpose and focus.

Closing Thoughts

There is no question that there is a powerful mind-body connection that can directly affect our health.

Simply stated, the way you think, feel and act impacts the health of your body. Any change in your life can disrupt your emotional health. Even changes that we think of as positive can be stressful. There are many illnesses and disorders that are "psychosomatic" – that is, caused by your psychological state. Unfortunately the Western medical community is not trained in this area. Even if the physician does recognize a condition as psychosomatic, the traditional medical solutions they have at their disposal offer no way to treat it. So it seems, at this point, that each of us holds our psychosomatic health in our own hands.

The best first step to taking charge of your mind-body connection is to learn about how it works. Do some research and read books on the topic so that you can be confident that you're applying mind-body techniques properly. This will help you avoid the problem that our friend Rose experienced when she applied only a portion of the mind-body connection theory to her life.

In the meantime, it can't hurt to set your focus on having a positive outlook. Try to focus on things that make you happy. You might also begin to incorporate relaxation techniques in your life such as meditation or yoga. Most importantly, make sure you're caring for your body in other ways. Enjoy your mind-body research and implementation journey. Implemented properly, mind-body connection strategies can unlock the magic inside you and make a world of difference in your healthier life.

RESOLVE TO LIVE

"Wherever you go, go with all your heart."
~ Confucius

"Lydia, come on! We've got to board now."

My husband was almost as excited about the trip as I was, and the kids were bouncing up and down. My older daughter, Crystal, was a lot like me and loved the idea of New York. Maybe that was my fault; I'd been talking about my dream of going there for the entire fourteen years of her life. My son, Ben, just liked to travel and, at eight, thought it was fancy to fly on a plane. James, my husband, was very supportive and had surprised me with this trip a month ago for my birthday.

I nodded and followed down the tunnel of the jet-way to the plane, but the feeling of dread grew in my gut and my lungs seized as I swallowed back the tears in my eyes and throat. It wasn't supposed to be like this, I thought as the attendant smiled and handed me a seat belt extension. I was still thrilled to have the chance to see New York. I'd dreamed of it since I was about Ben's age, watching movies about Broadway and Times Square and Chinatown. I wanted to see every last square foot of the city.

I was 38 years old now, and in many ways, life had been good to me. But I'd married young, right out of college, and James and I had a wonderful relationship. I'd had two kids, and over the years, I'd struggled with weight. But when I'd graduated from high school, I'd been a scant 120 pounds. I was part of the homecoming court my senior year and I'd even been nominated for prom queen, though I hadn't even come close to winning.

College had been rough and though I had stayed in good shape by walking almost everywhere I went and going to the gym every once in a while to blow off steam, I'd still put on the freshman ten, and it hadn't fallen off. In fact, over the next three years as I dated James, I'd put on ten more. I was 140 pounds at our wedding, and while I would have liked to wear a size two wedding dress, I was just fine with the way I looked.

I dieted when I got up to 160 and it helped for about a year. Then, I'd gotten pregnant and it was all over. I never lost the baby weight from having Crystal and I'd continued to balloon out of control afterward. It had been a hard pregnancy. I'd grown depressed and tried to compensate by eating, which turned into a disaster. James was a wonderful husband through it all, and I knew he still loved me very much, so I tried to lose weight for him. More than once, I'd tried the diets that nutritionists and celebrities alike swore by on various talk shows and I might lose five or ten pounds, but shortly after I gained back twice what I lost.

By the time I got pregnant with Ben, I was already over 200 pounds, and I put on forty more during the pregnancy. He'd been delivered by emergency cesarean and I'd gone into a total funk. I hadn't crawled out of bed for nearly a month and had to be heavily medicated and go to therapy to recover. I felt shame and guilt, especially since I hadn't been a mother to either of my children during that time. When I found out I was weighing in at 262 pounds, I wanted to punish myself. I went on a crash diet, eating nothing and drinking nothing but water, tea, and unsweetened fruit juice for two weeks.

Of course, I had eventually crashed, passing out in the floor of my bedroom one day while Ben was sleeping, Crystal was at school, and James was at work. I woke up starving and barely able to walk. When I got to the kitchen, I gorged, eating everything I could find. I was done trying, done caring. I would rather hate myself than fall down and drop my infant trying to get thin.

Now, eight years later, I was an embarrassment. I weighed myself just before leaving for the airport and I was 322 pounds, 200 pounds heavier than I'd been twenty years ago. I had wept in the bathroom, silently, where no one could hear, wondering how I was going to fair on this trip. I was too fat to fly with a regular seatbelt, for goodness's sake and I was disgusted with myself. I was shocked my kids weren't too ashamed to be with me, and as I sat down and connected the seat belt extension, feeling morbid, my husband leaned over and planted a kiss on my lips.

I stared at him in shock. He just smiled. "I'm excited, Lydia. All I can think about is how long you've wanted to go to New York and I can't wait to watch how childishly excited you get. You know, your eyes glitter when you're happy."

He was so wonderful, and he was right. I'm not sure how he remembered my happy face; it had been so long since I was truly happy. I thanked him and took out a book and my iPod, determined to huddle in on myself so I wouldn't notice how people looked at me. I also ignored the hurt look on my husband's face at my withdrawal. I didn't need the guilt on top of the feeling of worthlessness. I concentrated on my music and the story, trying to put my children's giggling and chattering out of my mind, and eventually, the plane came in for a landing.

I should have been jumping for joy, but there were enough people staring at me already, and I didn't want to embarrass my family any more than they already were by me. I kept my head down and pushed through the crowd, joining my family at baggage claim before heading to the subway system that would take us to our hotel and my first view of New York City.

Once in the hotel, I managed to clear my head a little and not be so worried. I took one look out our window and squealed with joy. The entire city was lit up almost like daylight in the darkness, and I couldn't wait to go exploring.

"Hey, Mom, the best pizza place in town is supposed to be three blocks from here," Crystal told me as she played with her phone. "I think that should be where we go for dinner."

"Sounds good to me," James told the kids, clapping his hands as he did when he made a decision. With my daughter as the tour guide, we headed out, stopping for pizza before heading to the Empire State Building, not far from where we were staying. It was a lot of walking for me, but the night air was cool and crisp and I enjoyed being with my family. I had control of the camera and took lots of pictures, making sure I stayed behind the lens rather than in front of it. I didn't really want to see myself in photographs right now. I hadn't taken one in over a year and I didn't intend for that to change now.

We were a little jet lagged, so after visiting what was probably one of the most famous buildings in the world, we went back to the hotel and put the kids in their room connected to ours and settled in to watch a movie and fall asleep. My husband cuddled close to me, but I wouldn't let him put his arm around me. It no longer reached, and I hated the reminder of how much I'd changed.

The next day was filled with excitement and shopping, my daughter insisting we had to go to Chinatown and bargain. There were clothes, fruits, trinkets, electronics, and just about anything you could imagine. I snapped shot after shot of my kids playing around, and even my husband got into the game. I took several pictures of all three of them, cherishing the happy smiles on their faces and glad, at least, that I had them with me on this trip. I don't think it would have been any fun had I just gone alone. I would have been too embarrassed to do anything.

We picked up some gyros for lunch, but I could barely eat. We ate on an outdoor patio, and I felt like the throngs of people walking by stared at me every time I took a bite, their expressions telling me they thought I shouldn't eat another bite. "Are you okay?" James asked quietly in my ear.

I gave him the best smile I could and nodded. "Of course. I'm here in New York with my three favorite people and I'm having a blast. My appetite just isn't very big right now. Maybe I'm just excited about being here."

"Well, I think we should make the trip out to see the Statue of Liberty next," Crystal said as she wiped her hands, having finished her gyro in no time.

Ben frowned at her. "Come on, Crys, this trip is for Mom. Why don't we let her decide what to do next?"

Crystal rolled her eyes. "Because I'm the planner here. I already know everywhere that Mom wants to go and all the things she wants to see and do, so I'm trying to make sure we do it all in a way that she doesn't miss out on anything."

I held up my hand to stop the argument. "Thank you both for caring. I think Crystal's right. Let's go see the Statue of Liberty and when we get back we'll go to Ground Zero and pay our respects."

The boat ride over was somewhat relaxing and I was thankful, still taking pictures. Crystal tried to convince me to have one of the staff members on the boat take a picture of all of us together, but I refused. I wanted to commemorate my trip here as happily as possible and that required not seeing what I'd looked like while I was here.

I was relieved that the stairs up to the top of the statue were shut down; I couldn't have made the climb, and I didn't want to disappoint my family. We strolled through the museum and listened to the tour guide, and my kids bought souvenirs before we headed back to the mainland and took the subway to Ground Zero. It brought tears to our eyes as we read the lists of people who died and saw how much work still needed to be done after all this time, so we needed a pick-up as we left.

Ben suggested we go to Central Park and find the zoo and everyone agreed. By the time we got back to the hotel, I was exhausted, and I worried about being ready to go the next day. In fact, the more we did, the more I worried about myself.

The day we went to Times Square, I'd finally convinced my family to stop asking for me to be in the pictures. "Come on, you guys, I'm taking great photos. I don't think anyone else could record these moments better. Now, move together," I told them in front of the MTV studio. It was a really warm day, and there were a lot of people, so I started to feel flushed, and with as much walking as we were doing, my heart was pounding.

"Guys, can we stop and sit for a minute?" I finally asked, completely winded. We were near the three-story McDonald's, and by the time I sat down and James went to get me some water, I thought I was going to have a heart attack. My left arm was even numb, and I was sweating up a storm. It took several long minutes to recover, and even when my heart rate felt normal, I was so tired that I'm sure the rest of my family cut the day short so I wouldn't get sick again.

After my husband fell asleep that night, I went into the bathroom and wept. I couldn't believe it was happening this way. I felt the life draining out of me as I explored the city I had longed to fall in love with for so many years, and I was dragging my family down with me. It wasn't fair.

I had to do something about my weight. I was going to kill myself,

100

not to mention tarnish the memory of this perfect trip. We had one more day in New York before we went home, and I decided that, when we got home, I was going to buckle down and lose the weight, even if it meant not eating.

Of course, it was easier said than done. When we got home, everyone was tired for a week. I really felt like I'd spent all my energy for the rest of the year. Rather than cooking, we ordered out for three nights and after that I made frozen lasagna and pizza rolls. It was incredibly unhealthy and since I didn't feel like going to the store and being stared at by everyone there, I munched potato chips and other greasy and sugary stuff for breakfast and lunch. I felt bloated and insecure and it made me more tired than ever.

It was almost two weeks before I had the energy and drive to start posting pictures of the trip on Facebook. They made me smile as I tagged and captioned them, adding them to my "I Love New York" album. I was probably about three hours in and powering through it when I started to get 'likes' and comments. I didn't read them at first, trying to get as many posted as possible, but about 200 photos in, it was time for a break.

I grabbed a soda and sat back down to read some of the comments, and I swallowed hard. The first one said, "Your family is lovely! Wish you were there." There were a couple more, then another that read, "Maybe next time you can go, too." And then one of James's coworkers saying, "I hope Lydia's well…didn't she go with you?"

I couldn't hold back the tears and I knew it looked bad for me to not be in a single picture. I'd gone to New York, the Mecca of America, the one place I'd always dreamed of, and now I had nothing to show for it, no way to prove it. It was as if I was invisible, a ghost in my own life, despite being too large to miss. I hated it, and I hated myself for letting it happen.

I cried for hours as I sat there alone, wondering what I was going to do. Obviously, things had to change, but I didn't know where to start. After all, dieting hadn't worked for me before and had only caused me to bounce back heavier than before. I couldn't get any heavier – I knew I'd be too far gone for any help that anyone could offer.

Knowing I didn't have long before my kids got home from

school, I forced myself to get into the shower and clean up, washing my face more than once to try to hide the fact that I'd been crying, and then I went back to the computer to search for help. This time, rather than looking for the latest fad diet, I clicked on the name of a nutritionist in the area. I made an appointment for the next day and decided I'd do this the right way.

After my family left the next day, I got ready and drove myself to the woman's office. She taught me a lot about changing my lifestyle. She taught me that a "diet" wouldn't help anyone. A diet wasn't a temporary thing—it was the way you ate on a normal day. So, changing your diet was about changing your lifestyle. She showed me a few simple things, like how to count calories and how much I could burn with several different low-impact exercises.

She also taught me about calorie deficiency and how that's a necessity for losing weight. We set up another appointment so she could give me a few more details. When I left, I didn't exactly have a bounce in my step, but I felt metaphorically lighter on my feet. I stopped at the store on the way home, buying several of the healthy snacks she suggested and putting them in a corner of the pantry, where they were not auspicious, but could be easily accessed.

Over the next several weeks, I worked hard and I found that the more I focused on the prize and the harder I tried to stay away from heavy fried foods and sweets, the better I felt. It wasn't just physical, either. It was mental, as if the grease that clogged my arteries also clogged my brain. I smiled more and I was more interactive with the children. Every day, I went for a one-mile walk around the neighborhood and I did other cardio exercises inside, using homemade weights and things to assist me.

I barely even noticed the weight loss until the first eight weeks were over and I was down 12 pounds. That put me so close to the 300 mark that it drove me harder, and I increased my walk to two miles, cutting back my calories by another 200 a day. I wasn't hungry like I used to be and I didn't have cravings for ice cream anymore.

Things kept getting better and the more positive I felt that I could lose the weight, the happier I was. I took my first picture four months into the new diet at my son's Spring Fling. I was down to 284, and even though I still hated what I saw in the mirror, I loved what I felt, inside and out. I could breathe easier and my clothes were baggy. I had to buy a few new things, just to look human when I did go out.

At the nine month mark, I hit a plateau. I was down to 203, but I couldn't seem to get below it. I hadn't talked to the nutritionist in months, but I had been doing so well, I thought I was going to make it alone. After two weeks of no results, I was frustrated and starting to spiral again. I knew I couldn't let it happen; I was loving my new life far too much to lose control. I set up another appointment and the nutritionist told me I needed a reset; that my body no longer realized it was supposed to make use of the fat on my body for fuel.

For a week, I increased my calorie intake enough to put on two pounds, which wasn't a lot, but the numbers made me uneasy. However, just as the nutritionist had told me, when I returned to the stricter intake, I started losing again, and the motivation returned. I went at it full force, and I even asked my husband on a date. It was the first time I'd wanted to be seen in public in nice clothes in years and it was a very romantic evening.

After that, I made a new resolve—even if I didn't get down to my goal weight, I could be happy with myself. I'd gotten back down to a reasonable size that I could manage and maintain and while I still wanted the size four body, I didn't have to have it if I was healthy and comfortable in my skin. The heart flutters had long gone away, and the doctor had just given me a clean bill of health. I wasn't giving up.

It took a year and a half, but I counted down a pound at a time and I continued to increase how far I was walking each day until I hit ten miles, but the day I stepped on the scale and weighed in at 123 pounds, I cried. I cried for a good hour, all the tension and hard work coming out with each teardrop. I looked in the mirror and, maybe for the first time since I started losing weight, I saw what I looked like. I hadn't really seen myself all this time and now I saw the thin woman I'd once been. I was older, sure, but I was beautiful, and my skin glowed with happiness.

I threw out all the too-large clothes, taking them to Goodwill, and I promised myself that I wouldn't let my mind or my body get that out of control ever again. I made a celebratory dinner of baked chicken breast, cheddar-broccoli casserole, and brownies for dessert, and I sat with my family and laughed while they told stories about their days.

I approached my husband that night when the kids were settled in their room, and I put my arms around his waist.

"James, thank you for being so supportive of me for so long. I couldn't have lost the weight without a husband who loves me this much. I wondered, could we renew our vows?"

He smiled and kissed me. "I love you, Lydia, whatever your size, and of course I want to renew our vows. In fact, I think I'd like to do that in Hawaii." He pulled something out of his pocket and I gasped, seeing four tickets to the islands in his hands.

I kissed him hard and hugged him tight, and with a smile that shone with all my renewed happiness, I told him, "That's perfect! I'll wear a bikini."

Closing Thoughts

If you have fought being overweight for years and years only to become more obese after each diet attempt, there is still hope.

Oh yes, I already hear your excuses – how? Because I have expressed them all myself. You've tried everything, it doesn't work. Well I'm here to tell you the cold hard facts that you haven't tried everything because you still have weight to lose. We are all looking for that quick fix, that magic diet pill that we will swallow and wake up skinny, but none of it exist. If you look at the plethora of diet pills, programs, soups and drinks you will see that they all require you to cut calories and spend at least 30 minutes a day being active.

Why? Because that is the answer! Eat right and exercise. All the added pills, drinks and soups are the placebos that promise you will lose weight *faster*. And sometimes it works – why? Because you BELIEVE that the placebo addition will get you the results faster never realizing that it is the right diet and exercising that is getting you the results.

I challenge you to do what Lydia did, take that first step. Take that first step and then follow it up with another step. Your weight wasn't gained over night, so it won't come off over night, just stick to it. Soon you will start feeling great, full of energy and the numbers on the scale will take care of themselves.

FIND HEALING IN HOPE

"Never affirm or repeat about your health what you do not wish it to be true."
~ Ralph Waldo Trine

I sat in the patient room, tugging nervously at my shirt while I waited for the doctor to come in. I'd been feeling a bit under the weather lately and I had no idea what was wrong. So far, I'd been cleared of flu and other infections, conditions like fibromyalgia, and even told that all my hormone levels were normal. There was literally nothing wrong as far as the typical tests showed.

My doctor had finally taken some additional blood for testing and sent me for a complete body scan to see if it caught anything they might have missed. I was losing my mind now, waiting for the results, and I had decided they couldn't be good if it was taking this long for the doctor to come in. Was he avoiding me?

When he opened the door, his face was grim, and though he smiled, I could see the concern in his eyes. "Good morning, Ms. Collins. How are you feeling this morning?"

I laughed nervously. "If I was better, I wouldn't be here."

He nodded. "Well, we've identified why you haven't been feeling well, Ms. Collins. That's the first step in resolution, right?" My hopes sank, what little I'd had, and I nodded, swallowing past the lump in my throat, waiting in silence. He sighed. "There's a mass on your right lung. Right now, it looks like it's contained to the one area, but we'll need a PET scan to know for sure. We'll also need to do a

105

biopsy. I can't tell you if it's malignant or not until we do."

I almost choked, my whole body stiff with disbelief. I was only 28 years old. I was in good health, had been all my life, and I had two babies at home, one of whom was only four months old. I couldn't have cancer. It wasn't possible. No, this wasn't happening. "Could the images be wrong?"

He pulled what looked like a photo out of the file and pointed to a particular area. "These are your lungs and this is the bottom of your right one here. See that dark spot? It isn't normal and shouldn't be there."

I shook my head. How was this happening? I wasn't a smoker. I didn't eat foods that were high in mercury or anything else dangerous. "How is this possible?"

He shrugged and gave me a piteous look that I hated. I had never enjoyed sympathy. "Sometimes, this just happens. Like I said, I think we caught it early enough that it hasn't spread anywhere else yet. But lung cancer is very aggressive and we'll need to get you in for surgery quickly. In fact, since you have to be sliced open for a biopsy anyway, I think you should just go ahead and remove the mass while you're at it."

He was talking about moving so fast that my head spun. "Surgery? We don't even know it's cancerous yet."

"Ms. Collins, I hate to be the bearer of bad news, but I've only seen one mass like this come through here that wasn't malignant. I'm going to refer you to an oncologist, who might be a little more experienced in this. He may have better information for you. In the meantime, I've gathered information for you about the options you have after surgery. I've got an entire bag of pamphlets for you, along with your referral." He cleared his throat. "There's also a referral for a counselor, just in case you need someone to talk to."

I nodded, not knowing what to say and not trusting my voice. I also knew that, as soon as I opened my mouth, I would also open the flood gates and the tears would fall. Instead, I took what he offered me and drove home, wishing I'd let my husband take off work and come with me today. I stopped by my mother's house and put on a brave face so I could pick up my baby girl, Gemma, and my two-year-old son, Matt. I didn't want to tell her until I'd told my husband.

I broke down sobbing when I did, burying my face in Clay's

shoulder as my body was racked with convulsions. I just knew I was going to die, and even if I didn't, I couldn't imagine caring for my young children while going through chemotherapy or radiation. Clay held her and cried with her, and he tried to soothe her, telling her everything would be okay. But I couldn't believe it, not yet.

I went to the oncologist the same week, who told me that he couldn't give specifics without a PET scan or surgery, but that he thought we'd caught it in stage two, which meant we could take care of it with surgery and some serious aftercare. He wanted to schedule the surgery immediately, but I asked for a little time to research the subject. He reiterated that the majority of growths on the lungs were cancerous and that they spread quickly, so he told me we couldn't wait more than a couple of weeks without risking the spread to other organs. I spent the next week, looking through the pamphlets, talking to my mother about the children and the help I would need, and crawling the internet for the best and most recent information on treatment options. But every time I got started, I fell apart again, seeing no way out of this situation. I ended up calling to schedule the surgery for the following week instead and then I began to get my affairs in order.

Clay reassured me there was no need to contact the lawyer to update my will, but I was determined. "Sandy, I'm not going to lose you. People survive this every day. You'll be fine. You're a strong woman."

I frowned, fighting the beginnings of tears for the fourth time today. "I know, honey, but I can't go into this surgery, and I certainly can't face treatment or the potential that treatment won't work unless I'm prepared. I can't think about leaving you and our babies alone unless I know everything is protected." He stopped arguing with me and just watched. I couldn't look at him, couldn't stand the sad expression on his face.

After I dealt with the lawyer, I spiraled downward, until I couldn't crawl out of bed. Clay had to drop the kids with my mother, who left them with my sister to come check on me. Even she couldn't drag me to my feet. I just pushed her away, listless and sleepy. I didn't eat, and I drifted in and out of sleep until my husband carried me to the car and took me to the hospital for my surgery.

I was scared, and I was shaking out of control as they wheeled me

107

into the operating room. My oncologist looked down at me, just before they put me under, and he said something I didn't quite understand at the time, but those words would register with me somewhere between the twilight and the unconsciousness, changing my outlook entirely.

"Ms. Collins, I'm going to get this tumor out of you, but that's the easy part. I can't cure you. You can have surgery and chemo and radiation, or whatever else you want, but nothing is going to heal you without your mind and soul being in sync with the desire to stay alive. Think about that, and fight for life while you're under anesthesia, okay? If you do that, everything will come out just fine."

The last thing I remember thinking was that I did want to stay alive, and then the lights went out.

I was groggy when I opened my eyes, and the lights around me were so bright I groaned at the sharp pain that went through my head. "Lights off," I croaked, not even knowing if anyone was there.

To my great relief, the lights dimmed, and my husband's face came into clear view above me, his smile the best thing I could remember seeing in a very long time. "How are you feeling?" he asked, pushing my hair back from my face.

I grunted. "It hurts to take a deep breath."

He nodded with a sympathetic look. "Everything went great, honey. The doctor says they removed the entire mass. Now, it's just a matter of follow-up treatment."

While I wanted to cry with joy because the surgery had been successful, I was still reeling over having the surgery to begin with. I wasn't ready to talk about other treatments yet. I'd just woken up. "How are the kids?" I asked, changing the subject.

He laughed. "They've been with your mother, getting spoiled. We're never going to be able to discipline them after this." He kissed my forehead. "But I don't care, as long as I have my whole family."

I was released from the hospital the next day, with a prescription for pain medication and strict instructions not to lift anything for a few days. I went to a follow-up visit with the oncologist a week later, and he was pleased with how I was healing, but wanted to discuss treatment options. I told him I needed a little more time; I hadn't done all the research I wanted.

"Fair enough. Just know that we can do chemo, or we can do

108

radiation. Or, if we choose a combination of the two, you'll have less of each in your system."

I nodded, thinking about the horrors of those treatments, and went home. That night, I put my children to bed and watched them sleep for several minutes, just glad to be there, and then I headed to the computer. I thought about radiation therapy, and all I could think of was nuclear winter. It wasn't a healthy option. But then, chemotherapy was literally putting poison in your body to kill the cancer. I was convinced that, with either or both, I'd be too ill to take care of my family. I couldn't stand the thought of handing my children over to my mother for weeks while I lost my hair and hung my head over a toilet.

But those were supposedly my options, and thinking I had no choice, I wanted to cry more than I had before. I turned to the internet, looking for anything and everything I could find to tell me what the right answer was. Which choice would be the least toxic and allow me to live the most normal life over the following weeks and months?

Something caught my eye. I wouldn't normally have paid any attention to it, but wasn't I looking for some other way to heal myself? The words *alternative therapy* sounded very new-age and not exactly reliable, but an alternative was exactly what I needed, so I was willing to grasp at straws. I clicked into the article and read several suggestions for therapeutic foods and practices that could replace the need for chemo and radiation.

I was skeptical, but there were several links to follow to stories from actual people who had followed the regimens and succeeded. From there, I followed links to other resources, including articles on the power of positive energy and thought. I remembered back to my doctor's admonition as I went under for surgery, his words were I needed *to want to live* and had to think about my wants. Maybe, if I'd stayed in the funk I'd been in for so long as I went under the knife, I could have died, or maybe the doctor wouldn't have been able to remove the entire mass.

It was hard to believe that positive thoughts and energy could really make that much of an effect on anything, so I spent the next few days testing it out in small ways. My two-year-old son, Matt, came down with a cold, and I gave him some medication for the

109

symptoms and had positive thoughts about a quick recovery. He was better overnight. My husband had a big meeting at work that made him nervous, thinking he might be going in to get laid off. I put positive energy out there, thought hard about it, and when he came home, he had gotten a raise.

They may have been isolated incidents, but at the same time, just being this positive was making me feel better, lighter, and healthier overall. My attitude began to change, just using the philosophy as a tool. The first time I climbed out of bed and felt dizzy and weak, I told myself that, after a cup of tea and a granola bar, I'd feel much better and be ready to face the day. It worked, and I felt better throughout the day than I had in months.

I also decided to grab a couple of the herbal supplements they suggested at the local health food store. Within three days of the regimen, I felt like I could run a marathon. It was empowering to think that such small measures, without the toxic waste of traditional drugs, such as antidepressants, could take me so far. And the largest part of it was a positive attitude.

With further reading, I came across information about cleansing and healing yoga practices. I read further, and when I'd gathered enough information, I sat down to talk to my husband. After all, we were a couple with children, and that meant family decisions were made together. I knew what I wanted, but I wasn't going to force the issue. I was going to present my case to him reasonably and see how he felt about it.

The discussion went well and while Clay had his reservations and concerns, he also understood where I was coming from. "The important thing to me is to have you here long term, Sandy. I want to spend a long life with you. I want Gemma to know her mother and I want you to see Matt grow up. But it's just as important for you to be able to enjoy them now, in the early years that you can't get back. I've always supported you and I'll be behind you in whatever decision you make here."

I was glad, and I hugged him, telling him my mind was made up. I spent the next two days showering my children with love and attention so I'd be in a happy, healthy mindset when I went to the oncologist's office to discuss my decision.

"I'm declining both radiation and chemotherapy at this time,

110

doctor. I've been looking into alternative therapies for cancer patients and I'd like to give that a go." He didn't seem incredibly surprised by my words.

"Ms. Collins, we tested the mass and the type of cancer you have is very aggressive. I can respect your decision, but I want you to be sure. In these cases, I always try to convince my patients to at least try a short round of radiation treatments. That would have the least impact on you." I shook my head. "I appreciate your concern, doctor, but I've made up my mind. If...*when* I come back in three months for a checkup, these therapies aren't working, I'll reconsider. But I want to be able to take care of my small children." I paused. "When you told me that I had to want to live, I took that to heart, and I feel that a strong will to live and get better, coupled with herbal supplements, diet, and exercise are the right tools to heal. If I'm wrong, we'll do it your way in three months."

"Very well."

I left the office, scared and excited at the same time. There was always a chance the cancer would still return or spread, but I had burdened my soul with the need to fight, and I was determined to win this battle. My diet became simple – very little red meat, lots of soy and fiber. I also switched out unhealthy snacks like potato chips for fresh fruits and vegetables, and I continued taking supplements that would help flush toxins from my system and keep my organ function at full blast.

I went to a yoga class for healing that helped me connect mind, body, and spirit three times a week. It worked wonders on my self-esteem, as well as my willpower and determination. It taught me that instead of only being happy when I felt good, I should equate feeling good with being happy. It became a mantra for me and every day that I woke up with a positive attitude was a good day. I lived for the present and worried less about the future, watching my kids grow and learn day by day.

I had romantic interludes with my husband that boosted my serotonin levels and we laughed a lot. I spent time with my mother and my sister, whether it was just a walk through the park with the children or a day of intense cooking for a gathering with the rest of the family.

Day by day, I felt healthier. The more positive thought and energy

111

I put into the universe, the better I felt. I shoved negative thoughts out of me and let nature recycle them. There was something healing about the earth as well and I meditated in a place every day where I could touch the ground or a tree, just to feel connected.

My husband looked at me funny over the dinner table, a couple of weeks before I was supposed to go back to the doctor, and told me, "You look radiant. You've always been beautiful, but now you have a glow about you that you didn't even have when you were pregnant."

I laughed. "I was sick when I was pregnant, not radiant."

He rolled his eyes. "You still had a glow about you, like despite how sick you were, you were insanely happy."

"I was."

"Well, you glow even brighter now."

I thought about it for a minute. "I am happy, truly happy. I've got the most beautiful children in the world and I have a loving, supportive husband. I'm healthy and positive, and I'm strong enough to face the truth if the test results come back that I still need chemo or radiation. I know even on that road, if I go into it with a positive attitude, I'll get through it with minimal problems and come out with a clean bill of health on the other side."

"I'm proud of you, Sandy. Even I've learned to be less negative and fatalistic watching you these past few weeks. You've done such a good job of sticking to your guns and I love you more than ever for your conviction." He hugged me tight. It brought tears to my eyes to hear those words. It hadn't been easy, but I knew I couldn't give up as I had just before the surgery. I would have died in weeks.

I waited in the doctor's office for the results of all my tests, incredibly nervous but believing I'd get good news. Just as it had worked with everything else, I was certain that being positive, coupled with the regimen I'd been on for the last three months would make all the difference.

The oncologist walked in, staring at some papers with a frown on his face, and my heart dropped. What did that expression mean? He started shaking his head, and asked, "Ms. Collins, have you seen another doctor since you were last here? Or is there something I'm missing on your chart?"

I shook my head. "No, I haven't seen a doctor at all. Why?"

He pushed his glasses up and looked at me across his desk. "Your results came back great. You're in remission and there is no evidence anywhere of active cancer in your system."

I couldn't believe it. That was better than I'd hoped for. "Are you sure?"

"I'm quite sure. I don't know how you did it, but I know you're a strong-willed, healthy woman, and I hope you keep doing whatever you're doing. I want to see you back again in six months for a reassessment, but I have faith it will be just as good as this test."

I practically ran from the office, calling my family with the news. I was ecstatic and I intended to do exactly what the doctor said. I loved the positive outlook on life, as well as how good I felt with healthy food, vitamins, and exercise, and I wouldn't give it up for the world, especially with these kind of results. It wasn't just my health that was better; it was my life. I'd beat the odds and come back stronger.

Fifteen years later, I sat with my husband on one side and my daughter, Gemma, on the other at Matt's graduation ceremony. I was so grateful to be there. I'd continued my healthy lifestyle – and healthy attitude – and not once in fifteen years had there been any sign of cancer returning. I remained in remission and I lived my life. As Matt walked across the stage, my husband recorded it on his phone and I cried. There had been a time when I didn't believe I'd see this day, but because of the changes I'd made in my life, this day was far from being my last.

Closing Thoughts

Evidence suggests that the power of positive thinking actually does aid in healing, possibly due to a connection between the mind's power and the immune system.

I would never suggest that everyone in any stage of serious illness should shun traditional treatment and embrace only alternative therapies. There are certainly times that it would not be in a person's best interest to decline traditional methods. But using alternative therapies like visualizing yourself without any health afflictions and appreciating the systems in your body that are functioning properly can also aid in your healing.

It is the responsibility of each individual who has an illness to carefully consider all alternatives in order to make an informed, intelligent decision regarding their chosen path towards healing.

Regardless, it would seem rather foolish to completely disregard the possible benefits of the power of positive thinking. It is amazing that it worked post-surgically for Sandy, in combination with a healthy diet and carefully-chosen supplements. Even if you choose a more traditional path toward healing, it seems likely that positive thoughts combined with those methods can only enhance your body's ability to heal. No matter what your illness or what path to healing you choose, always remember that your thoughts are at least partially responsible for your healing. It is, literally, mind over matter. Healing does indeed stem from hope.

FIND YOUR POWER

"In the long run men hit only what they aim at."
~ Henry David Thoreau

I hung up the phone, still lying on the floor of my closet. As I tried to curl into a fetal position, I sobbed harder, realizing that the bulk I carried wouldn't even allow me that comfort properly. How had I let this spiral so far out of control? I hated my life. When I stepped into the closet to find something to wear to work today, I'd finally noticed that nothing in there fit me, that even my largest clothes were too tight.

I was glad my daughters had already left for school this morning, and I was relieved it wasn't my carpool day. I was lost and I couldn't find a way back out of this hole I'd fallen in. I lay there long enough to lose track of time, my tears coating my cheeks and making them feel stiff and dirty. When I finally convinced myself to get up, I was ashamed of how much difficulty I had, and I had to roll around like a beached whale to be able to lift myself to my feet.

It was even harder to reach down and pick up the phone where I'd left it after I'd called in sick to work, unable to face the fact that my body was out of control. I grunted as I drug my feet all the way to the bathroom, avoiding a glance in the mirror as I tortured myself by stepping on the scale. I grimaced as the digital output read 226. I didn't even remember crossing the 200 mark.

I should have gotten in the shower, cleaned up, and gone to the store to find at least a couple of outfits I could mix and match for work. It would be the responsible thing to do, but I couldn't seem to wrap my head around the idea of being responsible. I felt worthless, as if I was a big ball of blubber that my husband, my daughters, and the rest of my family had to lug around with them in life, like a ball and chain. I was beginning to believe they would all be better off without me.

Instead of taking care of business, I went to the kitchen and grabbed a bag of chips and a soda – after all, what difference did the calories make now? I took them with me to the family room, where the walls were covered with photos of my daughters, their grandparents, my husband, and the occasional shot of me, years ago. I pulled out one of my high school yearbooks and two of our old photo albums and began flipping pages.

Kristi Brennan was a different person than I was today. The picture of the cheerleading squad brought back so many memories it was hard to face. I remembered being fit, healthy, with lots of energy. I wasn't the top of the pyramid, but I wasn't the base, either. I'd been 135 pounds of toned muscle back then, and I'd had the boys fawning all over me. I'd also been in gymnastics, and I opened an album, finding a picture of me in my leotard, with a silver medal for the uneven bars event I'd won at a regional competition.

I'd remained that way through college, retaining an academic scholarship, but still participating in cheerleading and gymnastics. I'd been so proud of who I was, how I looked. I was never cocky, and I never thought I was the belle of the ball, but I was confident that I was a pretty girl. When Devon Fields had asked me to study with him for a final my junior year, I'd fallen instantly in love with the way he looked at me, as if I was the most beautiful woman he'd ever seen.

We'd married after college, and my wedding dress hung in a closet in the guest bedroom, mostly because I couldn't stand to look at the tiny little waistline and realize that I was about twice that size now. Of course, the wedding picture made me look like a goddess, and I missed that person. Today, I looked like I'd swallowed her, or that maybe she'd gotten lost inside one of my fat rolls.

When I'd become pregnant with Kelly, I'd put on a few pounds of baby weight, but I'd dropped back down to the solid 135 I'd been before in just a couple of months. I'd been so proud of myself and all I could think about now was how many times people told me I looked like I'd never had a baby. Devon told me every day how radiant and beautiful I was. I think that was really the highlight of my life.

When I'd found out I was having another baby, I'd been all for it. After all, my body hadn't suffered the first time around. I could do it again, and I couldn't wait to have a second child. But Bailey had been born and the weight hadn't come off so easily. In fact, I got down to 145 but couldn't seem to lose that final ten pounds. I think that was where the spiral started.

After six months, I wasn't just hauling around my 15-pound infant and towing my 3-year-old toddler behind me; I was still carrying ten extra pounds of my own. I went on a very strict diet, and a week later, I had lost five of those pounds, but I was famished and weak. I'd denied myself so much so quickly that I broke the diet and, the next thing I knew, I had gained ten more pounds.

Incredibly unhappy with how tight my clothes were and not liking what I saw in the mirror, I took it out on my husband. Devon had asked at the wrong time, as I stepped off the scale, if I might want to go out for a nice steak. "Is that some sort of fat joke?" I clipped at him.

He'd been blindsided. "No, I just thought you might like to enjoy dinner out. I even asked the neighbor girl if she could babysit for a couple of hours so you could take a night off from the girls." He'd come over and hugged me and said, "You're beautiful, Kristi. You are thin and gorgeous, and you have all the right curves. I love you."

Feeling terrible for jumping down his throat, I had pouted. "I'm sorry, Devon. I love you, too. Let's go out. It'll be good for us."

I had gone back to work shortly after that, finally feeling that Bailey and Kelly were both old enough for daycare. Going from an active life of caring for children all day to sitting at a desk didn't help me much. I tried to eat salads for lunch, but I found myself stressed and unable to get away for lunch at all. Instead, I would snack at my desk throughout the day, and before I knew what was happening, I had gained another ten pounds.

If I'd been unhappy at 150, I was miserable at 160, especially when I had to start buying new clothes in larger sizes. I felt like I was about to bust out of my skin, and I was uncomfortable all the time. I didn't want my husband to look at me and I traded in my sexy gowns for pajama pants to help cover up the weight gain. When he tried to make love to me, I told him I wasn't in the mood and he was good with me for a time. Eventually, though, he got frustrated and I told him I just couldn't. By then, I'd gone up and down in weight by five and ten pounds at a time until I was pushing 190.

After that argument, he'd stopped asking, and we'd become distant. Once again, I became determined to lose the weight, and I practically stopped eating. But again, when I watched my daughters eating ice cream cones at night or enjoy bowls full of pasta, my depression took over. I hated myself for getting into the situation, and I was jealous of everyone else. I refused to go to my parents' house for dinner on Sundays, and when Kelly would ask me to chaperone a field trip at school, I made excuses. I didn't want her friends or their mothers to look at me and laugh. My size was laughable. I was beginning to resemble a stuffed sausage. When I would make those comments, my relationship with my husband would go from bad to worse, his determination to ignore me suddenly flaring into indignation and rage so that he chastised me for my attitude.

I would cry and tell him, "That's how it feels, Devon. You don't look at me anymore and I can't blame you. I'm a pear instead of an hourglass, and I'm full and ripe. It's disgusting. I'm shopping in the women's section now, which is just code for fat ladies."

"No, it's not, Kristi. And I do look at you. I still want you, but I'm tired of being rejected. I shouldn't have to suffer because you're unhappy. That's not fair. I love you the way you are and I'm very much attracted to you. You've given me a beautiful family and a beautiful life and I just want us to be whole again. But if you can't do that as you are, I'll do whatever I can to help you lose as much weight as you want. I'm completely supportive."

Of course, I'd thrown it back in his face. "See? You think I'm fat. You're just trying to be kind about it." I would walk away and shake my head. "Don't worry, I'll take care of it." After the big blowout, I'd gone to the kitchen with a spoon and a half gallon of ice cream. I couldn't starve myself forever and I lost hope. I no longer felt it mattered how I looked. I'd already ruined my love life and I'd stopped being social long before.

Over the next two years, it only got worse. I knew I wasn't only miserable with myself, but also miserable to be around. I looked up at the family picture on the wall, taken on Bailey's fifth birthday. My girls were five and eight, and I couldn't even be a big part of their life. I'd positioned them on my lap in the picture, trying to hide as much of myself as I could. That was my MO – hiding. Just as I'd done this morning rather than go to work. Just as I did socially, always having an excuse not to go anywhere I was invited.

I was no sort of role model for my daughters. They came to me and wanted to do things, and I had to say no. I shopped for them online or sent them with their Aunt Jenna because Mommy didn't want to be seen in public. I rarely took them swimming in the summer because I refused to get in the pool with them, feeling that I'd displace so much water everyone would be forced out of the water.

My husband worked late most days to avoid the nasty conversations that tended to come about while I prepared dinner. My mother didn't call much anymore, unless she wanted the girls for the weekend, and I no longer had friends, having alienated myself dozens of pounds ago. This body was still foreign to me, five years later, and I cringed with every reminder that I wasn't the teenager in the cheerleader uniform anymore.

The chips were gone and so was the soda. I brushed a few crumbs off the precious albums before replacing them on the shelf where I'd found them. I threw away my trash, feeling bloated and dirty. Again, I told myself to take a shower, but as I climbed into the tub with effort and looked down at the water streaming over my body, realizing that I couldn't even fit all of myself under the spray at the same time anymore, I began to weep again, sobs that racked my whole body.

My sorrow was deep and ached, and I told myself how gross I was as I lifted my belly to scrub beneath the roll that had formed there. I had become everything I promised myself I wouldn't, and I had no real excuse. I'd been lazy and careless and completely misguided in how to handle life as a whole. Instead of dealing with stress, I'd eaten it. The same was true of pain and hatred. Every bit of what I felt had gone into my mouth, and I'd been punishing everyone else.

I decided then to stop pushing my problems on everyone else and I felt a modicum of relief that, while I would continue to suffer, no one around me would. After all, I deserved the humiliation of being seen in public, whereas my daughters didn't deserve to be put off on someone else when they wanted their mother. I deserved for my family to look at me in disgust at Sunday dinner, while my husband and children deserved to be able to spend time with their grandparents and cousins.

I pulled on a pair of sweats, since I had nothing else that fit, and I went to the store, where I picked up just a few blouses and two pairs of pants in a larger size. I needed to be able to dress if I was going to start leaving the house, not to mention that I couldn't call into work again and keep my job. I went home and put on one outfit, just in time for my daughters to come home. I could hear the bus rolling up and the chatter of children as they climbed out.

But as Kelly opened the door with Bailey at her heels, I realized their words weren't happy but angry. I heard Bailey tell Kelly in that sweet little voice of hers, "But Tara and Renee and Jessica all wear a littler size than me. And Renee's legs are really skinny."

I peered around the corner in time to see Kelly roll her eyes and place her hands on her hips. "You're still a baby. It's okay to have a little bit of difference in your size when you're five. I'm eight. I shouldn't have to suck in to close my jeans. I have a tummy that sticks out. I'm not skinny enough."

I realized in horror that my self-image issues had rubbed off on my daughters. Neither of them were large. As Kelly had pointed out, Bailey was a bit chubby, but only because she was so young. It was the typical baby fat that would grow with her as she got older and keep her healthy. As for Kelly, she sounded like an anorexic, considering that there wasn't an ounce of fat on her body. She was extremely thin, and the only time her stomach stuck out was right after she ate a big meal.

Coming into the room, I hugged them both and told them, "Neither one of you is fat. You both look great, and you're much too young to worry anyway. You are beautiful, and that's what matters."

Kelly frowned at me. "You don't think you're beautiful, Mommy."

She was right, and I wanted to cry again, though I seemed to be out of tears that would express the sadness she made me feel deep down.

"Mommy has a very hard time, yes. But I do weigh too much and

120

I want to fix that. I want to be thinner and healthier so I can go on your field trips and do things like take you to the park." It was a resolution I intended to follow through with and whether or not I made the goal weight I wanted, I was definitely going to be more involved in my children's lives. It was especially important since they were already suffering from misconceptions about their weight.

I didn't say anything to my husband about it when he came home; I'd hurt him enough and I didn't want to get his hopes up, nor did I want to see the doubt in his eyes. Rather, I just cooked a healthy dinner and after the girls went to bed I fired up the treadmill for the first time in a year. I did four miles that night and felt like I just might pass out, but the soreness in my muscles the next morning felt great, the burn reminding me of my younger days after a hard day on the gymnastics floor.

I continued on that path, not counting calories, simply eating better and being more active. On Saturday I called my mother to let her know we all wanted to come to Sunday dinner. It was a nice evening out. I was self-conscious about my appearance, but I enjoyed the company. I loved watching my daughters interact with their cousins and even my husband perked up at my change of attitude.

Weeks passed before I finally dug out the scale again, determined not to frustrate myself by weighing every day. I had noticed changes though, with my skin clearer and my clothes a little looser. I was also stronger, with more stamina, lasting for six miles in the evening on the treadmill. To my delight, I had dropped to 212. That was fourteen pounds, and it really didn't feel like I'd been trying. I could do this, I told myself.

In fact, the more I forgot to think about my weight, the more positive I felt. I volunteered at the library at my daughter's school for a book sale, and I didn't even notice whether or not anyone was staring at me or laughing at me. I took Kelly to get her hair done for a play their class was putting on, and I took Bailey to the mall for a mother-daughter shopping trip. Both times, I walked with my head up and wore a positive attitude. I realized as I walked past the food court that, a year before, I would have wanted to buy a heavy lunch after sampling every offering. That day, with my beautiful daughter and my clothes that were three sizes smaller, I wasn't even hungry and could wait to go home and make a salad of my own.

After six months, I took the scale out again, and I literally cheered when I saw I was down to 179. It wasn't a shocker that when I put on a nightgown I'd bought specially for when I'd dropped below 180 and engaged my husband, he was surprised and more than willing to be intimate with me. I wasn't as thin as I wanted to me, but I'd found peace with myself and the way that I looked. Plus, I felt so much lighter on my feet than I had six months earlier that it was a wonderful thing to rekindle our physical relationship.

Things continued to get better and my daughters smiled more. My husband came home and addressed me with a smile and a kiss every day. I worked harder and started socializing with my coworkers again. In fact, the more positive I was about everything, the better I felt and the easier it was to maintain a healthy diet and exercise schedule. That led to losing weight without even trying.

Losing the weight helped me heal myself, and as I became healthy in body, my mind returned to a normal state as well. I could be around people again, and I found that my other relationships were healed. My daughters started looking up to me again and stopped worrying about their weight. And my husband started telling me I was beautiful again, with my reply no longer a frown, but a thank you with a kiss.

My life blossomed, and it took me an entire year, but at the end of that year, I stepped onto the scale and made my own jaw drop. It read 137, and maybe that was two pounds heavier than what I'd maintained as a teenager, but being thirty, it was close enough. I couldn't believe that, with a positive attitude and a smile on my face even through the hardest day, I'd managed to bring back the 'me' I'd known before, only better. Now, I felt good, had a family that I adored and loved me in return, a career and life experiences I would never want to give back, and a better outlook on life in general than I'd ever had.

I knew who I was, and I knew who I wanted to be. Surely remaining that person would be easier than finding her had been. Everything was like magic, and I couldn't be thankful enough. I was happy, healthy, and secure. My mistakes had been that I'd been someone who wanted to please everyone else and reinforced the need to do so in a negative manner, always coming down on myself. Now, though, I did it for myself, and the results filtered down to those who mattered. I praised myself for successes, and the positive attitude was my saving grace. I would never become the depressed, beat-down person who had given up again. There was always a better way, and I would keep "positive health" as my motto from that point forward.

Closing Thoughts

So how many pounds would you like to lose? Five? Fifty? One hundred or more? You are not alone, but that does not mean you are in good company. Put plainly, being overweight is likely to shorten your life.

Of course, it is easy to forget the long term benefits of healthy eating when you have a doughnut staring you in the face. That pleasure surge you get from increased serotonin (the sugar rush) can feel awfully good, but makes us feel awful afterwards.

Regardless, beating ourselves up about the number we see on the scale is counterproductive. Choosing to focus on your weight number is essentially focusing your mind on a negative thought. Borrowing the lyrics of an old song, doesn't it make sense to eliminate the negative and accentuate the positive instead?

Did you notice all of the negative thoughts poor Kristi had on a daily basis?

My body is out of control
I can't think about being responsible
I'm worthless
I'm a big ball of blubber
I'm a ball and chain to others
I swallowed my inner goddess
I lost her in one of my fat rolls
I'm miserable, uncomfortable, and unsexy
I'm embarrassed by my laughable size, and I try to hide myself
I'm a stuffed sausage
I'm a pear
I'm a fat lady who is miserable to be around

I feel depressed just reading that list! My goodness, with that much negative self-talk, it's no wonder Kristi couldn't lose weight! Since she spent so much of her time mentally beating herself up, there was no way she could muster up the strength to work toward bettering herself. Kristi's inner voice repeatedly told her that she had no value because of her weight. With a mindset like that, it would be impossible to accomplish almost any goal!

So how did Kristi change her life? She made a resolution to be healthier. She put the scale away, and rather than focusing on her (negative) fat number, she focused on the (positive) future benefit of good health and worked toward that goal.

I challenge you to change your way of thinking to imitate Kristi. Stop thinking about your unhappy weight number; instead, focus on re-training your mind to think about having good health. Think that the power of positive thinking is all psychological mumbo-jumbo? Try this exercise. Think about what you weigh and how that makes you feel for about thirty seconds. Now imagine yourself eating your favorite, most decadent treat. Seems like a pretty realistic scenario, right? You feel a little guilty, but I bet in your imagination that treat tasted really good. Now, clear your mind, and then take the next thirty seconds and visualize yourself in a healthy body. Picture in your mind how good it would feel. Imagine your body running on reasonable portions of healthy food, feeling good after exercise, and putting on pants that are one, two, or three sizes smaller. Now go back and imagine eating that decadent food. Does it really have the same appeal, or does it feel even just a little slovenly and indulgent?

If you are honest with yourself when you performed this exercise, chances are that visualizing a healthier you reduced the desirability of sweets. This is the mindset you need to maintain every day. Picture yourself healthy when you wake up in the morning. Picture yourself healthy before every meal. Picture yourself healthy when you're tired after work and you'd rather go get a pint of ice cream than go to the gym. Picture yourself healthy before you go to sleep.

The brain is the most important muscle to flex when it comes to weight loss. I challenge you to engage it to focus on the positive. Weigh yourself once, and then put the scale away in the closet. I don't want you to focus on your weight number as you begin this journey. I want you to focus on how you feel as you begin making smarter choices for your health. Find your power, and self-motivate your way back to healthy. Keep up that mindset, and in time you'll be as pleasantly surprised as Kristi. You can do it!

EMBRACE YOUR BEAUTY

"Know first, who you are; and then adorn yourself accordingly."
~ Epictetus

There had been a time when I didn't care what others thought of me, but that was before I realized exactly what they thought. I'd always been into sports in school, and by my freshman year, I was well known for my athletic prowess, being on the swim team, playing tennis, and running track. I had a lot of friends, and I was beginning to think that Dale, a guy on the football team I was crushing on, might be interested in me. We talked a lot and studied together for two different classes.

I was sitting in geometry sophomore year – one of the classes we shared – finishing my homework, which hadn't gotten done the night before because I'd gone to the football game – and waiting for the bell to ring as everyone else in the class was milling around. I happened to overhear a conversation between Dale and Riley, another guy on the team, and though I wouldn't normally have eavesdropped, I was interested because I heard my name.

"You've been spending a lot of time with Margie lately," Riley says.

"Well, she's nice, and she's smart. It's easy to talk to her, and she's a really good tutor. I'm surprised you haven't butted in, with the way your grades are going. She's a good friend. I can ask her to help you." I smiled to myself. I loved how thoughtful Dale could be.

"That's all right, I'm already working on extra credit. But the two

126

of you seem really close. I mean, we do have a dance coming up, and you don't have a date. Are you thinking of asking her to be your date?"

My whole body seized. Could it be true? I wanted to hear the answer, and I squeezed my eyes shut in hope. But Dale laughed. "Who, Margie? No way! She's fat!"

I couldn't believe what I heard. As my heart sank, I curled in on myself. I'd never thought of myself as fat. No, I wasn't one of these skinny girls who wore a size double-zero and had no curves. I was an athlete and I had muscle and curves in several places. But fat? I looked around the room as inconspicuously as possible, considering the other girls and comparing myself to them. It was a foreign thing for me. I'd never much thought about how I looked next to other girls. The more I thought about it, the more I could see that I wasn't up to par. All these girls looked like twigs, with barely a curve to their bodies and waists the size of my wrist. I didn't particularly have a bunch of extra weight around the hips, but my stomach was firm and solid from my abs. I didn't have thunder-thighs like a couple of the large girls in school did, but I could see how the hefty quad muscles in my jeans might be mistaken as such.

Maybe I wasn't attractive, but did that mean I wasn't good enough for a date? The words from Dale cut deep, and I started to question everything I believed about myself. I wondered what others thought, if they looked at me with the same disdain as Dale had. It made me sick to my stomach, and I could barely even speak to my friends and teammates without feeling self-conscious.

My original intention had been to fill up my high school years with athletics and honest fun with friends. I wanted a scholarship based on my athletic ability, and that meant keeping my head down and out of trouble. At the same time, I'd wanted to make memories. This made me question how I could do that. If I couldn't socialize with others without being paranoid what they might think of me and my "fat," how was I going to create that experience for myself?

Rather than deal with this head-on, I started to hide behind my schoolwork. My heart was broken, and I didn't care about much of anything. Every time I put on my bathing suit to for a swim meet, I cringed, barely able to stand the idea that people were watching the fat rolls flop around in the water.

My insecurity made me a hermit. I stopped really caring about athletics. I still participated, but I didn't spark interest in college scouts anymore, never breaking out in a better than average performance at anything. With less physical effort, I found myself less driven to do much of anything, my whole life switching from tons of reasons for motivation and drive to nothing that made me even want to get out of bed in the morning.

I stopped coming in early to hit the gym for a jog or a workout, instead sleeping in and climbing out of bed fifteen minutes before I had to be at my first class in the morning. Instead of staying after school to get in a little extra training with my friends in the athletics department, I left after class and headed up the road with my allowance to the ice cream shop or the bakery. I suddenly had a sweet tooth like I'd never experienced before and the more sugar I ate, the less I really cared about anything.

At the end of my senior year, I'd become my worst nightmare. I had gained sixty pounds and when I looked in the mirror I now saw exactly what I felt Dale had seen all along – a lumpy, unkempt girl with stringy hair that dressed frumpy in sweats and jogging pants instead of the tank tops and shorts I'd worn in the past. Even worse, I didn't care about anything or anyone. There were several instances where an old friend would fall into step beside me in the hallway and ask if I was okay, or what class I was headed to, or why I'd quit track.

I'd roll my eyes and mutter some rude response, like, "Who cares?", or, "Whatever," or simply, "Leave me alone." I gave teachers attitude if they criticized my work in class or told me I was lazy. I may have been, but no one was going to call me that except me.

After graduation, which was a nightmare of walking across a stage in front of the entire graduating class and their families looking like an old lady in a moo-moo, I wanted nothing more than to sleep through the summer before heading to my college dorm to hole up and study for the next four years without interruption. Unfortunately, I had already signed on as a counselor at a summer camp for girls. I called ahead to try to get out of it, but the schedule had been made and my ten girls for whom I would be responsible already assigned.

With grave resignation, I drove up to the camp and readied my bunk a day in advance, taking my baggiest clothes to help hide my extra fluff. The following morning, I stood apart from the other camp mentors, not wanting to be berated. After all, none of them were anything larger than a size eight, and I was in a size fourteen. Role model indeed, I thought as I watched girls climb off a bus and out of cars where they hugged their parents.

I collected my girls as they came in, giving them the blue name tags that meant they were my charges before heading up to the cabin where we'd be staying. All the girls were between 12 and 14, probably the time that most girls are at the height of insecurity. I thought to myself that I couldn't believe I hadn't noticed my flaws back then. But now, these girls were the focus, and I realized that it was nice to get my mind off my own problems for a few days.

As I assigned bunks, I noticed that one girl hung back from the crowd, and as I took names of volunteers for things like trash pickup and morning alarms for the next eight weeks, she didn't step forward or volunteer for anything. Instead, she stood silently off to one side. She was a little heavier than the other girls, but not a lot, and I could see the beginnings of a beautiful young woman ready to blossom. She would hit puberty and turn out tall and thin almost definitely. I caught the name Jill on her name tag.

I assumed she would settle in, but throughout the entire first week, she seemed to make no friends, participated in no activities, and generally sat to the side and didn't interact with anyone, including me. I wondered about her, but I didn't want to address her in front of the other girls. Aside from camp rules about privacy, I personally didn't feel it was appropriate to air dirty laundry in front of the other young girls.

Finally, on Saturday evening when the rest of the girls had just come up from the lake to roast marshmallows in the dusk, wrapped in towels after a late swim, I saw Jill sitting alone at the end of the pier, staring across the lake, dressed in sweats. It was the first chance I'd had to get her alone and I asked one of the other counselors to watch over my group while I went to speak with her.

I approached cautiously and announced myself so as not to startle her. "Do you mind if I sit with you for a minute, Jill?"

She nodded and scooted over, as if she needed to make more room for me. I sat by her, my legs dangling above the water next to hers. "You don't seem to be enjoying yourself much here, Jill. Is there something I can do to help you have a good time?"

129

She shook her head. "I'm having fun."

I frowned and followed her line of vision but found nothing exciting in that direction. She must have been deep in thought. "Do you not like marshmallows? I have a couple candy bars in my bunk, if you'd like one of those instead."

She grimaced and shook her head. "I know what the other girls will say if they see me eating a candy bar or marshmallows."

My heart went out to her. Jill had a problem with her weight. I thought she was pretty, and I already saw the potential in her. But I understood the perception a girl could have of herself. I suffered the same issues, except I knew the truth – I really was too heavy. Trying to think of something else that might help, I asked, "You didn't go swimming with us earlier. Would you like to go for a swim?"

"No way," she adamantly refused. "What if one of the other girls comes down here? I can't let anyone see me in my bathing suit."

I thought back to sophomore year and how I'd felt when I realized how different I was from the rest of the class. Of course, looking at myself now versus how I'd looked then, something clicked inside my head, and I cringed. I looked at the girl beside me again. Jill was thick, and she had a lot of muscle, but she wasn't fat at all. I saw myself in her, and it struck me that, for the past three years, I'd let other people's opinions shape me, make me hate myself for something that wasn't even true about me. I'd never been fat.

Like Jill, I was thick and muscular, and like her, there had been nothing unattractive about me. I'd bought into the popular opinion of what a woman should be so quickly and so easily that I'd literally become what I was falsely accused of. If there was anything to hate about myself, it was that I'd been so easily brainwashed into believing the hype.

I'd wasted three years and probably blown a college scholarship, all because of what one miserable guy had thought of me. As I considered Jill, I decided I wouldn't let her experience the same thing. I wanted to help her, to make her understand what she was and why she should be happy with herself.

"You know, Jill, when I started high school, I looked a lot like you. You're a beautiful girl, and it doesn't matter that you don't look like a clone of everyone else your age."

"But I'm not pretty like they are."

I shook my head. "Pretty is relative. Not everyone likes the skinny runway model look. And on some people, it just doesn't fit. You have what they call an athletic build, like I used to have. Even if there wasn't an ounce of fat on your body, your waist wouldn't be a size two because you wouldn't look good that way. Every person is built differently, and this is the body you were blessed with." I nudged her shoulder. "You should take advantage of all that muscle. I'm sure there has to be a sport or two that interest you."

She gave me a sideways glance. "I was really fast when I was little. I think I might be good at track. And I'm pretty good at tennis."

I laughed and cheered. "Perfect! Tennis is my favorite sport. You know, if I hadn't listened to everyone else and let myself get fat, I could have had a scholarship for tennis." I looked at her again and knew what I had to do. I couldn't preach a word that I didn't follow.

Making a resolution, I told Jill, "I'll make a deal with you. I should never have lost confidence in myself because I would have still been as pretty as you. So I'm going to get back in shape. Every morning, I'm going to get up and go for a jog before breakfast for the next seven weeks we're here. You can join me any time you like, and we'll have those thighs of yours in great condition to make the track team when you get back to school. Does that sound like a plan?"

She looked skeptical. "Would you really do that for me?"

I rolled my eyes. "Of course! I'm doing it for us. You don't need to be thinner, Jill, but I do. And you want to take up track and field. So, we'll train together and both feel better about ourselves."

For the first time since I'd met her, a small smile traced over Jill's lips. "I'd really like that. Do you think we could play tennis sometime, too?"

I clapped my hands. "I would love to play a few sets with you! In the meantime, come up to the campfire with us. A couple of girls wanted to tell scary stories, and I'm sure you've got one up your sleeve somewhere."

Biting her lip to hide an even brighter smile, she nodded and got to her feet with me. The evening turned out great, and when she interacted with the other girls, they really seemed to like her. It only drove home that I'd been a great person before, and as I'd let negative thoughts and energy overwhelm me, I'd turned into a much more negative, unhealthy person. I'd liked who I was before, and I

131

wanted to strive to find that person again, physically, mentally, and emotionally.

The following morning, I was up before dawn, and I made my way to the trailhead nearest our cabin as I'd promised Jill. As I stretched, knowing how difficult this would be with as out of shape as I'd become, I saw her approach. I smiled, and she returned the expression. When she reached me, I said, "Good morning. You should probably warm up before we go."

She nodded and stretched her arms over her head. "Do you really think we're going to be able to do this?" she asked, sounding skeptical.

"Well, we won't be able to run ten miles today, but we'll build up over the summer. Come on, let's go." We started at a good pace, but after a mile, we were both winded. The trail was three miles and wound back around to the cafeteria, so we walked the rest of the way. I was tired, but I felt good, and breakfast tasted fantastic. I saw Jill devouring hers, too, all the while talking to some of the other girls from our cabin.

Over the next few weeks, we built up our strength and stamina, and I could see the difference in Jill, both physically and mentally. She was more interactive, starting participating in activities, and those muscles started to tone up and really show. She no longer looked like a young girl on the verge of puberty but a young athletic woman on the cusp of greatness.

It gave me hope for my own future, and as I really looked at myself in the mirror, I noticed a waistline start to appear again. It motivated me, just as much as being able to help Jill did, and we pushed harder and harder together, driven by results, until we were running the trail twice every morning for a total of six miles a day.

Three days before camp ended, Jill asked me as we headed to breakfast, "What am I supposed to do when I go home? I don't have this trail or a jogging partner."

I squinted and pretended to think really hard. "Well, you could always run circles around your backyard fifty times or so." She gave me a withering look, and I laughed. "I have internet on my phone. We'll look up park trails near your house, and you can find out how long the track around your high school football field is. Make use of one of those, or all of them to change it up from time to time. Make some friends with other kids in class who want to run track or play tennis, and partner up with them. I bet, if you set up a regular time, you'll have several people showing up to jog with you every day. Be the leader."

She seemed to think that over, and the brightest smile I'd ever seen from her crossed her face. "I like that idea."

Saying goodbye was hard, but I realized that she'd helped me as much as I helped her. I took my own advice and found trails near home to run, and when I got to college, I started using the track. By the end of the first semester, I still had about twenty extra pounds on me, but I was in good enough shape to make the track team and get into the tennis program. By the middle of my sophomore year, I was back to the old me physically. The best part was that I remained pen pals via email with Jill, so she sent me pictures of herself as the victor of tennis matches and running competitions that made me so proud of her. She looked great and was really coming into her own.

It was strange to me when I looked back and saw how far I'd fallen in my depression and what a struggle it was to crawl back out of that hole. It had taken seeing myself in someone else to find the mental strength that would allow me to repair my body and my heart. Jill had been my savior, and she saw me as hers.

With newfound confidence in my looks and fitness, I was sociable and made a lot of friends in college. On my twenty-first birthday, four of those friends decided it was time for us to go out. I didn't do a lot of dancing or partying, but you only turn twenty-one once, so I agreed and got dressed up. My roommate helped with my makeup, since I didn't wear any often.

I was sitting at the bar, waiting for a drink after dancing up a sweat, and I was a little winded but happy when a guy came up to me with a cocky smile. He was decent looking, but I wouldn't have noticed him in a crowd. He was far too average to stand out. His friend behind him, though, was sexy, and so I smiled back at the one approaching me. "Hi, I saw you sitting here alone and thought maybe you'd like some company."

I motioned toward the dance floor where my friends were still at it. "I came with them. I'm not alone, but I appreciate the concern."

He shrugged. "Well, since I'm over here, can I at least buy you a drink?"

The bartender came back with my order. I pointed to the guy beside me. "It's on his tab." The bartender nodded and walked away. I took a sip and told him, "Thanks."

He held out a hand in greeting. "I'm Dale. Would you care to dance?"

I nearly choked on my drink as I realized who it was. I couldn't believe it; this was the guy I'd had a crush on in high school, who had caused my life to spiral out of control in the first place. Now he was interested?

Feeling confident and justified, I smiled sweetly back but didn't hold out my hand. "I'm Margie. I'm sure you remember me. And thanks for the offer, but I'm really not interested." The shock on his face was priceless as I walked away, swaying my hips to the beat as I went to rejoin my friends. It was poetic justice and it felt amazing to wear the shoe on the other foot.

Closing Thoughts

No matter what your age, you must learn to embrace your beauty. Lovely advice, but easier said than done, right?

When it comes to embracing our external beauty, it can seem as though the world is against us. We all know that sex sells in the media, which means that we are constantly bombarded with pictures of people who have perfect figures and six-pack abs. We can remind ourselves that many of those images have been air-brushed and altered, but seeing these unrealistic images repeatedly can easily sabotage your self-image. So now your image is deflated from all those ads, and you see an ad for ice cream telling you that having satisfied taste buds will make you happy. Go ahead, indulge, super-size your meal – it will make you happy! All-you-can-eat buffet for $7.99? Awesome deal, right? In our more-is-better society, it is very easy to succumb to temptation like Margie did. Put together, the swimsuit ads and food temptations in the media pack a mighty one-two punch that can challenge, and even knock out, the strongest person's self-esteem.

But wait, you say – what about those mean girls in high school with the perfect bodies? They're not airbrushed! Indeed, they are not. Fair or not, a select few of us were blessed by the gene pool our parents passed on. These girls (and their male counterparts) always seem to have perfect hair, perfect teeth, perfect figures, and perfect lives. And yes, those mean girls aren't only in high school. They go to college, they get jobs where we work, and they go to our beach in their tiny little bikinis and thongs. Really, it seems like there are always a few wherever you turn!

Yes, it's true; men will always look at pretty women. It's how they're hardwired. But in all fairness, let's take a look at Margie. She was crushing on Dale, who was on the football team. What images did that conjure in your mind – ugly and scrawny, or big, tall, strong, and handsome? Now add to that the fact that Margie and Dale have been studying together. Be honest – you know you assumed that she was helping Dale, and when you put two and two together, he fit the "dumb jock" stereotype perfectly. So was Margie crushing on Dale for his beauty within? Probably not.

Okay, so maybe we're being a little hypocritical here, thinking it's unfair that the boys only want the prettiest girls. Regardless, you still think being the prettiest girl in the room would make you happy? Think again. Go ahead, do this Google search: pretty girls and self-esteem. As I write this, three of the top six results are about how pretty girls have low self-esteem. Girls and women who value themselves primarily for their beauty feel that they are constantly watched, so they feel unending pressure to maintain their exterior appearances. It may be difficult for them to make friendships because others are jealous of them. And when it comes to career success, it can be much harder for a pretty woman to be taken seriously. Let's think about this – if a man wants you only because of your external beauty, what does that say about his values? Does he really want you, or does he just want arm candy? Really, do you want to be with someone that shallow? Yep, maybe he's a hottie, but inside he's a nottie. In the long run, you don't want someone to be attracted to you only for your exterior. If you're going to be compatible with someone, it's what's on the inside that matters most.

All that having been said, isn't it time you embraced your own beauty? Maybe you're not the prom queen, but few of us are. We won't be judged later in life if we received that tiara or not. It's time, right now, to stop valuing yourself based on how you think others perceive you. The best way to present yourself, no matter what you have to work with, is to be as healthy as you can be. How good will you feel tomorrow if you drown your sorrows in a bag of chips today?

I've said before, the most powerful muscle to exercise for good health is your brain. Use it to make wise choices. Take time to exercise. Make healthy choices when you eat. Drink water. Get your sleep. The healthier you are, the more self-confident you can be. Honestly, nothing is more beautiful than healthy confidence. Be the best you that you can be, and your beauty will be projected to the world.

DON'T IGNORE THE CONNECTION

"And you? When will you begin that long journey into yourself?"
~ Rumi

Dang, Derrick had a set of lungs on him. From this far up the beach I could hear his voice carry across the sand. My son, the ever vigilant lifeguard. Always on the lookout for riptides, jellyfish and newbie surfers that didn't know how treacherous the waves could be. Behind me I could see my wife Lucy talking with another couple. I took a minute to catch my breath. Sitting in the sand, warm sun on my face, in a minute I was asleep.

I started dreaming one of the "reruns," combination dream sequences that were part flashback, part fantasy. For the most part, they were the same. Familiar threads running towards the same conclusion. Lucy admitted she still had them sometimes, too.

Lucy and I met during our second tours in Iraq. She was an Army doctor, the most skilled field surgeon I'd ever seen. She could save limbs from amputation, resuscitate soldiers from certain death. She was fearless and amazing. I was crazy about her long before she even knew my name.

"Forrester, right?" She asked me one day. "Think you can give me an assist?"

I was just a medic. I carried my weight but I found myself flustered and nervous in her presence. Her talents were legend.

"You do know a clamp from a retractor, yes?"

I nodded, lamely.

"Then get over here, you'll be needing both."

From then on we were inseparable. She was patient with me, as she was with everyone in our unit. I learned more from working with her than I would in a hundred nursing programs. Proximity, long hours, we became close friends, and despite the fraternization policies, lovers.

We were married as soon as we got stateside. She was immediately snatched up at the number three teaching hospital in the country. I finished a nursing program and joined the ER staff at a nearby hospital. We worked crazy hours and often, opposite shifts, but we managed to find enough time together to conceive three children, Doug, Derrick and Lisa. My ever-efficient bride delivered the twins four years after Doug was born, almost to the day. I used to tease her she had our kids on her dinner breaks, between surgeries.

My esteem for Lucy never wavered in all our years together, growing stronger as I watched her manage motherhood, marriage, and all the pressures of her job. I really paled by comparison. I made an okay nurse, but I wasn't publishing in medical journals three times a year. I was a good father, I suppose, a lot of the parenting duties fell to me, but I didn't have newspapers and magazines clamoring to interview me like Lucy did.

About the only thing I excelled at was eating. Before I joined the service, I'd been all-state tackle. I was a big guy, to be sure. I'd always had been a little chubby. Not quite the fat kid in junior high, but on my way. When I discovered football I suddenly could eat anything I wanted and it just went to muscle. My years in the service eradicated any fat cells that might have remained. When Lucy met me I was as lean as I'd been in my life.

Once we got out of the service, I led a much less physically active lifestyle. I started picking up weight from sitting in class all day. When I got into the ER I was keeping such odd hours it was hard to schedule regular meals. I became the favorite customer at the fast food joints next to work. Lucy and I used to laugh that every time she got pregnant, I was such a helpful husband I even put on the weight for her.

In typical Lucy perfectionist fashion she only gained about ten pounds during both pregnancies. She lost those within a month of delivery. Not me. The twenty-five pounds I gained both times stayed.

Soon, Lucy wasn't laughing about by weight, she was getting aggravated.

I knew she was trying to help, but each time she brought home another diet for me to try it felt like I was failing her, like I wasn't measuring up. The worse I felt about myself the more I turned to food for comfort.

By the time the twins were in high school, I weighed at least 350 pounds, that's as high as my bathroom scales could measure. I started experiencing a host of physical problems. The hospital made all employees have an annual physical. My doctor, Phil Bennett was a real nice guy I'd gotten to know from his occasional stints in the ER. He called me personally and asked me to come in so we could go over my lab results.

"Jason, we really need to have a conversation." He started.

We were sitting across the desk from one another in his office. He looked concerned, holding my file in his hands as he continued.

"I'll be brief. First of all, your blood pressure is elevated." He held up his right index finger. "Second, your cholesterol and triglyceride numbers are awful, much higher than a year ago."

He continued gesturing as he numbered the other areas of concern. "Third, you're presenting shortness of breath and lower oxygen levels. Fourth your blood sugar is out of control and you are borderline diabetic. We talked about that the last time you were in."

I interrupted him, holding up my hand. "Okay, okay. I get it. I'm getting older. Enough. Let's go get something to eat."

"It's not funny, Jason. But since you've opened the food door, I'm going to walk through it. What's going on with you? What's eating you?"

"What do you mean," I was going to force him to say it.

"I'm saying, this kind of weight problem, there's usually a mind-body connection. You've added more than one hundred pounds since your last physical. At 411, you are creating some serious health problems here. Almost all of these can be reversed if we can get that weight off. Which is why I've got to ask, what's going on with you?"

"I don't know, Phil, maybe I'm addicted to doughnuts?" I was still trying to use humor to alleviate the tension. I knew things were bad. When you put on weight there's no hiding the fact that you have. You have to buy bigger clothes. I was constantly buying new scrubs for the ER. I'd heard my own breathing. I knew my snoring was driving Lucy out of our bedroom at night.

"I don't know that a group like Weight Watchers isn't a bad idea, Phil. You know, a support group, meeting with people that are familiar with and share your issues, well that could be a good thing. I'd like to see you give that a try. But until we get this under control we're going to have to start some pharmacological measures to try to reverse some of the damage and prevent things from getting any worse."

I watched him feverishly writing out several prescriptions on his pad.

"This is going to bring your blood pressure down. We need to get that addressed immediately. I'm also writing two prescriptions to help with your cholesterol and triglycerides. They work a little differently. I think we'll get good results with the two of them. I'm going to put you down for a 90-day call back. Let's see what we can get done between now and then. Diane's going to come in and go over a diet plan I think you'll be comfortable with. It's nothing you aren't already familiar with – lots of fruits, vegetables, lean meats, grains, nuts."

"Spare me the diet, Phil. I know what to do. If it tastes good, spit it out."

He ignored me and continued with his instructions. "I want you to avoid alcohol altogether for the next three months. Lay off the beer. I want you to drink six to eight glasses of water a day and start walking. You can use the gym downstairs; they've got a walking track all set up. Any questions?"

"When are you going to stop talking?" I was laughing when I said it, but I would've rather taken a beating than listen to a professional colleague lecture me like this. I felt nine years old, sitting in the principal's office while he doled out my punishment for being a very bad boy.

"I care about you Jason. You are not a little overweight, Buddy, you are obese and your health is in jeopardy. I couldn't be more serious. We'll get this under control. I'll see you in three months."

He left me to wait for Diane and her miracle diet. I didn't wait. I took my wad of prescriptions and left. On my way home I stopped at Manny's and picked up "The Manny Combo." The menu described it as the perfect repast for a "Man's Man," triple meat, triple cheese all

140

the way with fries and a super-sized cola. "I am Man, hear me roar." I said aloud as I accepted my sack from the teenager manning the drive-thru window.

I ate my meal on the way to the pharmacy where I turned in my scripts. They said it would be about a half an hour. I went across the street to Real Deal and order a double-scoop butter pecan sundae. It'd been a rough day. Tomorrow I would start working out at the hospital gym. This was my last hurrah.

When the garage door opened I saw Lucy's Mercedes. I wasn't expecting her home. I shoved the fast food wrappers and other evidence of my afternoon's exploits beneath the bench seat of my truck. I'd throw it all out later. I grabbed my pharmacy sack and headed into the kitchen.

I walked into an unexpected surprise; Lucy and Lisa were at the stove cooking fried chicken. The house smelled wonderful. I gave Lucy a kiss on the cheek and asked what the special occasion was.

Lisa explained, "It was my idea, Daddy! I told mom we never eat fried food and I just wanted some. Mom said we could make it healthy, she pulled all the skin off, she says if we make good choices and eat broccoli we can have fried chicken once in a while."

"Well," my bride added, "I also knew you had your doctor's appointment today. I know how you hate those. What'd Phil have to say?"

"Healthy as a horse. Wants me to lose a few pounds, you know."

"That's it?" Lucy pressed. "Lose a few pounds? How many is a few?"

"We didn't get into that!" I snapped. "Does everything have to be so damn precise?" I walked away, but not before I saw my daughter's startled expression.

That night at dinner, Lucy gave me her world-class silent treatment, asking the children to pass the vegetables and tea. Ignoring me completely other than to shoot me disapproving looks when I went for seconds on the bread and chicken.

That night she slept in the guest bedroom. Usually when we were both at home she'd go to bed with me. Then, when my snoring woke her up, she'd move. I breathed a sigh of relief when I saw the light go out in the guestroom. I didn't want to share a bed with her either, what was the point.

141

We'd never discussed it, but Lucy and I stopped making love more than a year before. Well, even before that, there were problems. After the twins, Lucy seemed to have lost all desire for sex. She made excuses about being tired, having to heal, uncertainty about her birth control, problems with her cycle, cramps, and headaches. I got tired of asking.

And, the heavier I got the harder it was for me to maintain an erection. We tried different positions and then, again, because of my weight, it became uncomfortable for Lucy. It just got to be unpleasant for both of us. Without the tenderness and intimacy of sex, the divide growing between us just got bigger and deeper.

The day Lucy found the pharmacy receipts she went ballistic. She'd accidentally thrown out a telephone number of a co-worker she'd hastily written on the back of a store receipt. She'd thought she might have dropped it when she'd borrowed my truck. She found the receipt from Emerson Drugs under the seat and that had sent her on a snooping expedition. It didn't take much effort to go through my bathroom cabinets and find the prescription bottles. She reached me on my cell phone at the hospital.

"Did you think I wouldn't find out?" She was yelling and Lucy didn't yell.

She wanted explanations and promises and went on and on about the children and if I wasn't willing to change for her I should at least be willing to change for them. I promised her I was already working out at the gym. She didn't believe me. No reason she should have.

Over the next six months she begged, I made promises. I'd lie and she'd nag. I didn't keep my follow up appointment with Phil and my waistline continued to expand. One day Lucy came home before I expected her to. I was polishing off a dozen chocolate covered donuts from a new bakery that'd just opened. I hadn't had time to hide the evidence.

"Really? This is what you call trying?" She said, picking up the empty donut box and throwing it across the room. You are pathetic and I'm done. You want to commit death by donut, go do it out of sight of our children. I'm not going to have them watch you kill yourself you selfish freak. Get out. Go eat yourself to death, I don't care, but you aren't going to do it here. Get out. Now." She was right. The kids didn't need their fat father around. I grabbed my stuff and left. I picked up a case of beer, checked into a motel near the hospital and ordered a double supreme pizza delivered to my room.

The next day I found a furnished apartment close to work, close enough that I could walk. For about a month I made a real effort to watch my diet -- eating salads and protein shakes, walking, I thought I could tell the slightest difference in the way my scrub pants felt. They weren't digging into my rolls of fat quite as much.

I even made an appointment with a personal trainer at the hospital gym. I walked in and walked right out. I hadn't seen anyone from the ER that I worked with, but I saw several skinny minnies. A room full of Barbie and Ken dolls lifting weights and working out on various machines. There wasn't an overweight human in the place. I always said, the only people that used gyms didn't need them. I walked to a Chinese buffet place. All you can eat. I ate all I could.

Not long after that, Lucy dropped Derrick and Lisa over to go swimming at my apartment complex pool. It was summer and they were really looking forward to it. We had the pool all to ourselves that afternoon. I sat in the shade and read while the kids horsed around. Derrick was showing off his trick flips off the side of the pool.

I had just looked back down at my book when I heard the crack and then Lisa's scream. Derrick had taken a running leap, slipped on the concrete, slamming his head on the side of the pool before going into the water. He'd been knocked unconscious and gone straight down. I lumbered over to the pool and saw him face down on the bottom, motionless. I jumped in after him.

For many years I had denied my weight problem. I lied about it -- to my wife, my family, my doctor and myself. But in that moment, the gravity of my situation was abundantly clear. In the service I had been it optimal shape. I used to be an exceptional swimmer. Before I'd gotten obese, I'd taught both boys to swim. That day, my 450 pounds sunk like a stone. It was all I could do to lift my son's lifeless body. I was certain he was dead.

I don't know how long I struggled to hoist him up and out of the pool. I was out of air and my chest was hurting, deep, piercing pain. Finally, I got him up and over the side. All I could gasp was "911."

Lisa was hysterical; I could hear her screams as I found the steel pool steps. Climbing out, one side came undone under my weight. I managed to pull myself out. Derrick's lips were blue. He wasn't breathing. All my medical training kicked in. Ignoring the pain in my chest I started CPR, rolling him to his side and then onto his back. I alternated chest compressions and breathing into his mouth.

"One, two, three" I said aloud in time with the compressions on his chest. Then I puffed three times into his mouth, willing my oxygen to fill his lungs. I heard sirens. Where was everyone?

Derrick didn't respond. Nothing. I kept trying, my vision blurred from pool water, chlorine, sweat and my own tears.

"No. No!" I screamed. You will not die." With everything I had, I resumed compressions. I heard a snap. I went back to his mouth and was about to exhale hard when he sputtered, saliva and pool water spewing from his mouth.

I rolled him to his side just as the ambulance and paramedics arrived.

"Step aside, Sir, we've got this."

I collapsed beside my son, exhausted, my chest in agony. I heard one of the paramedics say, "The fat guy probably saved his life, but he broke a couple of the kid's ribs in the process."

That was the last thing I heard before I passed out.

They say, in order to recover from an addiction, you need to hit your personal bottom. I found mine that day at the bottom of a swimming pool fighting to save my son's life. In that moment, struggling to lift his weight, I realized he would probably die because I was so morbidly obese I couldn't save him.

Deep down, I never really cared if I was killing myself. That's the truth. But the thought that my selfish choices could harm my loved ones? It was a possibility I'd never even considered.

Derrick and I got really close. We were roommates at the hospital until they moved me to the cardiac care wing. I'd suffered a coronary. I was lucky it hadn't been much worse. My arteries were blocked but not to the extent I needed bypass surgery. The cardiologists were able to repair the damage with stents, although at my weight even that procedure was especially risky.

I lost twenty pounds almost immediately. My food intake at the hospital was severely restricted. Once I got home, Lucy brought me to the house to recuperate and I put myself on the recommended diet. I followed my doctor's orders to the letter.

144

"Terror is a powerful motivator," I told Phil. I also did something I never had done before. I admitted I had a real problem and asked for help. Phil hooked me up with a support group for overeaters. I also went into counseling to try and understand why I kept sabotaging myself. I realized I'd always suffered with self-esteem issues. Marrying a woman with so many capabilities just exacerbated my own sense of inadequacy. I was so certain Lucy would one day leave me I'd driven her away. A self-fulfilling prophesy.

Some of the members of my support group talked about their success following the principals of the law of attraction. Before I could become a thinner, healthier, more confident me, I had to see myself that way. I did lots of things to help promote that image in my mind. I bought scrubs in a smaller size. I used smaller plates to eat from.

I wrote the number 210, my ideal weight, in permanent marker everywhere. I had it screen printed on my favorite sweatshirt. I used Lucy's lipstick and wrote it on my bathroom mirror. I made an accountability chart and posted it on our refrigerator. Every day I weighed myself and every day I wrote the results on that graph in plain sight of my family. Every day, no matter whether the number was higher or lower than the day before, everybody clapped.

"Yeah, Dad!" Lisa said.

"Dad rocks," Derrick added.

My eldest son, Doug sent me motivational tapes from college. Lucy slept in my bed. She found all kinds of ways to reward my efforts. Derrick's and my near-death experiences brought the family closer and saved both our lives. It took two years, but I'm closing in on 210. Derrick's a lifeguard and every chance we can we spend family time at the beach. I can outrun Lucy now.

"It's nice there's at least one thing in this world I can do a little bit better than you, madam." I told her after racing her down the beach.

"No, Jason, there's two. When you set your mind you are absolutely unstoppable. You never give up. I gave up on you. I'm sorry. You've taught me so much these last two years. You are my hero. But I do want a rematch."

As she took off again down the beach I looked up at my son and waved.

"You're my hero too, Dad" Derrick yelled. Mine too."

Closing Thoughts

They say, in order to recover from an addiction, you need to hit your personal bottom. Who is they, and why do we always tend to believe them?

Okay, well, it did seem to be true for Jason. He couldn't even stop eating when his marriage fell apart. It took a near-death experience for him to come to grips with the fact that he had a serious health issue that needed to be confronted in a serious way.

Jason clearly had a propensity for being overweight, since he was chubby as a child before discovering football and serving in the military. Sadly, after Jason married his wife, he developed a negative mind-body connection that drove his desire for food way out of proportion. Jason felt he had less worth because his wife's career was more successful than his; subconsciously, as a result, he ate to appease these negative feelings. Unfortunately, once a person loses control of his or her weight the problem usually continues to snowball. Thoughts like, "One more doughnut's not going to hurt" allow a person to rationalize weight gain all the way to his or her grave.

Thankfully, Jason was able to turn things around before it was too late. When Jason went to counseling and support groups, he learned to eliminate his negative mind-body connection (his feeling of inferiority to his wife). Using techniques of the law of attraction, Jason adopted a positive mind-body connection. He visualized himself as a thinner person and surrounded himself with cues (smaller clothes, smaller plates, and the number 210) to remind him. Sure enough, with a positive mind-body connection and the support of loved ones around him, Jason was able to meet his goal and recover his life in the process.

So back to what "they say" . . . let's prove them wrong. Don't wait until you hit rock-bottom to come back to health and wellness. If you're 250 now, why wait until you're 350 or 450 to finally wake up and realize that you have to work your way back? It's easier to lose 10lbs than 100lbs!

Get yourself a good support group (and counseling if you feel that is warranted). Find a healthy diet plan that will work for you. Throw away negative thoughts like, "One more won't hurt me," and replace them with positive thoughts. Exercise, even if only just a teeny little bit to get started.

Only you can decide when you will finally realize that it's time to adopt a new lifestyle and create a new, healthier you. For *life's* sake, take freaking baby steps and don't get overwhelmed and quit! When you do and succeed, know that Justin and I will be cheering for you!

SECTION III

WEALTH

"He is richest who is content with the least, for content is the wealth of nature."
~Socrates

GIVE AND FORGET

"There is one word which may serve as a rule of practice for all one's life – reciprocity."
~ Confucius

"Mom, let's go." For some reason my oldest child Ronnie Jr. (I called him RJ) was anxious to get to school. I held up my index finger motioning I'd be with him in just a sec. I was on the phone with Glenn Collins, the loan officer at the bank where our home was mortgaged. He was explaining where we stood. I only absorbed about half the words. "...so sorry... delayed as long as we could, the directors want to get these problem loans off the books, it's been two years, we've made every allowance..."

"I understand," I said. What else could I say? It's not like this was unexpected. I'd been waiting for this particular shoe to drop for months. I'd felt like some sailor adrift in the middle of the ocean in a sinking vessel. I'd been bailing and bailing as long and hard as I could, but I knew it was just a matter of time. It was inevitable. This ship was going down.

I was almost relieved it was finally official. We had 30 days to vacate. The property would be sold on the courthouse steps a month from today. At least now I'd be force to do something. I'd been emotionally paralyzed since the children's father, Ronnie, Sr. left. He was my husband, but I couldn't stomach that word any more. "Children's father" was the best I could do. For the kids' sake I never called him aloud what I called him in my head, -- useless, rotten, selfish, cowardly, lying, cheating, deceiving, corrupt, conniving – there weren't enough derisive words for him.

Collins was still talking; I had to cut him off. "Glenn, it's alright. The kids and I'll be fine. Go do what you got to do." I sounded convincing. In truth, I had no idea if we were going to be all right. I couldn't imagine much more that could befall us. We'd lost everything.

Sure, we should have moved out sooner. But how much upheaval could I put my kids through? Kimmie was only seven and didn't have as many memories of her Dad as her brother did. I'd pulled RJ out of private school away from all his friends and favorite activities. For just a second I allowed myself a macabre moment. I got a mental image of the two kids and me, panhandling under a bridge, destitute. I shuddered. I couldn't afford self-pity. I channeled all that residual energy into my seething anger.

Ronnie and I'd met 14 years ago. I was working as a legal assistant downtown for a big law firm. I was in the market for a new car and one of the attorneys suggested I lease from the place the firm used for their company vehicles. I left Flexplan Leasing with a brand new Honda Accord, loaded, a three-year lease with no early termination penalty, and the business card from my leasing agent. "Call me if you need anything. Here's my cell number, it's at your service, as am I, twenty-four seven." I was less than impressed. Too smooth by half, I thought.

I should've trusted my instincts. A couple of weeks later, that agent, Ronnie Gessler, called to see how I was enjoying the vehicle. I assured him I was really happy with it. He said he was glad to hear it because a woman like me deserved to be happy. "He's a player" alarm bells went off in my head, I ignored them.

Not that I'd had that much experience with players or any other type of dating material. I was too shy and sheltered. My parents were especially strict. It was easier to avoid the dating scene altogether than to comply with all of my dad's curfews, rules and stipulations. That's what he called them, "rules and stipulations." An attorney that specialized in prosecuting drug dealers, my Dad found most people suspect. "Too many years watching scumbags in action," he'd explained.

150

A month after I'd leased the Honda, a deliveryman brought in a gigantic vase of mixed flowers. It was embarrassingly huge. "Who died?" My co-worker Gayle asked. The card read, 'It's our one month anniversary of the day we met. We should celebrate. Dinner?' RG

I would like to say I brushed him off. I didn't. I fell for his pitch, completely. I was head over heels from the start. To his credit, Ronnie was a good dater. He always had something new and clever arranged, handling every detail from the tickets to the venue to dinner reservations beforehand. He even recommended what I should wear, down to the length of the hem and the neckline. He was a meticulous planner and I found him especially thoughtful.

Gayle and my other girlfriends weren't convinced. Each of them used the expression "too good to be true" and "controlling." He was single, at least as far as any of us could tell. Owned a very nice condo on the top floor of one of the Uptown high rises, drove a new Audi. His office at the leasing company was crowded with trophies, accolades and certificates attesting to his sales achievements.

He consistently won the annual performance contests. We'd only been dating a couple of months when he won the coveted Platinum Club Award, the agency's top prize, a 10-day cruise for two to the Hawaiian Islands. He insisted I accompany him. My dad, as I expected, went through the roof. "No self respecting woman sails off with some man she's just met. I promise you, you do this Nora and you'll regret it the rest of your life."

That's when Ronnie went to work on my dad. He invited him to dinner with us. He pulled out all the stops, five-star restaurant, a table by the water, strolling violinist.

My dad didn't budge. "If you think all this," he said, waving his hands about the restaurant, "is going to get you my blessing on your little liaison with my daughter, you are sadly mistaken. I don't believe in putting the honeymoon before the wedding. You can call me old-fashioned, but I won't stand for it."

Which is when Ronnie replied, "Nor should you. What I'd like, Mr. White, is to ask you for your daughter's hand in marriage." Then, before Dad could collect himself, he rose from the table, dropped down beside me on one knee, and with ring in hand asked me to be his wife." I don't remember ever answering.

Suddenly, everyone in the restaurant was cheering and applauding, waiters were bringing champagne and my dad was sending me "what in the world?" looks across the table. Many times in the weeks that followed he tried to talk me out of marrying Ronnie. I was spellbound and just got swept away in a daze. My bosses, co-workers, friends and family weighed in with doubts and reservations. Everyone wanted me to wait. Ronnie used every comment or suggestion for delay as evidence why we should just elope. "We can't expect anyone to understand what we have, Nora. This is once-in-a-lifetime magic. We've trapped lightening in a bottle."

He took me out to dinner at another high-end restaurant. Waiting for me at the table was a heavy parchment envelope. It was from a company called Enchanted Occasions confirming our arrangements to be married aboard the cruise ship in Maui. "It'll be just us, what could be more romantic than that?" Ronnie said, raising his champagne flute in a toast. "To us."

So less than six months from the day we met we were married. No bridesmaids, no family. It was not the wedding I had always dreamt about, the one where Dad walked me down the aisle. "We'll show him the video later," was all the comfort Ronnie could muster.

He insisted I quit my job. "C'mon, baby. You've been working since you were 15; let me do this for you. Let me spoil you." Then we bought – well, he bought – this enormous house. It was far bigger than the two of us needed, with two stories, five bedrooms, two fireplaces, a game room, a swimming pool, and summer kitchen. He said he bought it for two reasons. First, to show my Dad he was going to keep his word and take care of me, and because he needed a place like it for business. "In sales, Nora, a lot of deals close away from the office." I would hear that expression a lot.

Ronnie arranged for a maid too, which was great, because even though I didn't work, I couldn't manage to clean it to Ronnie's satisfaction. "I can hire a maid, Nora. What I need is a partner." Ronnie had plenty of ideas what this partner should do.

Every morning before he left for his office he'd hand me a list of tasks he wanted taken care of. At the top of each list he always wrote, "Babe," and then listed about a dozen errands. In my head I called them his "Babe lists." They covered assorted tasks, specific instructions and scheduling details: 1) Morrie's Dry Cleaners (napkins, place mats, dress shirts, taupe pants) 2) Ben's Liquor: (See attached for Sworensen dinner Friday) 3) Michele's Uptown (buy something nice to wear for S Dinner Fri.) 4) Carrie's Salon (please have your highlights redone) 5) Danica's Flowers, order centerpiece and three matching table arrangements 6) Confirm caterer.

I stopped sharing the "Babe lists" with my friends. I didn't know if they were jealous or not used to having this kind of money, but they all thought the lists were bizarre. I just thought they were part of Ronnie's personality. I kind of appreciated his attention to detail, how he thought of everything.

He managed all our checkbooks, and he had several, "So I can better separate our business expenses and personal for tax purposes," he'd explain. To his credit, Ronnie made a ton of money, more than twenty grand a month. He'd leave his statements out on his desk and I'd see there were numerous deposits into each every month. "Yeah, we get paid per unit and per annum quota." Like I'd understand what any of that meant.

All I knew is we had plenty of money. He gave me a designated credit card to handle the "Babe list" items and anything I needed for myself. Although before I could ever think of something I might want it had usually already found its way onto a list. And so, for many years, that's how we rolled. I took care of the "Babe lists" and our two children, first RJ, then six years later, Kimmie. I stayed busy.

Ronnie's income only increased. Good economy, bad economy, it made no difference. We entertained constantly. Small dinner parties with two other couples, big soirees with live music and 150 people, Super Bowl celebrations; Halloween costume galas. Sometimes I really felt like a cruise director. It was never the same people, which I found odd; always new faces, week after week. "That's the name of the game," Ronnie said.

Sometimes, I'd wake up in the middle of the night, my heart pounding, like when you awaken from a nightmare. Only there was never a nightmare, just this vague sense of unexplainable panic. Usually, those were the nights I'd find Ronnie downstairs, sitting in the dark, drinking. His speech would be slurred. "Go, back to bed, Nora."

One night I couldn't shake the feeling something terrible was about to happen. I went downstairs and found Ronnie, very drunk, staring out the window, talking softly into his cell phone. "Don't threaten me." I heard him whisper. Then, "Ever."

The next morning he was gone. Never saw him again. Poof! Vapor! Never did get the chance to miss him and I certainly wasn't lonely. When Ronnie split I suddenly had a steady stream of all kinds of visitors to keep me company. There was the morning the local detectives showed up, then the guys from the Securities and Exchange Commission, FBI, Interpol, and my new best friends, the Internal Revenue Service.

Thank God for Dad. He found attorneys that specialized in tax and criminal law. There were multiple charges pending against Ronnie, if anyone ever found him. Rumors circulated that he was in Europe or Brazil. The IRS were betting it was somewhere without an extradition arrangement with the US.

Wherever Ronnie went, he'd taken his money with him. "Dumb, dumb, dumb" I raged to my father one afternoon in complete frustration. "What kind of idiot am I?" My name wasn't on one bank or brokerage account. My magic "Babe's list" credit card was one of the first ones frozen when the various government agencies swept in.

As official holder of the bag of everything awful, I never wanted to see the agent of my destruction again. For two years I struggled to put food on the table – and the table was about the only bit of furnishings not seized as part of the multiple investigations.

Two years after Ronnie's disappearing trick, the bank was finally tidying up their involvement in the "Gessler Case," a complicated, messy, duplicitous, international affair; involving identity theft, Ponzi schemes and money laundering. Everybody wanted Ronnie. Except me.

The irony was rich. Here we were, this sad sack abandoned and penniless family of three living in one of the nicest homes in the State. No way could I afford the mortgage. I never attempted to. Because of the complexity of the multiple ongoing legal cases, the bank wasn't even able to begin foreclosure proceedings until recently. Now we were absolutely at the end of our financial rope.

My former bosses threw some transcription work my way when they could, but it scarcely made a dent in the bills. I shut off most of the rooms in the house and let the pool turn black. Our maid and nanny left with unpaid salaries owed. I pulled RJ from private school with a year's unpaid tuition due. When I learned our life insurance policies had lapsed I realized I couldn't even die to take care of the kids, and that *had* crossed my mind.

I grabbed the kids' sack lunches and my car keys. RJ almost forgot his essay on the kitchen table. It was a long one. I asked him what he'd written about.

"Ms. Harris in social studies is teaching us about this law of attraction stuff. It's about how people can make their lives better or worse by what they think and how they act. We were supposed to write about an example of how we could apply it in our lives."

"Go on."

"I said it kind of works like karma, what you put out comes back to you."

His father was in big trouble, I thought.

"It's like, Mom, if you want to get something you need to give it away. If you want love, you need to love first. We don't have any money now. But I think if we gave away whatever we have left we'd get back what we need."

I blinked furiously, fighting back tears. Not once in the two years since the emotional tsunami leveled our lives had RJ complained. He never whined, and here he was all matter-of-fact and curious about the laws of the universe.

"I want you to tell me more about this tonight," I said. After I dropped the kids at their respective schools I pulled up to Cornerstone Coffee Shop. I used to stop there every morning and sip lattes while I planned my days around all the errands on the "Babe lists." Funny. I never used to even check the price of a cup of coffee -- or anything else. It came so easily. There was always so much... I sighed, "Easy come, easy go."

I didn't realize I'd spoken aloud until I heard the stranger in the corner booth reply: "Tell me."

I looked up to find a bedraggled man sitting alone. He was quite unkempt; hair in disarray, clothes soiled and stained. He looked like he lived on the street. Before I could acknowledge his comment, Wanda, a waitress that had been at the coffee shop for years, came up to the man and brusquely told him to leave. "C'mon, Ray, let's not do this. No money, no coffee. You've got to go. I can't have you tying up the table, not when --"

Maybe it was RJ's comments from this morning or my current

brush with destitution – I interrupted her. "It's on me." That was pretty hysterical. That used to be Ronnie's favorite expression. Everywhere we went he was always picking up the tab for the crowd. Here I was, offering to pay. I wasn't even sure I had enough change to cover two $.99 regular coffees plus tax.

"You didn't have to do that," Ray said.

"Oh, I have a funny feeling I really did," I said, smiling. I introduced myself and asked if I could join him. For the next two hours Ray and I talked and Wanda kept pouring coffee. Despite appearances, I found him intelligent and fascinating. He told me how he'd served and survived three tours in Afghanistan. Like so many vets, he suffered from PTSD. He had no problem getting hired on somewhere, but he couldn't keep a job. He'd have a flashback from the war or get a panic attack. "Employers hate it when you wig out on their dime."

Ray was easy to talk to and I found myself telling him all about my difficulties. Well, I left out the part out about the multinational manhunt. I just kept it to the deadbeat Dad, skipped out, leaving me with two kids, a mountain of bills.

"Any hopes of back child support?" Ray asked.

"They've got to find him first."

"Not necessarily. I worked for a while for one of the government agencies that tracks money. They have ways now to trace and seize funds through passport hits at the border. It's pretty complex and it takes a while for the funds to make their way through the system, but it's working." Then Ray asked me about the Cadillac. "I'm not being nosy, but your ride does kind of stand out. How come you haven't sold it? Surely, that would help you for a little while."

It was the only asset I'd been allowed to keep. Of course I could sell it. That hadn't even occurred to me, but it made sense. I asked Ray how I might be able to help him. He said I already had. "Just by taking the time to talk to me, like I'm a real person, that means a lot. You know, I'm homeless; I'm not an idiot, I'm just messed up in my head.

Ray had been staying at a shelter and resource center that helped vets get back on their feet. I gave him a ride there. I liked the sign posted out front, "No Vet Left Behind." I decided if I ever got on my feet again I was going to look into helping out at the center.

156

I drove straight to the Cadillac dealership, happy to be doing something, anything positive towards getting my life back. Not the life I had with Ronnie, the life I had before I gave up my life for Ronnie. All the way to the dealership I thought about Ray's situation and mine. It didn't really matter how you get there, when you land at the bottom of the pit it all looks and feels the same down there.

As I pulled up to the lot all I could see were row after row of bright unaffordable automobiles and SUVS like mine. Luxury vehicles. They weren't called "necessity cars." For so many years Ronnie and I had lived a life full of every material thing and I don't remember ever really appreciating them. I didn't need them. It's hard to appreciate what you don't need.

I threw back my shoulders and confidently approached the manager. He recognized me, mine was a familiar face; I'd been all over the media for months. I explained my situation. Once I assured him I could deliver clear title in good order, we negotiated a trade down to a used economy car. It was far less than the Honda I'd had when I met Ronnie, but it was all the car I needed and left me enough money to make a down payment on a small condominium. I was grateful.

Six months later, as I was leaving for work, I ran into our mail carrier.

"Hey, Mrs. Gessler, glad I caught you. I didn't want to leave these in your mailbox." She handed me a stack of official looking brown envelopes. My heart pounded. More IRS notices? Someone else suing for civil damages? My fingers trembled as I opened the first one. I read: "Pay to the Order of Nora White Gessler." Surely, not.

Each envelope held a check of varying amounts. They were issued from all over the world. Every time Ronnie crossed a border customs collected a "duty" which went towards restitution and child support. He'd crossed several.

Stunned, I drove to my job as Director of the Veteran's Resource Center. My legal background enables me to help Vets navigate through the tangles of bureaucratic red tape to get the kind of assistance they so desperately need. It's a rewarding job and it pays our bills, and now, this unexpected blessing. I close my eyes as I repeat my mantra – "Thank you, thank you, thank you."

Closing Thoughts

There are a lot of cosmic theories in this world. The one that RJ taught his mom about was the law of attraction. My definition of the Law of Attraction posits that our positive or negative energies attract positive or negative energies back to us.

Part of the Law of Attraction is giving and receiving. The Universe gives you back what you give others in return. Even when she couldn't afford it, Nora started giving with a simple cup of coffee. She believed that her positive actions could benefit all involved and it did!

I challenge you to do something good, just for the sake of doing well. Go out of your way to do something nice for someone today. Commit a random act of kindness. What have you got to lose, $0.99 for a cup of coffee for a homeless vet? If the Universe happens to return the favor, which it may well, that's awesome! The Law of Attraction certainly seemed to work for Nora. But if you don't think it ever does, be happy in knowing that you helped fill someone's belly or brightened their day. Maybe that should be all the satisfaction we need.

According to Mahatma Ghandi, "You may never know what results come of your action, but if you do nothing there will be no result." Go ahead, test the theory.

We have all been broke, searching for pennies and wondering how the hell we ended up this way. When is our next paycheck? Can we miraculously get an advance or a payday loan or borrow money from family and friends? We've all been there. And if you're there now, I'm here today to tell you that it will get better. If you pay attention to the theories behind the Law of Attraction their science is proven. I won't go into Quantum Physics, but I am here today telling you that I am proof that you can be down to your very last dollar and be rewarded with unexpected income if you believe that helping others helps you most of all. Everything has a way of working out at just the right time, I promise if you stop and think about it, you might come up with several examples in your own life. As you sit there discouraged, broke and maybe even hungry, like I was, I beg you to trust the process and watch varying amounts of wealth begin to accumulate in your life.

ATTITUDE IS EVERYTHING

"There is nothing good or bad, but thinking makes it so."
~ William Shakespeare

There were three familiar personnel files on my desk, a trio of talented folks, and the cream of this year's crop of management trainees. But I also knew all too well that these fast-trackers could be a handful. I called my assistant over the intercom. "Janine, please send in Ms. Hanson, whenever you're ready."

Lauryl Hanson was barely twenty-one years old, graduated early from a big name Texas school with a finance degree, big dreams, and cocky as all get out. That was okay. I could work with cocky. "Lauryl, thanks so much for making time for me." I stood, shook her hand, and gestured for her to be seated. I stepped around her to close my office door so we could have some privacy. Ms. Hanson and I were going to have a talk.

Not so many years ago, I was Lauryl Hanson. I was twenty-five and on my ninth year with Cavanaugh's, a high-end retail competitor of Macy's. At sixteen I began working nights and weekends for the Cavanaugh's in my hometown. I started as a part-time commissioned sales clerk in the men's shoe department. First thing I did was separate myself from the half-asleep tenured zombies that worked there.

Since I was on mostly commission, I figured I'd make more money if I concentrated on selling the more expensive shoes. I made myself a technical expert on all things loafer, wing-tipped and leather.

I could talk tongues and soles, laces and broguing. It was a good strategy. I beat all sales records for our unit, then region, then nationwide.

I moved into a position as assistant buyer, then head buyer. When I finally finished my degree, which took forever, I qualified for a transfer to the company's corporate offices. I accepted an entry-level position in marketing just to get to work there. Now I'd have a chance to really move up. Except, I didn't.

I joined the marketing department's copy unit, I was part of a five member team. I cringed at the very word. The "team" was made up of a bunch of lazy, been-there-forever types that lived for their next coffee break.

We were supposed to be designing product copy for the store's catalogs, mailers, newspapers, and magazines. The unit had reworded the same tired sentences and graphics for years. In the field, I'd never sold a pair of shoes because of their sterling prose.

My new boss, Dennis Abrams liked me. Probably too much, so I made sure I kept our communications very professional. Rumor had it that Dennis was in trouble with the higher-ups. He had the same inertia as his crew. I hoped it wasn't contagious. Dennis spent far too much time chatting when he should have been managing.

Our group had just been tasked with reworking all the copy of the top hundred movers. Those were the hundred products that Cavanaugh sold the most of and made the most profit from. Dennis had assigned each of us twenty product write-ups. We were to turn our drafts in at the end of the week.

I jumped on the assignment, completing mine in two days. I couldn't wait to show Dennis. He liked them so well he took them straight to his boss, Sam Halverson, who was similarly delighted. "Have your unit continue to generate this kind of work product, Dennis. That's all I've been asking."

When Dennis came back from his meeting, he gathered the team to share his good news. He made it sound like everyone got the credit. That was ridiculous. The others hadn't turned in one new piece of copy. When Dennis asked them for their progress reports, everybody had some lame excuse why theirs weren't going to be ready by deadline.

"Well, guys, how 'bout you each give five products from your lists to Melanie. Let McCrackle take a crack at them." He thought he was hysterical. His suggestion provoked eye rolls from two of them. With one line, Dennis had managed to utterly alienate me from the "team."

I actually didn't care. I hadn't moved to corporate to make friends. I had the fifteen rewritten by the next morning. Dennis was beside himself, moving his 300 lb. Girth down the hall to Halverson's office. Later that day Karen, the team member who seemed to dislike me the most, was throwing a fit in Dennis' office. I heard a string of expletives and, "she doesn't know an adverb from an adjective." Then, "Fine, take your little protégée and your precious copy and stick them. I quit."

The next day, her coven partner, Tamara didn't show up for work; that left just me and the two weak links, Gladys and Helen. Helen was in tears and Gladys was so nervous she'd broken into hives. The vestiges of the copy team were in Dennis' office. His face was scarlet and he was sweating.

Helen was babbling. All of her words running together. "I c-c-an't do all these. Don't make me. I can't handle all this pressure."

"Oh, for heaven's sake," I said, grabbing her pages of products from her. "Let me have them." I reached over and took Helen's from in front of her. Turning to Dennis, I said, "Go ahead; give me Mutt and Jeff's lists too."

Sheepishly, Dennis handed them over. I went to my cubicle and knocked out fifty-five original creative descriptions way ahead of Dennis' Friday deadline. Dennis' boss, as well as the department heads over publicity, sales and accounting, saw my work and were impressed. I got all kinds of kudos and commendation letters in my personnel file.

For a year I turned in every assignment ahead of schedule. I was good at my job but I was also willing to put in the hours – nights, weekends, it didn't matter. One day, Dennis had another spell. He turned scarlet and was sweating profusely. We called the paramedics. It was a heart attack. They were able to save him, but he wasn't coming back to work for some time. Sam Halverson called me into his office.

"Melanie, we're all aware of the contributions you've made to this department. First, taking over the lion's share of the product mover project, then covering for the two staff members we lost. You've got

161

incredible talent and lots of potential and I'm considering making some changes." He dropped his head down then and rubbed his nose with his index finger, up and down. He did that when he was thinking or very serious.

"No doubt, you've got the talent and energy to fill in for Joe, but I'm not sure you have the seasoning. What do you think? Do you think you're ready to lead the unit?"

"More than ready, sir. I run rings around them already."

A look passed his face. I couldn't quite read it. I felt like I'd said the wrong thing. I tried again. "I'm just saying, sir, if you'll give me a chance, you won't be sorry."

"Very well, Melanie. I have reservations, but let's see what you can do. I'm going to make you head of Joe's unit – on an interim basis. Just remember something, kid. Management is not just about getting results, it's about getting results through people."

Yeah, yeah, yeah. I thought. Blah, blah. Just give me the ball.

He did, and some would say I dropped it. To be honest, a promotion like that? It went straight to my head. I started behaving like a power-crazed jerk. Monday mornings, I was always the first one in the office. I usually was at my desk no later than 7:30. I expected my people at 8:00 sharp. Invariably, I'd find them huddled up, gossiping and sharing tales of their weekend exploits.

Everyone was polite and treated me with respect, even though I was much younger than any of them. Where a normal human might exchange a first of the week greeting like, "How was your weekend?" My first words were always work-related: "So where are we?"

Six months as head of the unit and I was building a reputation for excellence. Our copy was catching the eye of consumers and the media. People magazine did a short one-pager titled: "What's happening at Cavanaugh's?" It featured one of the old catalog pages next to a new one we had produced. The execs on the 12th Floor were ecstatic.

I was anticipating an outstanding review. Mr. Halverson watched as I read the one he'd written. He'd cited my initiative and commended me for doing more with fewer people than my predecessor. He wrote that I had good instincts and technical excellence without equal. Under the management section he'd commented that I was abrasive, lacked empathy, displayed impatience and an inability to coach my employees.

At the bottom of the performance review form were two lines with boxes next to them: "Promotion recommended" and "Salary increase recommended." He'd checked "not at this time" both places.

I couldn't even respond. Head down, I walked back to my office. My disappointment morphed into anger and then resentment. I couldn't get past how I'd been "screwed over." I whined and moaned and grumbled and complained to friends, relatives, colleagues, and stupidly, co-workers who weren't nearly as loyal as I thought they were.

Naturally, in no time at all, word got around that I was bad-mouthing the department and worse, my boss. Halverson called me in to his office first thing one Monday morning. I had the sickening feeling I was about to be fired.

"Sit down, Melanie." He said, closing his door. I want to commend you again on your high standards of excellence. Your work product has had a significant impact on the company. Now then, the reason I've asked you in this morning is to let you know I've cleared the way for you to participate in a high-level training program. It begins tomorrow and I personally recommended you for the slot.

It's a pilot program, one we think can really be the kind of management development seminar we've be looking for to groom our sharpest candidates. I know I can trust you to provide me with your usual candid impressions. It'll be held off-site at the Worthington Hotel and Conference Center. Very nice accommodations, I think you'll be pleased. Jackie has made all of your arrangements. Do you have any questions?"

I didn't. I shook his hand and thanked him for the opportunity. Jackie had a three-inch binder, map, and reservation confirmation numbers all prepared. Attendees were to stay on-site, no exceptions.

The seminar was being held in the Grand Ballroom. There were six long conference tables set up, four attendees to a table. I had intended to find a place somewhere in the middle of the room when I noticed the name cards. Assigned seating, ugh. I found my name card at the end of one of the tables towards the back. I was relieved. Suddenly, I didn't want to be there; an inconspicuous spot towards the back was perfect.

Looking around I didn't recognize anyone. There was already a guy seated next to my place, conversing loudly with a big-haired woman wearing too much makeup seated immediately in front of him. I didn't like her giggle, but I did like the sound of his laugh.

As I took my seat, he turned to me and announced, "My, what a big head you have." That was the opening salvo from Alan Belton. I knew him by reputation. Just 27 years old, he was already a company legend and a popular long-lunch topic. He'd been recruited away from the top international men's apparel company, supposedly for gobs of money. He was heading up some hush-hush special project predicting retail trends. He was assigned to the Strategic Planning group but purportedly answered to the CEO.

I remembered reading his profile in the company newsletter, "A Vision for the Future." His bio said he was married, originally from London. None of my friends at Cavanaugh's knew him personally, but everyone liked to share whatever morsels of info they had or could make up about him. Seeing him in person, for some ridiculous reason, I was flustered. He was dressed straight out of GQ magazine; monogrammed oxford shirt, sweater tied around his shoulders, and a tie bar that looked really expensive. He smelled wonderful. He made a blockbuster first impression.

I realized I'd been staring for way too long. He was smirking at me. I hated that. He obviously was the kind of man that knew his effect on women and relished it, played to it. Well not me.

"I'm sorry, I volleyed back, were you commenting on my obvious superior intelligence and extra-large brain?"

"Oh, I like that," he said. "No, I was referencing the fact we're hand-selected to have our heads shrunk. You do realize that's why you're here?"

I didn't. I hadn't a clue why I'd been chosen.

"Oh, yes." Alan explained. "Look around, you'll find each and everyone here is bright, driven, getting results. But we're all quite flawed. We're square little rebel pegs, refusing to go into our trusty round corporate holes. Watch. This is our last, last chance. They want to salvage us, reform us. See if I'm not spot on.

"Well, if they want us to do trust falls, fair warning. I dropped the last guy on his head."

Alan thought that was hilarious and knew exactly what I was

referring to. A lot of touchy-feely training programs used a bonding exercise where one person was blindfolded and was supposed to fall straight backward and "trust" some participant would be behind to catch them. I thought most training programs were a waste of both the company's time and mine. I just wanted to do my job.

Candace Stanton took the stage. She was probably forty, short, in a smart yellow suit, matching sky-high pumps and pale lemon bow-tie blouse. She had shoulder-length blonde highlights. Very sharp.

"Let's get started. I see before me the future occupants of the 12th floor of Cavanaugh's corporate offices. You've got it all – talent, ambition, smarts – every criterion to succeed at the highest levels. I am going to work you hard these next three days. I'll challenge you, provoke you, frustrate you and in the end, hopefully, help you. All I'm asking in return is your attention and participation. Even if you were coerced into coming here, I'm going to ask you to trust me, I know what I'm doing."

When she said, "trust me" Alan kicked me under the table. Great I thought. I'm sitting next to Ferris Buehler.

"How many of you have ever flown an airplane?" Candace asked.

I was surprised to see Alan's hand go up.

"Great. Alan, can you please tell me what the instrument is called that tells you how high the plane is flying?"

"Altimeter," he replied, carefully.

"Excellent! Now, what's that instrument gauge you watch that shows you where the plane is in relation to the horizon?"

"The attitude."

"Did you say, altitude?"

"No," Alan answered, "attitude."

"Really? So, your attitude determines whether you're above ground and rising, or crashing? Thank you Alan, appreciate that. Let me ask the rest of you. This morning would you say your careers are rising or crashing?"

Alan kicked me again, mouthing, "See?" I was going to be bruised before this week was over.

"My job this week is to provide you with all the information you need to keep your attitude adjusted so you won't crash and burn. I want to tinker with your instrumentation so you can you fly right and soar to the heights we know you are capable of climbing to. Who's on board?"

Alan and I were the last ones to raise our hands. Covering his hand he whispered, "I say you and me go get a drink."

The first day flew by. I had a headache by the end of it. We spent the entire day filling out a battery of psychological assessments. Fill in the blank. Scale of one to ten. Question after question. My head felt shrunk, to be sure. After class, most of the group ended up in the hotel bar, which wasn't discouraged. Candace had asked us to use our breaks and downtime to discuss our discoveries with one another. "Most of the learning will happen outside the classroom," she'd said.

The first night I drank way more than I should have on an empty stomach. One glass of wine led to another and I was enjoying the camaraderie of my fellow classmates. They were bright and engaging and for once I didn't feel like the Lone Ranger. Alan sat next to me. He had a caustic, sarcastic wit, but I enjoyed it. For the first time in ages I found myself seriously attracted to a man. I looked at his left hand holding his scotch and water, the one with the gold band. I saw his nails were buffed and polished.

He caught me looking. I saw his eyes follow mine. "What does your wife do?" I asked.

"Pretty much whatever she likes." He winked, swallowed his drink and went to the bar to order another round.

I could feel my lips numbing and didn't trust myself. I used the opportunity to duck out.

The next day we were all given the results of our assessments. We'd learned that we all have a personality style that makes us more or less social and more or less task oriented. I tested off the chart task oriented, but fairly low socially. Candace helped interpret our scores. To me she said, "Ah, yes. Yours was the scary profile. Your personality type likes to eat their young." The class roared. I didn't think it was very funny.

There were more jokes at my expense, but most of the class profiled the same way, strong on task, low on people. "It's not that y'all don't like people. You'll have lunch with someone. As long as you pick the restaurant, the time, the date..."

"You, my dear," Alan said to me, under his breath, "are a control freak. And I'd love to have you control me."

There were times I loathed my Irish heritage. I turned crimson

166

instantly.

The third day we role-played, worked in small groups and learned the impact of our particular management style on others. Candace paired the high task leaders with the high socials. We couldn't stand each other. At the end of the exercise Candace drove home her point that it takes all personality types to get the best results.

"Or," Alan whispered, "They could just fire the slackers and let us get the results. We're the only one's working anyway." At last, I'd found my kindred spirit.

That last night in the hotel bar it seemed everyone else was raring to get back to work all dewy positive and improved. The girl with the big hair was saying, "...well, my attitude certainly wasn't getting me anywhere. I'm going to try her approach. I've got nothing to lose."

"Let's get out of here," Alan suggested, taking my hand and pulling me with him.

We ended up in the gardens of the hotel, locked in a steamy embrace. My resolve was no match for his brains, accent, wit; penetrating brown eyes and intoxicating cologne, I was about to screw up royally. Thankfully, a couple of seminar attendees interrupted us and I fled.

The Saturday after the seminar I summoned my best friend Carla to an emergency brunch at our favorite haunt. I poured out all of the events of the past week, including the dalliance in the gardens. She listened thoughtfully and asked a lot of questions.

"Are you open to the possibility that you might be making some pretty poor choices?" She asked. That's why I loved Carla. She didn't sugarcoat. "I mean," she continued, "there's a lot of truth in that expression, as long as you keep doing what you've always done you're going to get what you've always gotten."

"Thanks, Dr. Phil."

"Seriously, girl. You may be smarter than anyone. Personally I think you're brilliant. But you don't have to hit everyone over the head with your talent. Don't fight so hard for the recognition. So, okay, maybe you don't have rocket scientists in your unit. Treating them so shabbily isn't good Karma. Why don't you try it their way? Do a fake-it-till-you-make-it makeover. Do you really think Cavanaugh's would have gone to all the time and trouble to send you to that fancy schmancy seminar for a week if they didn't think you were valuable?"

Carla, as usual, made a lot of sense. I went back to work and while I wasn't whistling in the hallway, I stopped my sniping and complaining. I forced myself to say positive things to my team members. I started reading, Stephen Covey, David Allen, John Maxwell. I came in on Monday morning and made myself ask everyone how their weekend was and then I made myself listen as they told me. I even started asking Gladys and Helen for their opinions on projects. Glady's hives went away.

In three months Mr. Halverson gave me a 10% increase. Six months after the seminar I received another raise and my promotion was official. I climbed to the head of marketing and then transferred to Personnel where I'm now head of Human Relations. I'm living proof that attitude determines altitude. Candace conducts her magical transforming seminars often.

"Lauryl, the reason I've asked you in this morning…"

Closing Thoughts

How is your attitude at work? No matter what your rank or position, your attitude is critical to your success. Attitude effects how your employees, your co-workers, and your managers perceive you. That perception drives whether they are going to for you or against you.

Not convinced? Think about how you think of others at work. Chances are you will be thinking things like: "Marilyn's a slacker." "Kelly is a kiss-up." "Nancy is snippy. I avoid her at all costs." "Bill is a gossip." "Jodi always dresses well and carries herself professionally." "I'd love to work with Bob, he seems to really know how to get things done." "John is dead wood." "Martin never has a bad word to say about anyone." "Martha will step on anyone to get ahead."

Open your eyes. You are judging your peers by their reputations, which have been created over time by – you guessed it – their attitudes.

The worst part about getting a reputation for having a bad attitude is that it can be incredibly difficult to change. And more importantly, your attitude can cost or earn you more money! You can destroy your reputation instantly by saying one wrong thing to the wrong person. When news about what you said spreads like wildfire at the water cooler or is discussed amongst higher-level managers, you can be instantly branded as a problem employee. With a slip of the tongue, your career at that company just became a dead-end job.

This is not to say that all career paths are irrevocably destroyed by bad reputations. Sadly, there are some people in the workplace with the (bad) attitude that a leopard can never change his spots, and you will never be able to do the right thing to win them back. But in a reasonable work environment, if you can demonstrate over time that your attitude has changed, the people around you will begin to adopt a new perception of you. Given enough time, you can reverse the damage that your attitude has created.

Thank goodness that Melanie's superiors were open-minded to the possibility of change. Melanie's boss and others in management were well aware of her impassioned work ethic, but they were also aware of Melanie's attitude of superiority towards her coworkers. However, management had faith that if they could convince Melanie to work on her interpersonal skills, she could become a valuable manager. Luckily, Carla's friend convinced Melanie to embrace the changes suggested in the training seminar, and things worked out well for Melanie.

Do you see any "Melanie" in yourself? Imagine a conference room with all your peers in it. You're out of the office, and someone brings up your name. Are your co-workers smiling at the mention of your name, or are they groaning and rolling their eyes? If the answer is anything less than smiling, it is imperative that you understand why and strive, on a daily basis, to earn smiles. It could be costing you money and the difference just might change your life.

DO WHAT YOU LOVE

"Your work is to discover your world and then with all your heart give yourself to it."
~ Buddha

"And here's another post from Jeremy. Oh my gosh, he's in Venice. He's acting like one of those gondoliers, he's just crazy, I can…"

My wife never took a breath. I'd long since stopped trying to respond. She was just talking out loud. I'm sure she did the same thing when I wasn't around. I sometimes wondered if she ever gave her computer a rest. I suspected she was somehow hardwired, tethered directly to her laptop through some invisible USB port in her arm.

I made a show of leaving. Noisily folding the newspaper. Was it asking so much for five minutes silence to enjoy my cup of coffee and the sports page? Yes, I still had the newspaper delivered daily. I was old school. I liked the feel of the sheets of newsprint between my hands and, unlike my wife, I wanted more out of my media and my life than snippets and sound bytes. I actually wanted a little depth.

Sighing, I dropped my coffee cup in the sink as loudly as possible short of breaking it. Then I laughed to myself. If I was trying to provoke her, I was wasting my time. She was utterly engrossed in her scrolling. "…Denise is having a ball with her dorm mates, they're hosting some sort of costume party. She's…"

I left without kissing Peggy goodbye. It annoyed me the way she'd half-turn her cheek to accept my peck, like some sort of perfunctory duty. Even those vestiges of affection were gone. I grabbed my briefcase, phone and the paper. I'd read it on the train.

The commute to work did nothing to lighten my mood. God. I felt like a dinosaur. The only people that rode the train anymore were my age. We dressed alike, suits and ties and worn wingtip shoes. No amount of polishing could get mine to shine like they once had. They were faded and tired. Damn, I felt like my shoes.

Looking around I saw my fellow foragers of income and benefits. Trudging off to the city from the suburbs, day after day after day. Once in a while someone made a break for it. "Went over the wall," my friend Larry called it. We thought Don would be the last to leave our ranks, but he decided after thirty years in banking to try real estate. Connie kind of fell apart when her marriage did. Bob had a heart attack and died at his desk. He'd been a stockbroker, 42 years old.

I never thought I'd be a suit on the train. Back in college I studied philosophy and literature. I was a deep thinker. I actually "got" Emerson and Thoreau. I planned to publish tomes of poetry and a novel or two. End up a Professor at some Ivy-league school molding minds. Now, I was just a man among the masses, a long way from Walden, living that life Henry David so eloquently described of "quiet desperation." I felt the tears pressuring up in my eyes and had to shake off those lost dreams.

The train lurched, signaling we'd arrived at Union Station. Along with the fifty or so regulars from my car, we fed ourselves through the long tunnel, up the ramp through the historic rail terminal. Then we funneled our way out into the bright smoggy southern California day. En masse, we traipsed to the bus station where we'd be shuttled downtown to our high rises offices, cubicles and dungeons. I broke into the song of the guards and the flying monkeys from Wizard of Oz: "Yo-eee-oh, Yo, Oh…" Sadly, few of my worker bees even noticed.

Well, one did. I heard a soprano start: "Yo, eee, oh…" then, "Exactly! I feel like that every day." She said, putting her hands to the sides of her mouth and yelling: "Moo-o-o-o-oo-ooo."

To my amazement she'd done a stunning rendition of a cow bellow. I told her so.

"Thank you," she said, curtsying.

171

She'd drawn far more attention with her cattle call then I had with the monkey mantra. The number 6812 bus pulled up. That was mine; apparently, hers too.

"Jane Cassidy," she announced. My pasture's at Sixth and Spring. Where's yours?

"A block further down, and my grass is concrete."

"Mine, too." She said. "But so far, no electric fence. I can still get out when I want."

We chatted to her stop. It was nice to talk to someone who had a pulse, I thought. I got off with her, not wanting to lose the connection.

"Didn't you say…"

"Yes, I'm down at the Turner Building, but I'm trying to up my steps," pointing to my pedometer on my belt. "It's about the only healthy exercise I work into my day, steps and stairs. I'm superglued to my desk."

"Hey! We match," Jane said, pointing to some similar step-tracking device on her wrist. "Doctor said it would help me with my anxiety. Well, this is me. Have a good day, Mr. You-Never-Told-Me-Your-Name."

Before I could, she'd disappeared through a set of revolving doors.

When I got to my building I took the stairs. Nine flights, eleven steps per flight, the automaton's aerobic workout. Waiting on my desk were four color-coded files marked: mail, for signature, read only, action required. I hung my suit jacket on the rack. Before I could sit down, my assistant Glenda was setting down a cup of coffee for me.

"Good morning, Dale."

Glenda was my office wife of more than twenty years. We'd lasted longer than most marriages and she was often kinder to me than my own bride. We read each other's minds; finished each other's thoughts and I would be decidedly lost without her. We'd never crossed any relational boundaries, I respected her too much, she was like family a close cousin and clearly, she'd never had designs on me. Though, I admit, I was quite drawn to her. No, we were strictly platonic. Just like my relationship with Peggy.

"We've a lot going on today," Glenda said. You've got a 9:00

172

intern candidate coming in, status update meetings at 10:00 and 11:00, Jim Fisk wants to have lunch with you at the Athletic Club around 12:30, and that leaves you to your own devices from 2:00 on.

"You know, Glenda, everyone would get a lot more done in a day if they'd just do the work instead of meeting about it."

"Amen. Let me know if you need me."

"I need you," I said. That was our joke. She shut my door as she left, smiling.

I thumbed through files she'd left for me. Reading, absorbing, signing, routing, making notes in the margins. I put the files in the out box and retrieved my yellow legal tablet from a credenza drawer.

Thirty-seven tasks. It was the to-do list I'd made for myself the night before. It was always the last thing I did before I left. I was the proverbial creature of habit, and my work habits were how I managed to churn out more work than my peers. Glenda and I'd had designed and developed our own operating system, matrixes and methods. The company newspaper even featured us in a piece on "Teamwork."

A lot of those habits were, like my newspaper fetish, "old school." Pen and paper lists, not computerized spreadsheets. Sure, there were probably all kinds of "apps for that" but I'd seen how effective physically writing down priorities could be. No one could argue with my productivity.

I'd been working at LPG (Liddy, Peterson, Garrison, LLP) since I graduated college 30 years ago. It was and still is one of the largest tax, audit and advisory firms on the planet. Like most LPG employees, once I came on board I never left. You couldn't see the electric fences rigged around their offices, but they were there. Between the LPG bonuses, benefits and salary packages, it was a corporate Hotel California; you could never leave.

I hadn't planned on working for one company every business day of my entire life. Heck, I hadn't even wanted to go into accounting. The emotions returning, thinking back I was going to be a great American writer, or a bad one. But I was going to spend my life writing.

But Peggy got pregnant our junior year. That changed everything. I guess I'd always assumed we would marry, but not that young. There's no way a struggling writer could support a family. The week we found out Peggy was expecting, LPG was on campus recruiting. They were offering contracts, signing bonuses, all kinds of deals if you were willing to commit to a three-year program. They were even helping with tuition and financial aid.

They sure seemed to want me. My recruiter gushed, "You've got exactly the broad base we're looking for." It was a bird's nest on the ground, as they say. I accepted their contract, changed majors, graduated and have been with them ever since. LPG proved to be a great training ground. It exposes new hires to all aspects of accounting. One of the big five firms, LPG has hundreds of office around the world; more than a hundred thousand employees. It was easy to find a place and stay there. I couldn't imagine where else I could have gone that would have provided so well for my sudden, instant family.

Our first child was a boy, Jeremy. He's now a journalist with one of the networks. Peggy and I were relieved when he was reassigned to cover feature stories in Europe. For eight years he served as a war correspondent covering the conflicts in the embattled Middle East. I attribute every wrinkle in my craggy face and all the silver in my hair to those years.

Now, he might be covering the papal elections at the Vatican or posing as a Venetian gondolier. He dreamt big dreams and is living them out. Of course, it helps that he had my financial backing while he earned his degrees, that I bankrolled him through the first years of his career. My money kept him financially solvent while he worked his way up the ladder.

Money is a fascinating commodity. When people say they aren't in a job for the money? They probably have someone paying their way. There weren't a lot people standing in line handing me money so I could go live in an artist's garret and write.

After Jeremy was born, Peggy and I held off on having any more children. Jeremy suffered with childhood asthma and a host of allergies. His medical condition was difficult, landing him in the emergency room numerous times. The hospital bills, even with LPG's excellent insurance coverage, were staggering. Even if I'd wanted to pursue a different career path, with Jeremy's health I didn't have the option.

When Jeremy turned nine, I was offered a transfer to the Los

Angeles office of LPG. The doctors said the climate change would be good for him. His health improved, our financial burdens eased and Peggy and I grew our family by two. Jennifer and Joannie, two years apart. Looking back, I don't think we realized that would mean financing two children through college at the same time. There was never any margin.

My intercom buzzed. It was Glenda.

"Your wife's on line 5."

"Great news, Dale. Jennifer got the art internship in Rome, but she says she needs the tuition paid by Friday. I'm not sure if a slot just opened up or they made one for her but isn't that the best news?"

"I don't even know what you're talking about."

"Well, maybe you should listen when I try to talk to you. It's fourteen nine and we can just put it on plastic, that's fine."

"Fourteen nine what? What's that number?"

"C'mon, Dale. You're the accountant. "Fourteen thousand, nine hundred dollars."

"We never discussed this!" I screamed. I couldn't breathe. My heart was beating out of my chest. "You call me at work and announce... I... Peggy, we will talk about this at home tonight."

I slammed the phone in its cradle and lost it. Enraged I hurled the phone across my office. Then swept everything off of my desk.

"When is enough, enough? All I am is some cash-dispensing ATM!"

Glenda had my door open. Alarmed. "Dale, Dale, what can I do?"

"Aw, damn it, Glenda. Look at this..."

I was grateful my 9:00 intern candidate hadn't come in yet. That wouldn't have given him the best first impression of life at LPG. It was especially difficult to sell him on the merits of the firm without cynicism creeping into my voice. I tried to keep my focus trained on him, not the company. He was a about the same age I was when I hired on. Part of me wanted to warn him, "Careful. Blink once and in thirty years you'll be standing in your office hurling coffee mugs and stationary."

I survived the two status update meetings, grateful for the distraction from the issues at home, and now, the bank. I was glad I could duck out and meet Jim Fisk for lunch. The timing was providential. Jim had been my fraternity brother in college, moving to LA when he graduated. He'd been instrumental in re-settling us when we've moved here. He was my best friend and right then I needed one.

"So, let me see if I can wrap my miniscule brain around this," Jim said, striking the perfect balance between sarcasm and sympathy. "Out of the clear blue, your wife makes a fifteen grand I love you call. Oh, I bet that made you feel all warm and fuzzy."

"Yeah, sure did." I said.

"Well, maybe it's about time Dear Old Dad started thinking about his wish lists before they all turn in to bucket lists. Seriously, Dale, I'm all about giving, but you haven't stopped since junior year. The girls get to study whatever – and wherever – they want and love, Peggy gets to do her volunteer neo-natal baby gig. Favored son is all over the globe while you toil under the fluorescent lighting. Sounds fair to me."

I sighed, heavily. I'm not sure I liked the mirror Jim was holding up to my life. Made me feel rather weak, like a victim of circumstance. Maybe that's exactly what I was.

I didn't see my new moo-calling friend on the commute home, I'd been hoping I would. She was like a breath of fresh air in my stale life. As I approached my front door, I paused. I realized, I really didn't want to go in and that brought tears to my eyes.

Looking back, I probably shouldn't have gone in. Not till I'd fully calmed down. I walked in and Peggy was at the computer, surprise, surprise. She called out over her shoulder, not even looking at me, "The tuition bill's in your chair. You can pay it online or send it overnight with the forms you have to sign."

All my earlier rage came back and then some.

"Peggy are you insane? Or am I?" How long do you expect me to keep signing checks and doling out the money for everyone else's fantasy worlds? You drop a fifteen thousand dollar bomb on my head – out of nowhere. I – It's unbelievable. Tell you what Peg," and then I really raised the melodrama.

I started hurling bank statements, credit cards, bills, tax files, checkbooks from my desk and throwing them on hers.

"Have at it, Sweetie. No big deal." I yelled. "Sign my name wherever you want. Spend every dime I make, I'll run right out like a

176

good little schmuck and make some more. You just be sure to let me know if I need to be working more than sixty, seventy hours a week. Oh, and if you don't mind?" I said pulling one of the credit cards from the pile, "I'm going to need one of these for a hotel room."

I grabbed my laptop, threw some toiletries and a change of clothes in an overnight bag and left. I'd never done that in thirty years of marriage but then in thirty years I'd never been that angry or that hurt. Halfway to the hotel I pulled over. I couldn't see for the damn tears. "So this is it. This is my *we-only-go-around-once* life."

At the hotel, I didn't answer Peg's texts or calls. I had nothing to say. Lying on the bed, I turned on an old black and white classic. The leading man had just gotten mired in quicksand. Huh, I knew just how he felt. One minute I was walking along, and then suddenly I found myself getting sucked down into the muck and couldn't get out. The more I struggled to free myself, the further down I went. I was being buried alive until there was no more of me.

Only, unlike the character in the film, I didn't stumble into the mire. I had to admit, I'd frog-marched myself straight into it. It'd taken years to get this stuck. No, mine wasn't quicksand; mine was tediously slow.

The next morning I checked out of the hotel and went to catch my train. I was happy to see Jane Cassidy already on board.

"Why it is a pleasure to see the good Ms. Cassidy this morning," I said. "I don't know that we were properly introduced, I'm Dale Keegan."

She took my outstretched hand. "My pleasure, ready to chew some cud?" We talked about her work in graphic design, the outlook for the Dodgers and my latest project at LPG. It was nice to have a change in conversation.

"I missed you on the train last night." I said as we were walking to our bus.

"I usually end up working late on some deadline. Most of the time I catch the 8:30 train. I usually finish up around 7:00 and just hang around at TJs by the station until then, have a beer, relax. You should join me sometime."

I didn't respond. It bothered me how tempting that invitation sounded. When I got to the office, Glenda was quiet. I guess I had her on eggshells now, after yesterday.

177

"Your files are on your desk, coffee too," she said softly. "Let me know if you need me."

"I need you," I replied. I went into my office and shut the door.

That night, I didn't see Peg's car in the drive. The lights were on in the house as I walked in and on my desk was my old IBM Selectric III from college. Lord, I didn't know we'd kept it. It looked like it had been restored, all shiny and clean. There was an index card taped to it.

In Peg's cursive it read, "Good as new. There's a ream of paper in the bottom drawer and new ribbon in the machine. I'm working at my happy place tonight, the nursery at St. Joe's. That should give you two some time to get reacquainted. Find YOUR happy place, Dale."

I was overcome with guilt. I realized I'd made everyone else responsible for the choices I had made and then blamed them for their outcome. I wasn't a victim – I'd used the pregnancy, my job, Jeremy's asthma, everything as an excuse for not following my dreams. That was always my call.

Switching on the Selectric, I heard and felt its familiar vibration under my fingers. Energy. Vitality. The power of possibility. I pulled several sheets of paper from the package, loaded one the typewriter and wrote four long overdue letters.

I wrote each of my children a letter of appreciation, letting them know much I loved them, how proud I was of them and the choices they were making. Then I wrote one to Peg. A letter of gratitude thanking her for all she'd done for me, standing by me, raising our kids, keeping a beautiful home – doing everything to support me so I could work to support us. I ended hers, "We really do make a helluva team."

Then I wrote one more to me – well, the 'me' of thirty years ago. I apologized for giving up on his/my dreams too easily. For selling out and caving in to expectations. I promised to do better. I got up the next morning and found Peg asleep beside me. I saw she'd opened my letter. As I was leaving, I said thank you, and kissed her on her lips.

On the way in to work I texted Glenda and asked her to set up an appointment with Personnel first thing. At 9:00 I met with Dan Harrison and he assured me they could adjust my schedule down to three days a week and I'd still retain all my pension and benefits.

Peggy hired on part-time at the hospital and while we had a lot less money coming in, we found we had all the money we needed. On my days away from LPG I scheduled time with Jim for racket ball and golf. I spent quality time with my family. I wrote. A lot. I wrote all about my midlife angst and what I learned about self-imposed limitations. I wrote about how hard it is to reach for something you want when you keep holding on to what you have.

A year later I was writing from home one morning when an overnight package arrived. It was from Compton House Publishing; inside was a contract and a five-figure advance check. Unbeknownst to me Peggy had submitted my manuscript for consideration, "Giving up Money to Find Your Wealth."

Closing Thoughts

Do you do what you love, or have you "sold your soul to the company store" for the acquisition of things, and for the benefit of others?

It's a common story. Many of us fall prey to the theory that greed is good, that more is better, that "He who dies with the most things wins." It can become hard to decide when enough is enough. A bigger house? Nice. A better car? Sweet. A grand vacation? Private college for the Kids? Are those your signs of success? That's all fine and good if you are earning the money for these things doing work that you love. But if you are spending your life slaving in a job that you hate, are you really happy with all of these acquisitions? Probably not.

And what if you've been a corporate drone *and* you've given up some of those material possessions that you wanted to make others happy? You have a relative who barely scrapes by, so you help him out. Your kid wants to study a semester abroad. A ten-thousand dollar wedding gown for your baby's wedding? A string of pearls for your wife for *your* anniversary? Something's wrong with this picture. But how do you draw the line? That can be a sticky wicket. Are we all as lucky as Dale? If you went into work tomorrow and told your boss that you wanted to halve your hours and retain full-time benefits, what are the odds that your boss would say, "Sure, whatever you want!" Okay, perhaps not, but that doesn't mean that you can't take steps to reduce the pressure that you feel and regain some quality time.

First things first. If you left your job tomorrow, how many people would it take to replace you? I once knew a woman who felt that she was basically owned by her company. She was given more and more responsibility and worked longer and longer hours, and why? Why didn't she push back? Because she feared the outcome. She had known what it was like to live without when she was a child, she never wanted to feel like that again, and she was afraid that she'd be let go if she pushed back. Moreover, she had worked for one company all her life. Retiring with the company and receiving her full pension and benefits – the thought of giving up any portion of those earnings was out of the question. But as it turned out, life had different plans for this woman. She had a stroke in her young fifties, and had no choice but to retire. And what did the company do? They replaced her – with four people.

If you are in this position, there are ways to manage it. If you're not sure how, hire a career counselor and get some coaching on how to handle the situation. It's your life, and you deserve time to live it.

In addition to freeing up your time resources, you will most likely want to examine your expenditures as well. What do you spend money on that is not making you happy? Whose endeavors do you support when they really should be supporting their own? Do you feel, like Dale, that you are a human ATM machine? Only you can fix that.

Sit down and talk with your family. Tell them how you feel. Explain to them that some changes need to be made. There is no need to feel guilty or narcissistic. Each of us deserves some happy in our lives, and if you need to simplify in order to find your happy, those who love you should support you. If they respect you, they should be more than happy to support you in the lifestyle changes you need to make. After all, how long have you spent supporting them? And if, in pursuit of happiness, you find that they don't love and respect you, then you most certainly did the right thing by cutting back.

In the immortal words of Andy Dufresne in the movie *The Shawshank Redemption*, "It comes down to a simple choice, really. Get busy living, or get busy dying." You only get one shot at this life.

Take time to do the things you love. Make some changes and get busy living before it's too late. Most times in life our wealth isn't measured by what's in our bank account.

PERSPECTIVE IS EVERYTHING

"If you are distressed by anything external, the pain is not due to the thing itself but your own estimate of it, and this you have the power to revoke at any moment."
~ Marcus Aurelius

"Hey, Dan! You think it's going to rain?" Bill asked. My best friend was cueing up a teaching moment for the crew. Many of them were brand new with us and still pretty green. We were just getting ready to frame the house. It was an excellent time to review the basics.

"Well, you know, Bill, it surely could. Then again, it might not. Right now? In this moment, the sun is shining; we've got a full crew and the Peterson's have a dream home we need to build. The task before us is clear. We've got a whole lot of timber to put up. And how do we do that?"

"One board at a time," Bill said.

"Why?"

"Because every board matters."

"That's exactly right, Bill, every board matters, why?

Everyone responded, "Because everything matters!"

"Exactly right." I affirmed. "So, we can all wonder about the weather or we can focus on making this job spot-on perfect. I say we frame this job, one board at a time, according to plan, because this is somebody's dream we're building and everything matters. Let's get to it. I'll check back on you at lunch break. Make it a good day."

I was chuckling as I got behind the wheel of my pickup. It really was that simple. It's hard to believe it could all get so complicated. I drove to the office a few miles down the interstate over land that was once covered by citrus trees and avocado crops. It seemed a million years ago that Bill Malloy, Megan Jones, and I went to Lemongrove High School together. We called ourselves the three musketeers.

Megan was the social butterfly. Man, she was in every school activity and ten on the side. Drama club, drill team, service groups. She was outgoing and fun and I was in love with her from freshman year on.

Bill was a woodworking and auto shop savant. Bill Malloy could do anything with his hands. He could take a toaster or a truck apart and put it back together better than new. All the trade teachers had him assist with their classes.

I wasn't especially social and I couldn't do anything that required patience or physical dexterity. I was okay with numbers, loved math, but mostly I lived in my head. I was a dreamer. I always had big ideas. I kept journals filled with sketches and notes for future projects and inventions. I wasn't very good at details but I could dream big dreams.

Growing up, Lemongrove was a middle-class, middle-American community that experienced exponential growth. The same climate that made it perfect for agriculture made it the ideal place to live; inviting throngs of people to its idyllic always-in-the-70s climate. Residential construction was in a perpetual boom.

Like most of our high school buddies, Bill and I both spent our summers working for Clifton Homes, the largest residential builder in the area. We started out as gofers, doing odd jobs and cleanup. It didn't take the site supervisors long to recognize Bill could do anything -- painting, carpentry, trim work. He could run a saw, handle a drill, plumb, wire, sheetrock. He dropped out of high school senior year to go to work with Clifton full-time.

I wasn't mechanically inclined but was willing to do anything. I "made a hand," my bosses told me, but that was as far as it went. After a few mishaps with power tools, I gravitated to safer pursuits, sacking groceries at the Model Market.

Megan got a scholarship and went out-of-state to study marketing. I was heartbroken when she left. I didn't have any idea what I wanted to do. I stayed on as night manager at the market and took business classes at the community college. That's where I met Don.

Don Davidson taught Real Estate 101. His lectures were very fascinating. A real estate developer, Don had interests all over the tri-county area – shopping malls, strip centers, condominium projects, and apartment complexes. He offered me a job as his runner and took me under his wing. I collected rents, typed invoices, opened and sorted mail. I took deposits, big ones, to the bank and posted checks in his ledgers and on his spreadsheets. He let me sit in on his meetings with zoning commissioners and city councilmen. "Watch, listen, learn," he said. And I did.

He took me to job sites and showed me everything that could go wrong at every stage of construction. He showed me how disreputable builders could cut corners to shave costs and he showed me the price they'd pay for doing so. I watched him supervise his crews, cajole reluctant investors, calm disgruntled buyers.

In five years I'd been exposed to every facet of his business. I saw how he handled land, material and people. He had great instincts. He paid me well and listened to my wild ideas. No one could ask for a better mentor and friend.

One of the best lessons Don ever taught me was to save 20% of everything I made. "Put it away, Dan," he told me. "Don't even look at it. One day you'll thank me. At the end of those five years with Don I had enough money saved to buy five residential lots in a new development he was starting in an exclusive wooded addition.

That turned out to be a fabulous investment. The real estate market was following the economy straight up, demand for housing was high, and Don's addition was one of the most coveted locations in Lemongrove.

With Don's blessing, I took the profits from the sale of those lots and set up my own construction business. I knew I had the drive, vision, and dreams to succeed but I was going to need some hands on talent. Bill Malloy and I had stayed great friends since high school and our paths crossed often when I worked for Don.

Bill had built a name for himself at Clifton Homes and worked on numerous residential developments literally from the ground up; from laying the streets and curbs, to pouring foundations; drying in to finish out. There wasn't anything Bill couldn't do and he had all solid contacts. He knew which subs to trust and how to oversee a

184

project. I knew we'd make a powerful team.

About that time, Megan moved back to Lemongrove to accept a position teaching Drama at the High School. I was very happy to have her back. We picked up where we left up and were soon married. Our son Brady was born the next year.

The next several years blew by in a flurry of projects and sales. Bill and I started out building reasonably priced track homes in modest additions for seasoned developers. The work was steady and we made good money. I always managed to put 20% back as Don had suggested. It should have been enough, I suppose, but I couldn't help wanting do to more with every house than the builders and plans called for. I'd make suggestions – add built-ins here, recess the ceilings, use more moldings, but that was beyond the scope of most starter homes.

Before long my aspirations were gnawing at me. With Megan's support, Bill and I started building residential homes on spec – speculation. That's where you build a home before you have a buyer, hoping you've created something that will attract one. We used some of the company profits from the track homes to build what we called the "Three Musketeer House." It was a compilation of what each of us said we would want in our own dream house.

Megan wanted a sunroom with a deck cantilevered over a garden. Bill wanted a home theater with the latest techno devices. I wanted a library with a wood-burning fireplace, and of course, my recessed ceilings and crown moldings. It was a gamble but it paid off. We'd put a lot of time and energy into finding an architect to bring our plans to life. The elevation was novel enough to attract a lot of attention and before we'd finished framing, a buyer.

That first Three Musketeer House was all we needed. We reformed our company into a partnership, "Three M Luxury Homes." We had all the work we wanted, almost more than we could handle. Our foray into high-end construction dovetailed perfectly with demand for larger homes.

We started hiring many of our subs so we would have the specialty talent available. As we grew also needed more help in sales and operations. Megan quit her teaching job and joined 3 M as broker and office manager.

Lemongrove National, our independent community bank handled

all our financing. They were integrally involved in our growth and success. Our credit was impeccable, our track record proven; we had all the line of credit we needed to operate. Still, in my heart I had bigger dreams.

I remember waking up in the middle of night with a vision so clear, so detailed, I knew it was meant to be. If we could make one perfect home why not build one perfect street?

It would take most of our resources and almost all of our savings but with the bank's assistance we could purchase the acreage, put in the streets, curbs, water, sewer and underground utilities. To save money we decided, okay, I decided, we should try some construction magic. I called Bill and Megan in to explain my big idea.

"If we can get Glenn at the bank to go with us, we can realize some economies of scale by starting four houses at once." I remember it got real quiet, real fast.

"Whoa, big fella," Bill said. "Let's not get ahead of ourselves."

"I'm with Bill," Megan said. "We're doing great. Better than great. I mean, come on, we're killing ourselves now with the pace we've been keeping. Why don't we all slow down, take a deep breath and enjoy the process. The climate's not going to change overnight. People will always want to move here. What's the rush?"

"Well," I countered. "Not to sound to cliché, but the time to strike is when the iron's hot. It's scorching now."

"Sounds fine, hon', but what if our homes don't move? We can't afford to build them and then have them languish there, all our money tied up in brick and stucco." The concern in Megan's voice was evident.

"When have our houses not sold?" I countered. "We already have waiting lists for the models. These are just going to be a little bolder and more expensive. This project will brand Three M as the premiere luxury builder in Lemongrove." I could be very persuasive, and I could see my partners moving closer to agreement.

Finally, Megan caved. "Whatever you decide, husband, I'll back you up."

"Well, good buddy," Bill said. "You're the dreamer. It's a whale of a project but I'm going to trust your instincts, if you think we're big enough."

"Go big or go home, am I right?"

186

We went home.

Even before the economy tanked our bank did. We'd only gotten the first four spec homes dried in when we learned Lemongrove National was in receivership. The new holding company was not nearly as likeminded or accommodating. We had no rapport, no credibility or leverage with them. Every day we were told to talk to some new name, another title in another division in another state. Landon McCaffrey, our latest liaison at the new bank was not sympathetic. "Our lending guidelines strictly prohibit these kinds of transactions."

He said "these kinds of transactions" like we were dealing cocaine.

"Mr. McCaffrey," I said, using every negotiating strategy I could remember from my days with Don Davidson, "I'm sure we can come to a meeting of the minds, an arrangement that will work in all of our interests."

He was unmoved. The next week we had different contact to deal with and then someone new name in corporate. In the end, the suits gave us thirty days to secure outside funding and refinance, which we were unable to do. Then they called our notes.

At my insistence we'd sunk everything we had into the project. Everything, individually and collectively was leveraged – our homes, cars, savings, even Brad's college fund. We had no other option but to file for bankruptcy. My attorney broke the news by phone one morning when I was alone in the office. I hung up and bawled like I never had in my life. It wasn't for me. I could shoulder that. I didn't care if I went under, but my family. Bill, his wife and kids, the families of our employees; so many people were getting hurt. Bankruptcy?

See, a lot of folks mistakenly think bankruptcy means you just walk away from your debts and go on down the road. That's not the case. Well, not in our case. Three Musketeer Builders merely got a reprieve, a little more time to liquidate. We were going to lose everything.

The judge granted our petition and I watched Bill leave the courtroom without a backwards glance. I couldn't blame him. We went into Chapter 11, which essentially gave us two years to try and crawl our way out. It was horrible. All except our most loyal tenured employees bailed. Our friends, for the most part, disappeared.

"They probably think bankruptcy's contagious, like leprosy." Megan offered.

"No, Megan, I think they all think we're crooks."

Our reputation tanked. Even if it hadn't, the economy did. Wall Street was searching for a cliff to fall off of. Projects everywhere were stalling. Unemployment figures nationwide were double-digit. For the first time in decades the influx of newcomers to Lemongrove stopped. People with jobs stayed put. It was like gremlins had pushed a cosmic pause button.

Thankfully, Megan was able to get her teaching job back; that kept food on the table. The day we settled with the bank we celebrated: "To us! We have nothing!"

We were down to one last custom home, the Standley project. They'd be willing to wait on starting. It gave Three M Builders ninety more days.

The only good news during this season of awfulness was I had time to spend with Brad. I chauffeured him to and from school and helped him with his homework. I was his number one fan at tee ball and slow pitch games. I never missed a one.

I was in the stands one Wednesday morning in June. School was out. The boys were on the field warming up. Looking around I was stunned to realize how many men were in the stands these days. It was a real reflection of the how hard and close to home the recession had hit.

It was hard not to overhear the conversation of two men sitting just below me. They looked about my age, but I didn't recognize either one of them. The guy on the left sounded pretty upset.

"So there I am, clients up the wazoo, working my 80 hours a week and BAM, I've got guys at the door with badges and briefcases and warrants. Can you imagine?"

I felt guilty for listening. Maybe misery does love company, I found myself leaning forward.

"So now, my clients of course, they're ghosts. And, I've got to bring in attorneys -- a team of them, and don't you know that costs a pretty penny. Then the wife takes the kids and goes to live with her sister, says she can't take the pressure. And, I'm like, what did I do?"

His friend was nodding sympathetically, not interrupting.

"It gets worse. So the wife's gone, the doors are shut, my bank accounts are pretty much frozen and here comes the IRS – full audit investigation. I'm telling you, those were some dark days."

I realized, as black as my situation was, it could be worse. Maybe that's a message I needed to hear.

The guy finished up his tale. "So. After all of that, after my life is turned inside out I get some postcard in the mail from the IRS. In the tiniest print I could barely make out the words, a case number and a little box checked 'concluded.' I'm thinking, what is that, concluded? My lawyers tell me the criminal allegations turned out to be unfounded. They had no case, so the IRS had no case. It was all a big, 'Oops, sorry.' And here I am at my kid's ballgame.

I heard his friend say something sympathetically about how he'd figured something was wrong when he never saw him at any of the lodge meetings.

"No, I sort of kept to myself. I mean, I never did anything wrong, but when you see your face in the papers next to 'indictment' – I couldn't face anybody.

"Have you and Noreen been able to work it out?"

"I don't know. Her leaving, not sticking by me, that was the worst. She probably thinks where there's smoke, there's fire."

"Well, I only wish I'd known sooner you were available. We've been looking for an accounting guru like you for the past six months since ours jumped ship and went to the competition. Unlucky for you, I know, but if you'd be willing to give up your solo practice, we sure would be glad to have you come on board with us."

Good, I thought. I was happy for him. What an ordeal. It made me really aware of my own situation. That poor guy hadn't done anything wrong. He truly was a victim of circumstance. It made me realize I'd been acting like a victim, when in truth, I knew better. I was largely to blame for what happened to the company. I'd gotten full of myself and ahead of myself, all caught up in the money and prestige. I hadn't listened to the counsel of my team. I'd been reckless and selfish. Right there in those baseball stands I decided if I could get another chance I'd start over and get it right.

That night, when Megan got home, I told her all about my eavesdropping, the story I'd overheard and how it had made me realize all of the mistakes I had made. I apologized for my pride and my ego, for costing us everything we had worked for. I told her how sorry I was for the pain I had caused her, our family. Tears flowed, I couldn't stop them.

I told her what it meant to me that she'd stuck with me. If anyone had a right to leave, she did. I asked her to forgive me.

"It sounds," She said, carefully, "like you need to forgive yourself. Billy and I both knew we were taking a big chance. We rolled the dice and it didn't go our way. The bank failed and then the bottom fell out of the economy. You know, Honey, crap happens."

"Yes, it does. But I put us in a position where we could be destroyed. I'm not sure…"

I couldn't finish, I was overcome. What I was trying to say is I didn't think we'd be able to recover. Per usual, my bride was eight steps ahead of me.

"You know, husband mine, it's not going to be easy digging ourselves out of this mess. We're going to have to take a hard look at how we operate. Change our perspective. But I want you to know, I believe in you. You keep on dreaming and Bill and I and the crew, we'll figure out how to make them work. Only, could we start a little bitty dream, at first?"We called together a meeting of the company, everyone on our payroll and those that we used on a regular basis. We needed everyone on the same page. I used old-fashioned flip charts and laid out exactly where we stood.

"We have exactly enough money and 90 days to complete the Standley house and – well, if we don't get another project, we're done. You all need to know where we are. I have faith that if we do what 3 M Builders does best, if we focus on our strengths, stay on task, we can attract the kinds of customers who want exactly what we offer."

I tasked every employee with drawing up the aspects of their job and key responsibilities that were critical to success. Throughout the Standley project, during each phase, we made punch lists – studying every step and how we could do things more efficiently.

We held workshops over lunch; we'd have our framers talk about their concerns and frustrations. Then the concrete guys and the plumbers got a turn. Everyone got to see how important each step of the process was, how a mistake in one step was going to negatively affect all the ones that followed.

And something amazing happened. We created a company culture

190

of symbiotic investment. Everyone cared about making this one house, perfect. The guys doing the grade work got suggestions from the rough in crew.

We succeeded, rebuilding our company mission statement: to be the premiere quality builder -- not the biggest, not the most expensive, the best quality.

Now we look at every house from the client's perspective, like it's our own. All buyers want their home to be perfect. My artistic bride painted our mantra in every room of our office and had it added to our letterhead and vehicles, it's simple but it works: "Everything matters."

Closing Thoughts

It really is true: perspective is everything. Let's take a look at perspective over the course of Dan's life.

Back in high school, Dan's buddy Bill ran rings around him in the construction business. After high school, Bill was a savant in construction, Megan was going to a four-year college, and poor Dan was a bagger at the local Model Market. If you were a fly on the wall at the Model Market at that point in time, who would you vote most likely to succeed? Would you have predicted that Dan would wind up being the leader of a building company, and that Megan and Bill would work for him? I don't think so.

Dan went to work for Don Davidson. When he first started working, he was doing mindless errands. Is it just me, or is anyone else reminded of the Karate Kid movie here? Wait, you're too young for that movie? Let me tell you about it. Poor Daniel (coincidence, huh?) wanted to be trained my Mr. Miyagi, a local karate expert, so he could defend himself against the school bullies in his new high school. Mr. Miyagi had Daniel come to his house and do chores for him. Daniel had to sand the floor, paint the fence, and wax Mr. Miyagi's car. After so much time, Daniel blew a gasket. From his perspective, what was the point of going to Mr. Miyagi's to do menial tasks? But then Mr. Miyagi let Daniel in on his little secret – the motion of each of the tasks he performed mimicked karate movements that Daniel would need to master! So . . . back to our Daniel. How do you think he felt, from his perspective, about the menial tasks that Mr. Davidson had him perform? Probably not so great, but from Mr. Davidson's perspective, he was taking a young boy under his wing and teaching him lessons that would last a lifetime. Ah, perspective.

It's years later. Dan, Bill, and his wife are sitting at a conference table. From Dan's perspective, his vision of building an entire street was a fait accompli – it was something that was meant to happen. From Bill and Megan's perspective, it was an extremely risky undertaking. Bill and Megan believed in Dan. If only he had seen things from their perspective. . . .

The market crashed. Three M was forced to declared bankruptcy. Bill left the courtroom without a backwards glance. He had no hope for the future where Dan and Megan were concerned. From his perspective, the future of Three Musketeers Builders was hopeless. His perspective also cost him a shot at rebuilding with his two best friends.

After eavesdropping at the ballgame, Dan swallowed his pride and begged Megan for her forgiveness. From his perspective, he didn't think they'd be able to recover. Thank goodness Megan's perspective was different.

So what's your perspective? Is your glass half-empty or half-full? Whenever you're in a tough spot in your life or you have a difficult decision to make, it is imperative to remember that incorrect decisions result from incorrect perspectives. Always examine the risks and benefits of every possible outcome before you commit to a point of view. Another lesson from Daniel's story is that as you succeed in building wealth, sometimes you need to step back and savor the spoils instead of taking your money for granted by chasing the next big thing. Perspective is everything!

DON'T BE AFRAID OF CHANGE

"Travel and change of place impart new vigor to the mind."
~ Seneca

When I arrived at the boarding area there was already a long line at the ticket counter. That was all right. I was more than an hour early for my flight. My baggage was checked, I had my boarding pass in hand. I could use this time to relax. It was going to be a long flight.

I saw a man about my age standing about third in line from the gate agent. He seemed aggravated; he was not enjoying the wait. He must have travel issues, I thought. He kept looking at the monitor and then his watch.

There was a time I was a lot more impatient than him. He reminded of me the day last spring when I'd nearly melted down in the grocery store. I smiled at the memory.

Between the checker moving at glacial-speed and the septuagenarian ahead of me I was confident I was going to die waiting in line. I was certainly going to be late getting back from lunch. I shifted from one foot to the other. Both of the snails ignored my withering glances and eye-rolls. Grandma was foraging through her enormous bag as she had been for some time.

She'd already tied up the line a good ten minutes presenting her coupons, one at a time. "I think I have just one more, it'd be a double-double." She offered by way of explanation.

The checker yawned.

I upped my non-verbal behavior to signal my seething annoyance.

193

I made a huge show of checking my watch. I sighed as loud as I could. Grandma must have found her prize, a stupid coupon that was going to save her, what, eleven cents? With excruciating care she started unfolding it.

Yes, I was going to die right here in line.

"Ma'am, may I help you over here?" The checker beside mine invited me to her lane.

Gratefully, I dumped my three lunch items on her conveyer belt. A greek yogurt, a package of mixed nuts, an avocado and a bottled water. I really was trying to eat clean.

"Bless you," I said. "I was afraid the yogurt would spoil before I got checked out." Okay, I may have said that louder than was absolutely necessary. "Honestly, there should be a special line for couponers."

On my way out I saw the tortoise twosome still transacting business, the clerk now discerning whether the elderly customer's coupon had expired. It was infuriating. I didn't have anything against seniors; I know a lot of them live on very fixed incomes. But if they were going to take all day to shop, the least they could do was avoid the noon hour when viable members of the work force were trying to get something done in a limited amount of time.

By the time I reached my office I had calmed down and even felt somewhat guilty for my impatience. I wouldn't want anyone treating my Nana that way. I finished my shift at the call-center where I supervised 47 customer service operators for a popular on-line retailer. Still feeling guilty, I decided to check in with Nana before meeting my girlfriends for dinner.

I dialed her from my smartphone as I drove to the restaurant. She answered on the third ring. I was going to have to learn to lie. Telling my grandmother how I spent my time or my money just led to arguments.

"You're going out to dinner again-en?" Honestly, my Nana could turn any word multi-syllable when she whined. "How many times does that make this week?"

"I don't know, Nana," I fibbed. "A couple..." I wanted to add, "but who's counting," but I already knew she was.

"Samantha Camille Piquet you know very well it's been more times than that, you just went out Saturday morning for brunch and

194

then turned right around and went out with your girlfriends that same afternoon, then, you went…"

"Nana, Nana, Nana!" I finally broke her recitation of events. "Okay, point made. Just because you don't like to go out --"

"Of course I like going out, I'm talking about being responsible. Eating out is expensive and you know perfectly well --"

"Okay, can we change the subject please?" I said, cutting her off again. "C'mon, Nana, please. I'm thirty. I have a good job, I work hard, I just got a promotion, I pay my way and I don't owe anything, except my car payment, and I only have a few months to go on it. I'm fine. Really, it's just ridiculous to cook for one person. Think of the money I save on energy and electricity not heating up the stove…"

While she was thinking of an appropriate response, I managed to escape, "Sorry, I'm losing our signal, Nana. Love you!"

I really did love her. But she and I were never going to see eye to eye on money. She had been born mid-way through the worst years of the depression. Her parents had struggled to keep their family of four fed. I'd heard the horror stories of her childhood often enough, I knew them by heart. She inherited her parents' fears, made them her own and would eventually pass them on to her son, my dad. Nana still saved rubber bands, like her own mother had. She hoarded plastic bags and reused aluminum foil. She wasn't being green; she was cheap. My grandfather past away a couple of years ago, but he'd been just as bad or worse. He wouldn't let her even run the dishwasher and kept the air conditioning off except for a few scorching days each summer. Even though he was gone, she still abided by his rules.

"That's how James was able to leave me so well provided for, Samantha Camille. He scrimped and saved for rainy days. I'm not going to squander his efforts. You never know when another depression could hit. Like my mom always told me, use it up, wear it out; make it do or do without."

My dad didn't hoard aluminum foil, but he was a third generation tightwad to be sure. That was part of the reason my parents had divorced. My mom had been his polar opposite. She was a spender, not that they had all that much. Dad was a firefighter and she was a stay-at-home mom. One way she expressed her affection, I guess, was to lavish all kinds of material things on me. In all my childhood photos I'm never in the same outfit twice. She dressed me in designer fashions from the best department stores. I had every toy I ever wanted and twice as many I didn't want.

When I was five, my parents divorced. Mom told me Dad had run across a credit card statement she'd been hiding from him. He didn't even know they had one. It was in his name and it had several thousand dollars charged on it. He found out she'd opened several department store cards too. It wasn't that he couldn't afford to pay them; he saw it as a big deception on her part. "I can't live with a liar." He'd told her.

When they split up, she got a job and continued to spoil me the way she always had. Nothing changed. In fact, it got better. Mom and I ate out all the time, lived in a nice apartment. She called us the dynamic duo. Every summer she took me on vacation and we stayed at really nice hotels right on the beach. She used to say, "Well, Sammy, you can't take it with you."

And she didn't.

When I was ten, my mom died, just before her 32nd birthday. She had just come home from work and had told me she needed to lie down for a minute, she wasn't feeling well. She went to bed and never woke up. The doctors said it was a brain aneurysm. Nothing anyone could have done.

My dad and I moved in with his parents, Nana and Grand Dad. It was just supposed to be a temporary situation, but I ended up living with them until I graduated high school. Dad still does. I know they loved me, but they were strict and they were so tight with money, I felt suffocated. I remember thinking they were dead broke. They weren't. They were just tight.

Even though Dad worked all the time, he always told me there was never any money for extras, for outside activities, like drill team. "If you want to join, you'll have to pay for your uniforms. Money doesn't grow on trees." Dad never let me forget Mom had died several thousand dollars in debt with a car note and several credit cards maxed out.

She'd had life insurance, but it didn't cover what she'd owed. It was several years before he had everything paid off. I know he resented her for leaving him with that mess. I was just grateful she got to enjoy what few years she'd had on the planet.

So maybe it was rebellion or I maybe I inherited most of my mother's financial DNA. From the moment I moved out on my own, I spent every dime I made. I got scholarships and went away to college, lived in the dorms, worked part-time. The first day of school one of the banks was offering credit cards to new students. I signed right up for one. I'd learned from my mom that credit cards let you get the things you needed right now but couldn't yet afford. "That's why God invented plastic," she's said.

Like mother, like daughter. I got in real trouble and over-extended myself. My grandparents found out and hit the roof. Then they told my Dad and he didn't speak to me for months. "You're as bad as your mother," he'd said. I haven't forgotten that. But I did learn my lesson. I graduated college and got a good job, paid off what I owed.

I learned to live within my means. I never used credit cards again unless I could pay them off within the month. I contributed to my 401K, enough to get the company's match, but that was all. I wasn't going to hoard my money worrying about some cataclysmic emergency that might never come. I knew far too well, life is very short.

I remember right after mom died and things changed, vowing to myself I was never going to let anyone – not my grandparents, my father, or some future husband – reign me in or control me. Money is power. It gives you freedom and it gives you choices. I liked what it did for me. I treated myself well. I wore beautiful clothes.

My philosophy was, if I see something I want and I have the money in my account I buy it. Who was I hurting? Spending made me happy. Okay, so sometimes I was careless or I bought just to be buying. If someone looked in my closet they'd find more black pants than I could ever possibly wear and don't get me started on shoes. Shoes were always my compulsion. I probably needed a twelve-step program for footwear.

Nana had really made me feel guilty. I cancelled my plans for dinner with my girlfriends and stopped instead at the whole foods store next to my apartment to pick up something for dinner. I thought I was going to just run in and run out. No, just my luck, I got behind a young woman about my age. She had a full cart. To her credit, she was nicely dressed, like she just got off work. I could cut her some slack; she was probably in a hurry too.

But, she wasn't. After she loaded her items on the conveyer belt, she pulled out one of those unmistakable coupon organizers from her day planner and then retrieved a thick wad of coupons from it.

"No-o-o" I thought, only I accidentally said it aloud. Both the checkout clerk and coupon queen looked at me. How embarrassing. I covered, quickly, staring at my watch.

"Wow, would you look at the time, I forgot about a meeting." I said.

The woman handed her stack to the clerk, "I think you'll find them all in order, none have expired; I double-checked. Thank you for taking the time to process them."

"Oh, my pleasure," the checker said. "It's not a problem when I get them neat and organized like this and you are going to save a bundle. "It must take you forever to clip all these."

"A couple of hours a week, but it pays off."

I admit I was mesmerized by the sound of the scanner beeping. I watched as the various amounts were subtracted from the woman's hefty three-digit sub-total. Minus one dollar, minus two, minus one, minus one. She wasn't saving pennies and dimes, she was really dropping her grocery tab. The store register hummed at a steady pace keeping time with the scanner.

The thrifty shopper's phone rang and she made the call brief, explaining she was checking out and would return the call from her car. "And, yes, Bali was wonderful. Just got back yesterday, can't wait to fill you in."

As she hung up, the checker beamed, announcing, "Well done! You saved yourself $63.00! Did I hear you say you just got back from Bali?"

"Yes," the coupon queen said, folding the receipt carefully and putting it in her hot pink day planner. "It was magical. I'm trying to do the whole 'Eat, Pray, Love' thing. Next I want to go to Italy, then maybe India. I'm almost at my goal for Rome! Thanks to you!"

The checker looked confused.

"What I save shopping I spend on travel. So I mean it when I say I really appreciate it when your store doubles the coupon amount."

I was flabbergasted; who'd have thought you could save that much grocery shopping. I had to hear more. I checked and there was no one behind me in line, so I asked.

"I'm so sorry to intrude, but you've piqued my curiosity. How in the world do you finance those kinds of trips with coupons? It'd take me a lifetime to save that much."

She laughed. "It's so easy. First, I research the cost of the trip. That's my goal number. How much I need to save. Then, every chance I get, whenever I shop, whatever I buy, I try to use a coupon. I keep track of my savings and deposit the exact amount I saved into a separate bank account. You with me?"

"I think," I said.

"So, as soon as I get to my car, I'm going to pull up my bank app, and transfer $63.00 from checking to savings. Then I keep a running total in my coupon organizer of how much closer I am to my goal."

She showed me. She had kept a handwritten tally, starting with $5,100 and I could see numerous amounts deducted from it. Her sub-total looked to be around $900.00.

"That's amazing," I said, clapping. "It's like you've discovered the secret to winning the lottery."

"Well, there are some secrets. I'm going to go grab a coffee next door, if you want, come join me when you're finished here. I'm happy to share what I know."

I checked out and went to the coffee place next door. She was already at a table, calculator and organizer out, working on her phone. She had a double latte in front of her, and another one next to her. She handed it to me as she motioned for me to take a seat.

"Well, thank you! I appreciate it. Hey, by the way, I'm Samantha," I said. "My friends call me Sammy. But I've got to say, doesn't buying a couple of four dollar coffees kind of defeat the purpose?"

Laughing, she answered, "Good point. I'm Jenny and look at this." From the back of her planner she pulled the smaller matching coupon organizer. Behind a BEVERAGES tab she showed me where she had several coupons for coffee houses. "This one was a BOGO, buy one, and get one free. Then, I used my punch card. After you buy nine lattes here, you get the tenth one free. They accepted both!"

"Won't most places only accept one coupon or discount at a time?"

"You never know," Penny said, brightly. "They accepted both

199

here, but I'm a good customer. That's part of the secret. Build a rapport with the managers where you regularly shop. They'll help you save even more money if you'll just ask them for help. The manager here told me most people lose their punch cards or don't bother to keep up with them. That's another way I use my organizer, so keep track of all these little cards. They stamp it every time I come in.

"So now, you'll transfer the $4.00 you would've spent on the coffee." I said, her process starting to sink in.

"That's right. Actually, I'm going to transfer $8.00, because I would've bought your latte anyway. See, one of the rules is you don't spend a nickel on anything you wouldn't normally buy. Me? I don't use peanut butter coupons because I don't eat the stuff. I only buy what I need and want and use, but I try to never pay full price. Take Italy, for example. I'm going on a trip that normally lists for more than ten grand. But I did my research. I found discounted airfares and special offers on the tour and I saved a bunch by booking early."

For the next hour, Penny generously shared with me her best ideas on bargain shopping and saving.

"Remember, you don't want to buy anything you wouldn't normally purchase. Keep track of the things you buy over and over. Gas, makeup, panty hose, food, cleaning supplies, clothes."

"Like coffee," I said, raising my latte. Penny found her BOGO coupon on the company's website.

"Exactly. Once you have in mind the kinds of things you regularly buy, start looking for savings at the places where you buy them. Check out the websites of your favorite grocery store, drug store and clothing stores. Most businesses reward loyalty. I even get some of my make-up free by buying directly from their product websites rather than the department store.

I thanked Penny profusely and went home. After I unloaded my groceries, I went into my bedroom to change out of my work clothes. I went to hang up my suit and could barely squeeze it in between my other suits; there were so many garments crammed onto the bar. There were beautiful blouses I had never worn; some still with tags hanging from the sleeves.

It dawned on me that I had been spending mindlessly. At the end of the day I really didn't have a thing to show for it all. Just a closet – okay, two closets – overflowing with stuff. I had a full wardrobe, gobs of scarves, hats, purses and accessories. I couldn't wear all it if I changed outfits twice a day.

Ever since I'd left my grandparents place I'd been trying to fill up some hole in my heart with material things. Things. Possessions were never going to fill the void. I wiped away the tears and decided I wanted to have more to show for my life – however long I might have – than closets full of stuff. I didn't need more stuff; I needed more memories.

Penny suggested I get on my computer to find out more about couponing. She said all I needed to do was enter HOW TO SAVE MONEY WITH COUPONS into my search engine. She said I could pull up tons of information. And I did.

It took some time to get the hang of coupons and to create good habits. Naturally, the first thing I did was spend way too much at a high end stationary store buying a designer day planner and matching coupon organizer. I would learn. Next, I started dreaming.

My boss and his wife had just gotten back from a ten-day trip to Germany. I had really wanted to go overseas like that but never imagined I would. I'd never been further than three hundred miles from my home my entire life. College had been just an hour away and the beach vacations mom had taken me on weren't much further than that.

I began by researching a river cruise down the Rhine River from Amsterdam to Switzerland. It was going to run about $10,000.00 I set that as my first goal. It might take me a hundred years but at least I had my goal.

It took much less. I found out that I could save a lot of money by being flexible with my travel dates. Some departure dates are considered out of season and are nearly half the price of peak season rates. I did my homework and it paid off big time. And here I am. It's been less than a year since I met Jenny, and I'm on my way to Germany.

Mr. Impatience Guy is at the front of the line now. He is kind of cute, maybe a little older than me. He's probably just on edge from the excitement of travel. Looks like he's by himself. When we board, I just might buy him a drink. As I reach into my trusty organizer I have to smile. Yep, just as I thought, I happen to have a coupon for that.

Closing Thoughts

See any Samantha Camille Piquet in yourself? Do you look in your closet and realize you overindulge, and rationalize your mindless spending by saying, "I deserve it?" Or maybe your budget is tighter than Samantha's, but you look at your friends and wonder how they can afford to take their kids to Disney when you can't?

Let me start by reinforcing one point of Samantha's story: the answer is NOT to make purchases on plastic that you cannot afford to pay off right away. I'm sure that many of your Disney-tripping friends are doing that, and it's a road to financial disaster. The only time to do that is in a dire emergency – and I do not mean a fashion emergency!

Now that we have that out of the way, it's time for you to savor the second morsel of my advice: coupons are not just for little old ladies on fixed incomes! Like Sam, if you put some effort into it, you might just be shocked at the money you save, increasing your wealth in money and life. Keep in mind that it doesn't have to be coupons either! There are plenty ways to save and find money for your trips, get creative. I literally don't have time to cut coupons in my busy life, so I began taking my bank statements each month and rounding each transaction up to the nearest dollar. I total all those pennies up from each transaction and put them into a saving account. I had to start somewhere! You're not going to get that $10,000 for the Rhine Cruise overnight; nevertheless, wouldn't it be an amazing goal to accomplish? I mean think about it, how much fun would it be to watch a savings account grow month after month knowing that trip is becoming a reality? Get on the web, do some research, conquer your fear of "change," and get going future Coupon Queens! Your dreams and growing bank account await!

YOUR WORDS CREATE YOUR REALITY

"Life is really simple, but we insist on making it complicated."
~ Confucius

"Have you given any more thought to where you'd like to go for dinner for our anniversary?" My husband and I were hurriedly drinking our coffees before heading to work.

"Not really," I answered, not especially enthusiastic about wasting a lot of money on another meal out.

"I was thinking the Rusty Pelican, we haven't had fish for a while."

"I don't know, it wasn't very good last time, remember? My salmon was dry and it was so crowded in there, all the tables squashed together. I could hardly hear myself think."

"Okay, how 'bout Surf 'n Turf?"

"What? Did you win the lottery and not tell me? There isn't one entrée on their menu that costs less than $25.00 and all the sides are extra. I think a baked potato costs –

"Helen! Enough. Don't spoil this. It's our 40th wedding anniversary. I think we can splurge one night."

My husband's voice was getting an edge to it. "I was just pointing out how ridiculous it is to spend a bunch of money on a mediocre meal. Besides, I don't have anything to wear to the Surf 'n Turf. You know how fancy that place is. Heck, we haven't finished paying off Christmas yet."

Ben picked up his car keys and walked to the door.

"You're leaving? We haven't settled anything."

"You know, Helen, you have a way of just taking the joy out of everything. Maybe we should just skip the anniversary celebration and throw a wake instead." He slammed the door behind him.

Just because I voiced my opinion, he has to get all bent out of shape. He sounded just like the kids. Everybody always wants a big party but no one wants to foot the bill. Sure, Ben was generous and would have come up with the money somehow, but that wasn't sensible.

I got so tired of always being the responsible one. I'd always handled our finances, keeping track of our household budget in a twelve-column ledger. I know exactly how much it costs to run the house I'd been a damn magician stretching almost nothing into just enough to keep food on the table and clothes on our back.

Ben was a good man and a hard worker, but he never made a lot of money and sure didn't understand what to do with it. He'd eked out a living managing Harper's General Store. Ben started out in his father's hardware store and then when it merged with Glenn Jackson's grocery store it became Harpers.

Harper's was where everyone shopped until that big mega store All-Mart moved in to Jamestown ten miles away. Most of the businesses in town were hurt, but Harper's was hurt the worst. Rather than lay-off any of the employees, Ben cut everyone's hours, cutting back his own the most to help the younger guys with kids and families to take care of.

I understood, sort of. All of our kids were grown, married, with children of their own. Still, it meant I had to find employment. I went to work answering phones at the big medical clinic in Carson. It barely paid minimum wage, but it was a paycheck and they did provide discounted health care. It wasn't my dream job but I didn't know what a dream job for me would even be. All I'd ever done was raise kids and take care of my husband. I suppose I should be grateful just to have a job in this economy, but a doctor's office is no picnic.

Mothers come in dragging three and four children with them, screaming and running around the lobby. Half the walk-ins don't speak English or pretend they don't. The seniors, they're the worst, forget their appointments, come in at the wrong time and they always forget their insurance and Medicare cards.

The phones never stop from the minute I sit down. Every phone call is an emergency. No one wants to wait, they have to be seen right away. No one wants to make an appointment. Patients get mad at me because the doctors are so behind, which they wouldn't be if people would just make an appointment and show up on time.

I really wanted to make more money and the clinic was expanding. There were openings in medical records and pharmacy but you had to have all kinds of computer skills that I didn't have. I didn't even know how to book appointments on the computer. I just answered the phone and routed the calls to the scheduler, the nurses, or a specific area like the lab or insurance.

The other girls in the office thought my job was a piece of cake, but they didn't have any idea how many calls I handled or what it was like trying to keep track of what's what when ten lines are on hold and more calls are coming in.

Ben didn't have a clue. Oh, he sees people at the store, sure. But he doesn't have to handle any of the pressure and problems I do. And he wondered why I wasn't all happy-go-lucky about spending a hundred bucks on dinner. I had to work a day and a half to earn that.

Sometimes I thought our kids were abducted by aliens and returned to earth. Those three couldn't be the three I gave birth to. Ben and I have never had any extra money for fancy vacations or new cars, but the kids? Every one of them was driving some brand new truck or SUV. They travel all the time and are always laying out money for uniforms, extra-curricular activities at the school, field trips.

Every one of them graduated college. Something no one on my side of the family or Ben's ever did. Benjamin, our oldest, is a software engineer. Beth's an ER nurse, and Beverly's a paralegal working for several attorneys. I guess all three of our kids found the money tree. I was never that lucky.

Growing up, I didn't have anything. College was not an option. Daddy worked at the mine and we managed on what he made. He always said he worried about me. "If you were a boy, I could get you a job, you better hope you marry well."

I didn't. He would. My mother died of cancer my junior year in high school. Daddy got remarried the next year to Carrie Stevenson, a widow in town that lost her husband in a mining accident. She'd received a big insurance settlement. On the way to my high school graduation Daddy broke the news he had put our house on the market. He was going to move in with Carrie and her three kids. "You'll be fine, Helen. You'll figure something out. Best be looking for a place to live."

I didn't have to look far. As soon as I told my boyfriend Ben the news, he proposed to me right on the spot. He was a couple of years older than me. He had his own trailer. "Don't you worry about a thing Helen. I'm going to take care of you. We eloped that night.

After Carrie's kids were grown, she and Dad bought an RV and took off. I'd get postcards from them once or twice a year. Those two were always off on a cruise or visiting one of Carrie's kids or grandkids every time I turned around. They're still together; I haven't seen them in years.

I finished dressing for work. It was a Tuesday and Tuesday's all the employees wore bright yellow scrubs. The doctor's office supplied everyone with different colored scrubs for each day of the week. Our office manager, Lola said it helped break the monotony and made a cheerful impression on the patients. I was going to need more than yellow scrubs to cheer me up.

Driving to the office, I kept hearing Ben's angry words. How did I end up being the bad guy? I should apologize for being honest? Or, maybe I should just let him spend every dime we made just like the kids did. The argument brought back the whole big family scene we'd had over the holidays.

Yes, yes I did. I hit the roof when I got the emails from the children with their kids' Christmas wish lists. Between our three children we have eleven grandchildren ranging in age from 7 to 17. I love them to pieces but if you ask me their parents have spoiled them rotten. Most of the items on their wish lists were expensive electronics and designer clothes. Ben thought it was cute. I thought it was pathetic.

Smart phones, video games, tablets. I didn't know what most of the items even were. I just got my cell phone a couple of years ago. I only had a computer because one of Ben's customers returned it. We were able to get the manufacturer to refurbish it, but Ben couldn't resell it at the store. He brought it home for me. I can barely turn it

206

on and off. My granddaughter Jenny set it up so I follow the family on Facebook. She keeps promising to show me more.

I was looking through some of the department store catalogs I got in the mail and I saw a pair of jeans one of the grandkids wanted. Seventy-five dollars for a pair of jeans she'll grow out of in ten minutes. I wasn't sure what upset me more, that there were actually jeans that cost that much or that my grandchild actually imagined I would spend that kind of money on them.

I stopped at a place that sells the games for the machines my kids all have. One game was fifty dollars. I thought the whole system cost that. Those gizmos cost more than three hundred. I had just found all that out when everyone started arriving for Thanksgiving. I always have everyone over to our house for the holiday. We have a big dining room table with extensions and there's room for everybody. We have the space, but we certainly can't afford to feed that many people. When we're all together there's nineteen around that table. Ben and I buy the turkeys and everybody else brings a side dish, then we don't have to take a second out on our home just to have a meal together.

Well the girls, my girls, and Ben's wife Joanie, were already starting to tease me about that. They'd all brought a pie and wanted to know if I had whipped cream. I didn't. "That's right," Beth said, "Mom can't afford whipped cream!" And everyone started laughing.

It went on like that. "Do you have salt? Or can we afford it?" Beverly chimed in.

"Well, looking at your Christmas lists, I gather you all can afford anything you want." I said, louder than I'd meant to.

That didn't go over well, so my kids and their spouses decided to just draw names so we'd each only have to buy one present. I didn't think that was a very good idea either and told them so, but I was overruled.

When I told Ben the arrangement he was disappointed. "It's taking the fun out of Christmas. It's just so structured. Don't you want to give everybody something?"

"How could we manage that, Ben? You cut your hours to nothing and I make nothing. How are we going to buy gifts? And, have you even looked at what they want? I may be a magician when it comes to stretching our dollars but I'm not a miracle worker."

Christmas went even worse than Thanksgiving. First, my daughter-in-law, Joanie thought it'd be a good idea if we picked up some honey-baked hams. "That's an idiotic waste of money," I said. Those are so much more expensive than turkeys." Well, she got offended, but I was only trying to educate her on feeding a large group like ours.

Around the table I just couldn't manage to keep the conversation going. First, Bev asked how I was enjoying my job, so I told her. I told her how little I earned, how many calls I was expected to answer, and the annoying patients. No one said anything. Then Bonnie wanted to know if we were going to go on any vacations. I was starting to explain how we couldn't afford to and then everyone stopped talking altogether.

After dessert, which was okay, my daughter-in-law had brought store bought pies and they're just never as good as homemade, we had the gift exchange. I tried not to show how disappointed I was with mine. Benjamin's daughter, Jenny had drawn my name and she'd gotten me a book. A paperback. What had she been thinking? The title was "Thoughts Matter, Words Matter." Flatly, I said thank you and put it on the coffee table.

Jenny's face fell. "It's the number one best seller, Gramma; just out in paperback. I think you'll really enjoy it."

"What I needed was a book on how to use a computer. Now that would have been a thoughtful gift."

Then everyone stopped talking again and just stared at me like I had two heads. Then, for some reason, everyone suddenly had to go home. I went to start cleaning up the big mess in the kitchen and I heard Benjamin say to his Dad as he was leaving, "You're a saint, Dad. That's all I can say, you're a saint."

"What did he mean by that?" I asked him after everyone had left.

"You really don't know, do you?"

As I pulled into the employee parking lot at the doctor's office and naturally my assigned parking was the furthest from the building, I realized that Ben had been acting moody and disagreeable for months. Maybe All-Mart's arrival had him more upset than I thought.

When I walked in, Lola, our office manager, was already making coffee. She greeted me cheerfully. She was such a morning person, "Good morning, Helen. Beautiful weather, isn't it?"

"For as long as it lasts. The weather report says a cold front's coming. We could get nasty weather with both rain and sleet. That's going to be awful to drive in. Ice."

"I hadn't heard that, but right now, it's surely beautiful. I love February."

"Not me. It's too cold. The cold weather makes my joints ache something terrible. Then before you know it, it'll be spring, ugh. Allergy season." I reminded her.

"True, and in our business, that's a godsend. Have a good day Helen. Be sure to put the sparkle in your voice when you answer the phones. Everybody needs sparkle."

I didn't have time to sparkle. It took forever, but my lunch break finally rolled around. I was starving. I found Carla from billing in the break room. She motioned me over to her table and I sat down.

"What's up?" she asked, smiling.

"Oh, it's been a day," I said, rubbing my temples. I was getting a headache. I told her how from the time I woke up things had just gone from bad to worse. I told her about Ben's insistence on going out to some overpriced restaurant and how we'd ended up arguing over that. Then, even though it was a Tuesday, how crazy the phones had been, and how I almost missed my lunch, my stomach was growling, my head hurt and all I had brought for lunch was leftover meatloaf.

When I finished, Carla was just staring at me. Finally, she motioned me to continue, "And? And? I'm waiting for the good part."

"What do you mean?" I didn't know what she meant.

"Get to the good part, Eeyore. You know. Blah, blah, blah. We all have sad stories and troubles and problems and times when things aren't all sunshine and roses. But no matter what, there's a good part. Where's the good part, Helen?"

"Well, there isn't a good part, Carla. That's what I'm saying. I quarreled with Ben, I worked all morning with morons, and now I'm eating last night's meatloaf."

"So let's recap. You have a husband who wants to take you out to celebrate your marriage, an interesting job to keep you busy, and satisfying food to eat. Wow, Helen. You do have it tough. You know what? Right now? There are people praying for what you take for granted. You need to find the good part, girl." Looking at her watch she added, "This moron's got to get back to work."

"B-b-but that's not what I meant."

As I drove home all I could think was no matter where I went, people were so touchy. When I got home, Ben was in his recliner, reading.

"Interesting book?" I asked.

"Very. It's the one Jenny got you for Christmas. She called. Wants you to call her. She asked me how you liked the book. I know you haven't read it, but you should. You really should. I just finished it."

I got up and returned Jenny's call. She was all excited. Breathlessly she said, "Gramma, HCC is offering a six week computer class for dummies. It's one night a week for six weeks. I enrolled us. I'll get college credit for it and we can do it together. It starts tomorrow night. I'll pick you up at six, we can grab a bite, my treat, and you can tell me about the book!" She hung up before I could respond.

I stayed up all night reading the book. I couldn't admit to Jenny I hadn't even picked it up. What I'd read had my head spinning. This psychologist was writing about the power of the spoken word. He maintained that what we think about comes out of our mouth and then we somehow start bringing more of what we think about and talk about into our lives. If what he was saying was true, every time I complained about anything, I was attracting more of what I complained about into my life.

Well, if that was true, all I had to do was talk happy talk and I'd win the lottery by Friday afternoon! I ran into Carla first thing and told her about the book. "Have you read it?"

"I have," she said. "Many times. I believe we have the power to improve or negatively impact our situation by what we think and say."

"So, if I talk all positive my life will be perfect?" I said, my skepticism evident.

"No, what I'm saying, Helen, is if nothing ever changes, nothing ever changes. Even a moron knows that."

I stood there, mouth open. Stunned. The book had me thinking about all the problems I was having at work, at home, in all of my relationships. Could it be that I had actually invited them in? Right then I became determined watch my words. The book had this exercise that was supposed to help me become aware of how much I complained. I wore a rubber band on my wrist and every time I caught myself complaining, I was supposed to snap it. I snapped it a lot. I had an angry red welt around my left wrist.

The book also suggested coming up with one word to remind myself to think and say positive things. I made myself say, "Blessed" whenever anyone asked me how I was doing.

For six weeks I wore my rubber band and took the computer class with Jenny. Every night I reread a chapter in the book she'd given me and added one more thing to the list of things I was thankful for in my life. I kept my list in a pretty silver journal and every night I added to it. The book also suggested reframing complaints as blessings. I learned to take every complaint and rewrite it as a statement of gratitude. So: "The phones at work drive me crazy," became, "I'm so blessed to have a job that makes it possible to help so many people in just one day."

Not only did I complete the computer course, I aced it. When I turned in my certificate of completion to Lola, I thanked her for hiring me and giving me a chance. I told her I was really concentrating on my sparkle.

Not long after I turned in my certificate, Lola called me into her office. She said she had received a call from one of the patients who had wanted to tell my supervisor how happy it made her to call the clinic, because the receptionist's upbeat voice always made her day.

"I'm torn, Helen. I'm not really sure what to do with you. I'd like to keep you at the front. You've really turned around and our patients love you, but I've gotten a request from Carla. She says she needs your positive energy and attitude and wants to bring you over to billing. I think you can handle it. The choice is yours, but billing would mean a promotion and a $5.00 an hour raise."

Did I ever have a lot to write in my journal tonight! I made dinner reservations at the Captain's Table, the nicest restaurant on the water in Harper. I kidnapped Ben and drove him there. We got to our table just as the sun was setting. It was beautiful. The waiter brought over the champagne as I'd requested and I handed Ben a card.

"Happy anniversary my darling. Thank you for taking care of me, for never giving up on me. I promise, our next forty years will be blessed."

Closing Thoughts

Poor Helen. Her life was so overcome by negative thoughts and words that this became the reality of her world. She thought that so many things were unfair or unjust that she became utterly incapable of finding positive in anything!

Let's look at some of the problems with Helen's thought process. What parent in America isn't happy that the next generation is better off than they are? Isn't that what we all want for our children? Isn't that part of the American dream? How is it possible that everyone else besides Helen is chronically idiotic, annoying, or moronic? No one in Helen's world could possibly measure up to her standards. Moreover, Helen's thought process was so mired in negativity that she couldn't even enjoy the simple blessing of a beautiful day; instead, she chose to focus on when the weather will turn bad again!

Sadly, the ultimate irony in this situation is that Helen isn't even aware of the worst problem in her life – that her negative thoughts and words in and of themselves make her life worse because they are driving all of the people around her away. So when we say "Poor Helen," we're not commiserating with her about her woes – instead we are sad for her because she is utterly blind to how unpleasant and abrasive she is.

It's so sad to know someone like Helen. No matter how many good things befall them, they always have a way to turn them into negatives. To make matters worse, people who find this many things wrong with life are generally narcissistic as well. Doesn't that sound a lot like Helen?

We all have bad days when nothing seems to go right. You may have some days when it seems like you are the only person for miles that has a clue about anything. Being aware of your budget and living within your resources is a very smart thing unless you force negative energy on it and then it becomes your shortage. It is easy to have moments when you feel jealous of those who have more than you, but if you examine your thoughts and actions and realize that these thought patterns are creeping into your life too often, then please, for the sake of yourself and others, take measures to find your bright side again.

Unfortunately, there is no book called, "Thoughts Matter, Words Matter." Perhaps that's what I should write next after I complete this book! But honestly, if you take the simple measures that Helen did, you can begin to live your life in a positive manner again. Put that rubber band on your wrist and take note of how many times you snap it over the course of a day. If you are disappointed with the number, then plan some ways to reinforce your speech with positive words. When you find yourself thinking or, even worse, getting ready to spew a negative thought, do your best to cut yourself off and re-spin your thoughts in a positive light.

If you find that this approach doesn't help in the least, it may be time to seek counseling. There is no reason to live in such a negative gray funk all the time, especially when negative energy is contagious. Believe it or not, there are good things and beauty to enjoy, even in this troubled world. It's time to get out there and find your wealth again.

MONEY GRATITUDE

*"He who knows that enough is enough will always have
enough."*
~ Lao Tzu

I looked around, nervously. There was no reason to think anyone
could see me, but I couldn't lose the knot in my stomach I got every
time I tried this. I couldn't risk getting caught. Not at this stage. This
was when I really had to have my wits about me. It was 5:30 in the
morning. The first rays of sunlight were barely breaching the clouds.

I had to hurry. I couldn't risk calling attention to myself. Get in,
get out; that was the only way this worked. Please, please don't let
anyone catch me doing this. It was my own deepest secret, I hadn't
even told John. I'd been getting away with my, uh, hobby, for several
months.

As I drove away from my latest rendezvous with risk, I thought
about my life before it all started to snowball. I remember exactly
what I was doing when the adventure began.

I had woken up early, before the alarm went off at 6:00 a.m. The
room was still dark. I reached across to John's side of the bed and felt
the empty covers. Then I remembered.

My husband was gone, working out of town, on day eight of his
twelve on/three off schedule with the pipeline. People always said to
me, "Oh, he must make tons of money." I always answered, "Yeah,
but with three children it takes two tons to get by."

I debated which activity I wanted and needed more—another hour's rest or a few minutes quiet time all to myself? I opted for silence and privacy, walking into the kitchen, turning on the computer and coffeemaker. While the coffee brewed, I pulled up Facebook to see how the rest of the world was faring this early on a Wednesday morning.

Sometimes I wondered why I looked at Facebook at all, but it was a great way to keep in touch with my mom, my sisters, and my friends from high school. Almost all my friends had moved away from Liberty Falls after graduation. I had gone to beauty school and gotten a job right away doing hair and nails at a popular salon in town. I knew everyone, everyone knew me, I had great clientele. I was good at it. It never occurred to me to leave.

I met John when he walked in for a haircut and the receptionist, Dennie, sent him over to me. As he walked towards my station I could see her waving at me from behind him. She was a hoot, making all kinds of gestures, hugging herself, acting like she was swooning, mouthing, "He's cute!" He was.

John and a couple of his friends had transferred with the pipeline from another project upstate. They were renting a place together. He was probably no more than five years older than me. He seemed so different from the boys I'd gone to high school with. I found myself nervous as all get out when he sat in my chair.

"I hope I don't screw this up," I thought to myself, not realizing I'd spoken my thoughts aloud.

"Well, I surely hope you don't screw this up either. I'm already as thin as I want to get on top, don't you be making a bad situation worse."

He had nothing to worry about. I couldn't see he was losing any hair and I didn't notice any receding at his hairline.

"You look great to me." I said, which wasn't what I meant. "I mean, your hair. It's great, uh, fine. Healthy. You have very healthy hair.

"Wow, woman, you're going to make me blush."

We introduced ourselves and just started talking like we had always known each other. It was weird like that, right from the start. Natural.

He told me how he'd just moved to town six weeks earlier, how

215

he'd been working with the pipeline for five years, how he hoped to go back to college, get a degree and move up into management with the company. He volunteered that he was single and not involved.

"Not that I haven't had my chances," he said. Laughing. "It's the male-patterned baldness. Chicks fall for it every time."

I thought I could hear his laugh the rest of my life. I watched his eyes in the mirror. He had pretty eyes.

The only problem with cutting men's hair, especially John Phelps who just needed a trim? It didn't take long enough. In a blink I was pulling the plastic styling cape off him and blow-drying hair from around the chair.

This was the part when I absolutely froze. I wanted to say something clever, like I hoped he'd be back to see me, or I hope he was satisfied and I got so tongue-tied I said something like "I hope you'll see me satisfied."

To his credit, he didn't take the opportunity to make fun of me, although he did turn red.

"Uh, ma'am, I think you did just fine. Thank you." Still red, he walked away until the ever-clever Dennie came to our rescue.

"Would you like to go ahead and book a standing appointment? Brandy always gives a discount to her regulars when they do. Shall we go ahead and schedule for, say, three-weeks?"

Nice! Good job, Dennie. But then, I heard him say something about schedule…varies… out of town. I couldn't turn off my blow dryer and just stand there and eavesdrop. I watched him walk away.

Before I could ask Dennie what he'd said, she was already shrieking! "He likes you. Wants to take you out, I told him you were single and not seeing anybody at all. So, he's like, great, I'll just give her a call and I said no, just leave your number so she can call you and he said he was going out of town tomorrow for a couple of weeks and so I said what about tonight and he said he hoped you'd call."

Dennie always strung a hundred words together before drawing a breath. I was surprised she didn't suffocate herself. She was more excited than I was and I was pretty excited.

"Here's his number, call him, call him, call him!"We'll be married eleven years this June and we have three kids: Rory 10, Barry 7, and Kenny, the baby, 4. We were on an every-three-year pregnancy roll, but I miscarried my last one. It was early on. We'll probably stop at three. Lord knows we can't afford the ones we've got. I can't imagine how we'd swing a fourth.

I got up and poured myself a cup of coffee and started scrolling through the recent Facebook posts. It always amazed me what people put on a website for all the world to see. I stopped on a picture of a castle on top of a hill overlooking a beautiful seaside village.

"Oh, no," I groaned. Had to be Marnie. It was. Good old Marnie Fitzpatrick, my song leader co-captain at Liberty Falls High. We had been inseparable from kindergarten on. Well, until graduation, anyway. Marnie got a scholarship to Stanford. I never even knew she was some sort of brainiac in chemistry. She went pre-med and then her junior year took some sort of special semester in Europe. That's where she met Phillipe. Oh, I'm sorry, Phillipe. Now she's Countess Marnie Genoa over some tiny principality in France.

Further proof that the Universe is still quite capable of granting favors and conjuring miracles. I hadn't talked to Marnie in years, but she sent me postcards, presents from around the world. I kept scrolling. What a weird idea, Facebook. Who came up with the idea of creating a perfectly permissible means of cyber stalking classmates, lost loves and celebrities.

Was everybody on the planet better off financially than I was? All I saw were posts of exciting places – gourmet restaurants, exotic island vacations, destination weddings. Someone had always "just gotten" their new dream car, job, home. Judging from the posts, I was the only person not enjoying perfect health, raking in millions, working out seven days a week, globe-trotting and skipping the light fantastic.

I should post some selfies. I could just see them. Here's one of me in my housecoat, dark circles from staying up all night with a vomiting toddler. Oh, look, how 'bout this one, here I am on the phone with the electric company explaining why our payment was late, don't I look cute? Or, I could take a picture of me scouring toilets, cleaning the oven, folding the laundry.

John always came home to a clean house, I made sure of that. And, I was always dressed nicely and had make-up on. But that was just a few days a month. The rest of the time I was RoboMom, on autopilot trying to make a good life with my family. I cooked

217

nutritious meals, or tried to. The kids were well-dressed, in hand-me-downs and seconds, but they were always ironed and clean. I stretched our budget every way I knew how, cut coupons until my fingers cramped. We got by.

For just a moment I pictured that on my gravestone marker. Brandy Phelps 1983-2014. She got by.

"Moooooooooooooooooooom! Rexster wants out, he's scratching at the door!" My middle boy. He had one volume, really loud.

"Okay, okay, Barry. Let's let him out. We need to take him for a walk. Remember, you said you were going to do that morning, afternoon, night. Remember? At least let him outside a minute, okay. Watch him. Dogs need to go outside once in a while or they'll go crazy."

Maybe I needed to go outside for a while, I thought.

I got the kids ready for another day. That was a job in itself. Everybody piled in the car, and we headed off for the elementary school. As I pulled out of the driveway, I heard the familiar tone of the car's low fuel warning. The indicator was all the way to the left, below the reserve. Dang it, I didn't have time to stop. I didn't have any choice. Surely, I could get to the convenience store. I did, barely. The car was making that weird knocking noise it made that time I ran out of gas completely.

I pulled up to the pump, inserted my debit card and nothing happened. I tried it again the other way, again, nothing. The station was busy, a guy in a new Honda had just pulled in behind me and already he was waving his hands, gesturing me to hurry up. I swiped my card a fourth time and the pump started beeping furiously. The digital readout said, "Please See Attendant."

The guy behind me honked. What did he want me to do? I stood in line at the attendant's window behind three other people paying cash. The lady ahead of me was counting out pennies. Been there, done that.

I got to the front of the line just as the Honda guy with anger management issues sped off, tires squealing. Another car pulled in behind me. I explained to the attendant my card wasn't working. He tried it on his machine and reported it had been declined.

I got in our car, and fortunately, it started up. I pulled up enough that I was no longer blocking anyone behind me, but I was starting to panic. I forced myself to think. I was sure I had $57.00 left in the account. I balanced my checkbook almost every day; things were that tight. John would get paid Friday, his check was automatically deposited to the bank, but it was only Wednesday. I started to call John and thought better of it. What could he do from there?

"Mom, we're going to be late, it's 8:00 already." My eldest announced.

"I know, Rory, I know. Do me a favor. Check around the seats. Check the glove compartment. See if you can find any money, okay? Barry, you check in the backseats; see if Kenny's holding out on us." I distracted them with our familiar game of find the money while I racked my brain. Then it hit me. The light bill. I had been so glad the utility company granted a reprieve I forgot to deduct the payment and late charge. I was probably overdrawn now.

The kids found $ .71 in change. As sweat broke out on my face, I tried to figure out a solution. The kids were already late. I could go inside the store and try to explain my situation. That wasn't going to work. Okay. I could just stand there and ask for money. When that thought hit my brain it unleashed a torrent of emotions.

How pathetic was this. Stuck in a car with three kids, not a dime to my name, my husband's out of town, I have no one I can call. John had been transferred here last January to start a new pipeline project. I still hadn't made any real friends. I had barely gotten to know the kid's teachers by names. Suddenly, I felt more alone than I'd ever felt in my life. All the responsibility felt like it was crushing my chest, I was dizzy, I felt my pulse running away and then –

"Hey, lady, are you alright?"

The stranger tapping at my car window scared the life out of me.

"Wha-a-what! What? I pulled up, I pulled up."

"No, you're fine." The guy didn't look like an axe-murderer. He was well dressed, wearing a suit and tie. He had a nice smile. Good hair. I still noticed hair. He was holding up a twenty-dollar bill.

"What do you want?" I said, still unnerved. Strangers didn't just come up and start talking to you.

"I think you must have dropped this, I found it by the pump."

"No, you didn't."

"I did." He insisted. "It was right there," he said, pointing.

"Trust me, if there'd been a twenty anywhere around here I

219

would've seen it, and I can assure you, I mean I can absolutely assure you it is not mine."

"Mom, take it, let's go!" Barry called from the backseat.

"Very well," I said, accepting the money. "It's very kind of you to—"

That was odd. Not only did the guy walk away, he drove away. Never got gas. Very odd. I didn't have time to think about it. I put $10.00 in the tank, dropped the kids off at school, and spent the remaining $10.00 on milk, bread, eggs, and peanut butter.

I put the groceries up and sat back down at the kitchen table. My computer was still on, Facebook was still on the screen with a new post from Marnie. A selfie on a yacht with her duke or count. He wasn't as cute as John. She was beaming in a red bandeau top and capri shorts.

"Seriously?" I said aloud and alone. "Ever run out of gas, Marnie?" And then, I just collapsed. I never imagined I'd grow up and party on a yacht but I thought I'd be living better than paycheck to paycheck. I got mad and then sad and then sobbed until I couldn't cry anymore. I was wiping the last of my tears and mascara away when I say that one of my Picasso-wannabes had marked up the kitchen table with crayon.

For crying out loud, I thought. Can't we have anything nice? The kitchen table was a $25.00 yard sale steal. It was one of the first things John and I bought for the house. It was round and hardwood, mahogany or cherry. When I polished it, it would gleam. Our little tribe of five ate every meal there when John was home. Tears started to well up again but there was no point in having a pity party. As Mom would say, "You don't have the dress for it."

I got out the furniture polish and started cleaning the table. I could see the marking was the letter K. Kenny was just learning his letters. We'd been working on his name. I couldn't get upset about that. When I finished, the table just shone. It was so beautiful. I was lucky to have it.

Don't ask me why, but as soon as I thought that? How lucky I was to have a beautiful table and a beautiful little boy to draw on it, eat from it, sit around it with his awesome brothers and my wonderful husband, I started crying all over again. This time I was crying tears of gratitude.

I might not have a yacht. I might never travel anywhere, but I was married to the hardest working man on the planet, and he adored me. If I had called him from the gas station, the crazy man probably would've left work that minute and rushed home. He did everything he could to provide for us. It wasn't easy, but who said life was supposed to be easy?

We had discussed our options many times. John always said it was my decision if I wanted to go back to work and I was the one that insisted on staying home to raise our family. It seemed foolish to me for us to pay other people to watch our kids when I could do it. It looked like it cost more for daycare than whatever I could contribute. In all honesty, John always wanted to take the family somewhere for a nice vacation. I was always vetoing that idea. I thought maybe when Kenny was seven or eight we'd take the whole family to Disneyland. No, John was a prince. His paycheck was direct deposited right to the bank and he spent almost nothing on the road.

The almost-out-of-gas caper was a turning point for me. That man, showing up out of the blue for some inexplicable reason just when I needed him to. It was my own little miracle. I was so grateful that he had come along and helped me. Instead of looking at what I didn't have, I started appreciating everything I did have. I was thankful I hadn't run out of gas.

I realized I was lucky to have a car that was in good enough condition to put gas in. Everywhere I looked, I saw another blessing. The more I counted my blessings, the more blessings I had to count. It wasn't just that I was focusing on my blessings, I mean, truly, blessings started raining down on me.

One of John's four days home, he arranged for a sitter to watch the kids for a couple of hours and took me out for a steak dinner. As we were eating, he said he had big news. Those online college courses had helped. He was given a promotion to regional supervisor. It meant a nice raise and he would be home more. He was going to be doing more office work and have an almost normal schedule. I was thrilled.

He said, "So you are going to have to reassess how much you want me to be depositing each week with the raise."

I didn't understand what he meant.

"I mean, how much of the raise do you want to put in checking?"

221

"All of it, of course." I said. "We're barely making it."

"Why didn't you tell me? I'll stop contributing so much to the kid's college funds, my retirement, and 401K. You do so well, I just assumed we were doing fine. You never complained about needing anything."

The next day John and I sat down and went over our budget. His payroll deposits each Friday were after tax and after his contributions to retirement and savings. Those were optional contributions. With his raise and some adjustments, we were able to increase his weekly deposits 40%. I felt like a countess myself!

The extra money gave me all the breathing room I could want. I was so used to managing on less, I never spent all the money from each paycheck. One day I was grocery shopping and was deciding between a pork roast and steak and realized I could have both. Out of the corner of my eye I saw a young woman staring at the last chance meat bin. She'd been there a while. I'd been there before.

"Excuse me, I believe you just dropped this." I said, handing her a twenty-dollar bill.

She started to protest and I insisted it was hers and walked away. That's how my compulsion started. Random acts of kindness are seriously addictive. Once I started, I've been unable to control myself. Now, several times a week, I just have to sneak off and do something for someone. They can't know that I've done it either. If I'm caught, it doesn't count.

Sometimes I pick up the cost of the meal for the person behind me in the drive-thru lane when I'm getting my coffee. It makes me especially delighted if the car behind me is an older model car and there are several kids in the car. Sometimes I leave money under windshield wipers of cars parked at the bus station. I stalk harried, exhausted moms at the boy's elementary school and leave gift cards to department stores and day spas where they'll find them.

The more I give away the more blessed I am. John's division recently won the company's coveted safety award for the first time ever. John was awarded a big prize for that achievement, five tickets to Disneyland—one each for John and I, the boys, and their baby sister.

Closing Thoughts

222

A few chapters back, I wrote about the Law of Attraction, which defined another way is that the more you visualize good things happening or the more you focus on positive energies, the more good things will happen that you want. Did you notice how these theories were woven into this story?

Brandy made do on her husband's deposited earnings week after week after week, barely scraping even. When she ran out of cash for gas that fateful day, luck came around in the form of a gentleman with a "found" $20 bill. Did this work because Brandy was a good budgeter? Not necessarily. Brandy deserved stroke of luck because she never complained to her husband about finances. To make do in the face of hardship, to not take a job for the sake of being with your children, and to never complain to your husband – clearly, this woman deserved some cosmic good for her selflessness.

After Brandy received the $20, she began, unknowingly, to apply the Law of Attraction to her life. She changed her attitude from being resentful of the success of others to being thankful for the blessings she had in her life. Everywhere Brandy looked, she saw another blessing. What happened as a result? The more she counted her blessings, the more blessings she had to count and that included an increase to her wealth. John got a promotion, his hours became more family-friendly, and Brandy suddenly found herself with 40% more to spend each week.

It serves to mention that it seems as though Brandy had no direct knowledge of the Laws of Attraction or karma. At least there was no mention of her knowledge in these stories. Still, they held true. What did Brandy do as a result? She paid it forward. Brandy began to create more cosmic goodwill by committing random acts of kindness as often as possible. Once again Brandy did this act selflessly, to symbolize out her never-ending thanks for that man with the found $20. What happened? John's division won an award and the family was rewarded with a family vacation!

Are you still saying to yourself, "Uh huh. All coincidence. If we all started doing good deeds tomorrow, trips to Disney won't fall out of the sky for everyone!" Oh, you poor cynical person. Well, you know, you could be right, but in the end, which is a better way to live – with your black heart full of wishes and wants, or with a grateful and giving heart with endless possibilities being returned back to you from the Universe? Do you want to be the Grinch before he stole Christmas, or the Grinch after he gave it back? The choice and consequence – positive or negative – is yours.

REVIEW

"I can no other answer make, but thanks and thanks."
~ William Shakespeare

I want to take this time to review some of the actions you can take to overcome any hardship you might be experiencing in this moment. I call them my 9 Universal Steps to Triumph. Whether it has to do with your happiness, health, or wealth, use this process to manifest your destiny of a life of abundance.

1. Resolve to Change

In order to make a real change and improve your life, you have to want it.

You have to *want* it.

Let's look as some things people may say when they want to change.

- I'm not sure this law of attraction thing works, but it would be nice to have a more positive attitude about it.

- I wish I was thinner, richer, and happier.

- I'd like to have a better figure so my kids won't be embarrassed of me.

- I know I should quit smoking, eat right, exercise and save money.

- I'd like to find a way to take a vacation someday.

All of these statements are lovely, but they are woefully inadequate. It would be *nice* to have a more positive attitude? Not much of a commitment in your heart with that statement. You *wish* something? Never wish for something – always *will* it – wishes are for fairyland dreams that may never come true. Using the word *wish* makes your goal feel unattainable. Using the word *will* makes you feel stronger and more powerful. Doing something for someone else? No, no, no! You need to want to do this for *you*, because *you* are the one who has to make it happen. You want to do something because you *should*? Please. You've known for quite a while now that you've had this problem, and you've failed at remedying it in the past. No, *should* is not good enough – you *will!*

You will never accomplish a goal if your want is in the form of a wish, an inclination, or a hankering. Your want must be a desire, a passion, something for which you hunger. You need to crave your goal more than you crave the next cigarette, drink, or doughnut. Your want must be a never-ending fire that burns in your heart. This is the mindset you must have to begin achieving the life you desire.

2. Identify the Problem & Question Yourself Honestly

Once you know you want to change your situation and you are emotionally charged, you need to find out where you are now within your hardship. In order to be successful with your new direction, it is important to explore the behaviors that got you the wrong results.

Are you trying to improve your figure? Your attitude? Your bank account? Maybe you grew up in the wrong household with an acceptance-of-struggle mentality, and you simply need a new plan. Usually, there's much more to the story.

More often than not, there is an emotional driver behind your behavior. When you push yourself further under the covers, reach for that cookie or cigarette or glass of wine, it's easy to think that you're just doing it because the short-run gratification feels good and easy. But if you need to do these things to feel good, then what bad feelings are you trying to cover up?

Do you have insecurities? Problems in a relationship? Problems with your extended family? Troubles from childhood that haunt you? Weight constricting your body? Unexplained depression? You might be surprised how these issues impact how we choose to take care of ourselves. Dig deeply within yourself, find your underlying pain, and work through it. If you can't do it by yourself, then seek counseling. This process is imperative. With negative energy flowing through a person due to underlying problems, it is nearly impossible to summon the positive energy required to accomplish the goals you want to achieve. If you fail to identify your problems then you can't move on to step 3.

3. Visualize Your Future

It is time to think about where you would like to be a year from now. This could be an easy step to bypass, so I'm going to ask you to take it one step further. I want you to write a letter, dated with the target date that you have set to accomplish your goal. In this letter, you should write how happy you feel now that you've attained your goal. Describe what you look like, how you feel, what you are doing, your financial status and family life. Also, write all of the positive changes in your life that have occurred because you have accomplished this goal. You ran a marathon, you took a trip, or maybe you published your first book or received that giant raise?

You can use this letter to support your efforts in two ways. First, I would suggest reading the letter every day when you first wake up. Don't look at it on day 100 and say "Pshaw, I've read it 99 times, I know what it says," and set it aside. Read it every day, and visualize it being true. Actually take the time to *FEEL* the feelings as if you have already accomplished your new life.

You can also keep a copy of the letter at a "point of determent" to help keep yourself from slipping. If you're trying to improve your figure, tape copies to the fridge and pantry doors. (If you don't want your letter to be quite so public, then find a small box for each location and place a copy of the letter in each box.) If you're trying to eat right, pursue your purpose or save money, put a copy in your wallet by your cash or credit card. If you're just trying to change your attitude, put a copy in your shirt pocket or tuck it into your bra, near your heart.

4. Create a Plan of Action & Test Your Beliefs

Now it is time for the plan! The plan must be as specific and measurable.

If you are working to improve your physique, it is time to decide how you will approach both caloric intake and exercise. Will you count calories? Will you keep a log? How will you decide how many calories is appropriate? How will you make sure that appropriate foods are in the house? How will you deal with dining out? How will you chose a form of exercise that you feel you can stick with? How will you ensure that you build up slowly enough to avoid injury? Whatever you choose, I strongly suggest that you take physical measurements of your body rather than relying on the scale alone.

Are you trying to find peace and balance? Will you study yoga, meditate, or will you eradicate the stress in your life? Will you forgive and change perspectives or find a way to let your anger go? When are the times you are most likely to be stressed or emotionally unstable, and what strategies do you have to conquer those moments? At what point will you consider your goal accomplished?

Is your goal to save money? What are you saving for? What can you do to reduce your spending? What is your goal date? What is your strategy to keep from splurging on that next perfect pair of shoes, or that next golf club you've wanted that's on sale?

If you are pursuing a more intangible goal such as "more positive thinking," because you realize this Law of Attraction "stuff" is legit, what goals will you set and how will you chart your progress? Perhaps you will keep a log of your thoughts throughout the day, documenting your successes and failures. For less concrete goals like this, you may have to think a bit outside the box to determine a way to quantify and measure your goal. However, if you're a believer in the law of attraction, then you and I both know that you *can* find a way to detail your goals and measure your success.

Now that you have your plan, do you have faith that it will work? First and foremost, you must truly believe in the law of attraction. If

228

you are new to the Law of Attraction and still have doubts, I dare you to visualize and ask the Universe for a front row parking spot next time you go shopping. Create a small test to reinforce the strength of your beliefs.

Not only must you have faith in the law of attraction, you must also believe that your plan will work. There is a simple way to test this. Imagine it is day one of implementation, and you wake up. Are you nervous or excited? If the answer is nervous, then go back, revisit, and revise your plan. There is something amiss that you don't quite believe will work. Find it and fix it. If, however, you are excited at the thought of waking up on day one, you know for certain that you're good to go.

5. Decide How to Measure Progress

How will you be sure you are staying on track? Every long term plan needs benchmarks for review. At regular intervals on your journey, you need to assess your progress.

Your interval of assessment can be as short or as long as you want, as long as it is commensurate with the goal you are trying to accomplish. While assessing your progress hour by hour for a smoker may be the best place to start, it would be absurd for someone wanting to shed weight. Whatever interval you choose, use these benchmark moments as opportunities to assess what has been working well, and not so well, over the course of your plan. Tweak your plan as needed to make it even better. If you don't know how or where to start measuring your progress, don't get discouraged. I recommend this one measuring tool to start: after some time, ask a friend or family member if they have noticed any difference in you. It really is that simple.

6. Build a Support System

Yes, you will feel bad if you do not stick to your concrete plan, but it also helps to have an accountability support outside of yourself. Once you have clarified your new destiny share it with somebody you can trust. There are a number of characteristics to look for when choosing people to support you.

- Choose someone who will have faith that you can do it. Avoid anyone who rolls his/her eyes because they know it's the Nth time you've set out to accomplish this goal.

- Choose someone who will be true and faithful. Can you imagine your friend saying, "Oh, I'm sorry you broke your diet. Here, have an Oreo."? If so, look elsewhere.

- Choose someone who has accomplished the same goal or have been through the same hardship and has overcame the adversity.

- Choose someone who can give you the support you need when facing a challenge. Of course, you must be realistic with your expectations. There aren't too many friends who will understand if you call them because you're tempted by your kid's birthday-cake-flavored ice cream at 3:00 am. And if you feel compelled to call your friend ten times a day for help, then stop bothering your friend and get a therapist for support instead. You still want that friend to be your friend after you've accomplished your goal, and wearing out your welcome is not the way to do it.

And here is my favorite one:

- **Choose someone who understands the Law of Attraction. Even if it is just a book that explains it - you will never find a better supporter anywhere!**

7. Lookout for Obstacles

You know the negative energies you identified while questioning yourself honestly? It is time to give those one more look.

It may seem a bit odd that a proponent of the Law of Attraction would ask you to dwell on the negative again, but really, it's necessary. These obstacles are the devils that keep you from attaining your goals, and the devils that you know are much better than the devils that you don't know.

If you are intimately familiar with your temptations and triggers for failure, then this time around you will clearly see those obstacles coming and be prepared with strategies to fend them off. With your devils subdued, your goals are yours for the taking.

8. Take Action

Finally, it is time to put your future plan into action by starting now. You know what you want, you know how to get it and you have a way to track your progress.

With the power of the Law of Attraction and common sense, getting to your goal will be easy, right? Well, not exactly. But with the Law of Attraction in your grasp and the plans and strategies you have at your disposal, this effort will be, without a doubt, the easiest it has ever been before. You have the tools and the power to accomplish your goal and overcome any hardship no matter how bleak it may seem now. You *can,* and you *will*, accomplish the life you desire.

9. Pay It Forward

Wow, you did it! Congratulations! I'm so proud of you!

But now, I must alert you to the fact that you are the bearer of karmic debt. The Law of Attraction has served your needs, and you must repay the favor. That may sound like a heavy burden, but here's some good news: this will probably be the easiest debt you have ever paid off. I bet you feel so happy from accomplishing your goal that you could practically shout your strategies from mountaintops, right? If so, then repaying your karmic debt will be a breeze.

You and I both know how miserable it is to be on the other side of the fence, feeling like you will never be able to change your situation, right? But we did. WE did it. We have BOTH benefitted from the Law of Attraction. We have used it to overcome our obstacles and successfully meet our goals.

Now is the time to share. Return that positive energy to the Universe by telling others *how* you accomplished your goal. Share your story, share this book, and let people know that you are available to mentor them if they should choose to challenge themselves to reach goals the way you have. Remember, every time someone you mentor has success, you have success as well. By helping yourself and helping others, you have doubled your own success and made the world a happier place. And if the two of you then mentor others and this pattern continues, your personal success could end up having an amazing impact on the lives of an exponential number of people in this world. I preach about the Law of Attraction daily and for those millions that I don't come into contact with, I wrote this book for.

Change yourself, and then change the world. Really, I cannot imagine a better accomplishment than that. One day you will look back at the memory of whatever hardship you're currently going through or have been through and whisper to the Universe a silent thank you. Because now, you are that strong, happy, healthy, and wealthy person you were always destined to become.

With this book, I hope you have started to recognize your individual path to put the *LIFE* back into your life! I know you will succeed.

ACKNOWLEDGMENTS

There are so many people I would like to thank today. First and foremost, I want to thank my husband, George, my three children, Kaitlyn, Kaimy and Kade, and the rest of my family for standing proudly by me while I live out loud and pursue my dreams of publishing this book. I wouldn't be here today without the instrumental help received from Ellen Lambert and Gail Morrison – may you both experience a life full of happiness, health and wealth! I want to thank Elizabeth Johnson, my copy editor and one of the best up and coming professionals out there – may you be blessed with the abundance and recognition I know you deserve. Finally, I want to express my sincerest gratitude to all my beta readers out there who gave me encouragement and the constructive criticism from a reader's perspective. You guys rock! Your kind words and suggestions were the hope and motivation I needed to keep going. Thank you. Thank you. Thank you.

ABOUT THE AUTHOR

Kahla Kiker is a writer who doesn't write to impress the proper usage of words taught by English professors everywhere. Rather, Kahla writes to elicit usage of imagination and feelings experienced by all mankind worldwide. She writes for the adventurer, the romantic, and the secret curiosity hidden in all of us. No genre left behind…

Kahla Kiker lives in Midland, TX where outside of work and writing, she enjoys spending time with her husband shooting competitive sporting clays and cheering on her three very active children.

Connect with Kahla Kiker Author!

If you want to view chapter excerpts from Kahla's other books or want to get an automatic email when Kahla's next books are released, sign up to follow her blog or Facebook page below. Your email address will never be shared and you can unsubscribe at any time.

Word-of-mouth is crucial for any author to succeed. If you enjoyed this book please consider leaving an online review, even if it's only a line or two; it would make all the difference and would be very much appreciated.

Publishing Blog: http://PenNameK.blogspot.com

Twitter: @PenNameK

Facebook Page : https://www.facebook.com/pages/Pen-name-K/681092721932866

Email: KWorldVentures@Yahoo.com

www.ingramcontent.com/pod-product-compliance
Lightning Source LLC
LaVergne TN
LVHW051044080426
835508LV00019B/1700